D0914953

RAWLYK, GEORGE

REGIONALISM IN CANADA

Regionalism in Canada:
Flexible Federalism or Fractured Nation?

CANADA
Issues & Options

A series designed to stimulate
intelligent inquiry into crucial Canadian Concerns

Regionalism in Canada:

Flexible Federalism or Fractured Nation?

George A. Rawlyk
Professor, Department of History, Queen's University

Bruce W. Hodgins
Professor, Department of History, Trent University

Richard P. Bowles
Associate Professor, Faculty of Education, University of Toronto

PRENTICE-HALL OF CANADA, LTD.
Scarborough, Ontario

Canadian Cataloguing in Publication Data

Rawlyk, George A., 1935-
  Regionalism in Canada

(Canada, issues & options)

Bibliography: p.
ISBN 0-13-770917-X

1. Regionalism — Canada. 2. Federal government —
Canada. 3. Canada — Politics and government.
4. Canada — Economic conditions. I. Hodgins,
Bruce W., 1931-   II. Bowles, Richard P., 1927-
III. Title.   IV. Series.

JL27.R39   321'.02'0971   C78-001508-8

Prentice-Hall, Inc., Englewood Cliffs, New Jersey
Prentice-Hall International, Inc., London
Prentice-Hall of Australia, Pty., Ltd., Sydney
Prentice-Hall of India, Pvt., Ltd., New Delhi
Prentice-Hall of Japan, Inc., Tokyo
Prentice-Hall of Southeast Asia (PTE.) Ltd., Singapore

Composition by CompuScreen Typesetting Ltd.

Cover illustration by Doug Martin.

ISBN 0-13-770917-X

1 2 3 4 5 W 83 82 81 80 79

Printed in Canada by Webcom Ltd.

Contents

4 The Contemporary Problem

5 Historical Background

6 The Future

Acknowledgments

The authors are particularly indebted to Professor John Weaver of McMaster University and to Mr. Douglas Smith of Edmonton for their great help in collecting some of the basic material for this volume. In addition, the generous assistance and advice provided by Mr. Rob Greenaway, Associate Editor, of Prentice-Hall was very much appreciated.

The authors would also like to thank the many writers and publishers who have granted them permission to use various materials. Source references are provided with the documents.

Preface

The *Canada: Issues and Options* series focusses on a number of vital continuing Canadian concerns. Each volume probes the nature of a complex issue in both its contemporary and historical contexts. The issues were chosen because of their relevance to the life of the Canadian teenager as well as the general Canadian public.

Every volume in the series provides a wide variety of primary and secondary source materials. These sources are interdisciplinary as well as analytical and descriptive. They embody many divergent points of view in order to provoke critical in-depth consideration of the issue. They are arranged in a manner designed to personally involve and confront the reader with the clash of opinions and options inherent in the various issues. The historical sources have been carefully selected to provide a better understanding of the roots of the issue under consideration. It is hoped that this method will establish in the reader's mind a meaningful relationship between the past and the present.

The organization is flexible. If a chronological study of the development of the issue is desired, this can be accomplished by treating the historical sources first and later examining the contemporary manifestations of the issue. By reversing this procedure, the reader can first deal with the contemporary section. This approach will provide the reader with a brief overview of the issue, a case study designed to put it into personal and immediate terms, and a more detailed examination of the issue in its contemporary setting, prior to examining its historical roots.

Questions designed to stimulate further research are also included. These questions do not limit examination or prescribe answers, but raise more questions and suggest aspects of the issue which might be further investigated.

Throughout these volumes, a conscientious effort has been made to avoid endorsing any one viewpoint. No conclusions are drawn. Rather, the reader is presented with information which has been arranged to encourage the drawing of his own tentative conclusions about the issue. The formation of these conclusions involves the use of the skills of inquiry and the examination and clarification of personal values.

Introduction

The Fathers of Confederation faced a major hurdle in forging a new nation in British North America: how to overcome the forces of disunity and create one nation out of several different colonies. This struggle between the forces of strong central government and regional forces is still being waged today. It is a conflict that has greatly influenced the course of Canadian development since 1867 and is basic to the study of almost every aspect of Canada's history.

The November 1976 victory of the Parti Québécois in the Quebec provincial election has served to focus even more attention on regional forces in Canada. The threat of Quebec separation and continuing regional protest in other parts of Canada raise some central questions about Canada and Canadian federalism, questions which will be examined in this volume in some detail. However, it is almost impossible to deal with all issues in one book. Issues relating directly to Quebec and the Canadian North are not treated in great depth here, since there are already two volumes in the *Canada: Issues and Options* series which deal with those two areas of Canada exclusively. For those interested in a more detailed examination, we recommend a look at *Canadiens, Canadians and Québécois* and *The Canadian North: Source of Wealth or Vanishing Heritage?*

As you read through the documents in this book, you will be exposed to some of the issues surrounding regionalism in Canada. By focusing on the political expression of regional concerns, it is to be hoped that you will gain a better understanding of the origins of regional discontent and of what measures can be taken to deal with these grievances in a fair and mutually satisfactory fashion. What is regionalism? Why does it exist? Can regionalism be a unifying force in Canada? For you is regionalism a healthy or unhealthy phenomenon in Canada? Why? What can be done to counteract regional protest? What alternatives face Canada if regionalism becomes a dividing force? In asking these questions and in dealing with the issues they raise, you will, in a very real sense, be dealing with Canada's future as a nation.

The Issue:
Some Opinions

The following documents present various views of regions and regionalism in Canada. Why is regionalism an issue in Canada today? What
effects will it have on the nation in the future?

WE MUST PULL TOGETHER

*On December 13, 1976, Prime Minister Trudeau responded to remarks
made by Premier Lévesque of Quebec at a federal-provincial first ministers' conference.*

Our situation in Canada is one of challenge, and also, I believe, one of
opportunity. I view our task as being not the defence of all that has come
before, of an immutable status quo. Our task is to build a more enriching
federalism, to guarantee even more firmly the liberty, self-realization, and
well-being of the people and communities of Canada.

When I speak of Canada, I do not have in mind an "identity" which
competes with that which a French Canadian and Quebecker, conscious of his
or her specific history and roots, holds dear.

I am not speaking or thinking of the fostering of some higher-order
Canadian personality, in which would be absorbed or subsumed the culture,
values and sense of identity of the Quebecker, the British Columbian, the
Albertan, or the people of the Prairies, Ontario, the Maritimes, or Newfoundland, or of Canada's native peoples.

I think, rather, of a political society, the ideals of which are liberty, equality, and, yes, fraternity. I think of a society which, by securing the cooperation of our people, by pooling the resources of our different regions, by making possible the free development of the different cultures of our communities, makes our individual liberty, capacity for self-realization and well-being more secure and better guaranteed than they would be if each community were to attempt to achieve this alone.

"Unity" exists in so far as we are inspired by like ideals, and pursue these in common and in concert. "Unity", for us in Canada, cannot mean "sameness".

WHO SAYS WE'RE NOT UNITED?

*On December 15, 1976, this cartoon appeared in a number of Canadian newspapers. (*London Free Press. *Reprinted with the permission of Charles Tingley.)*

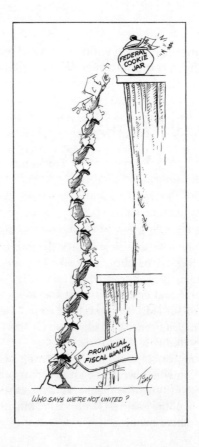

AS A PEOPLE WE DON'T LIKE EACH OTHER VERY MUCH

Writing in Saturday Night *in July 1971, Robert Fulford made the following observation about regionalism in Canada.*

As a people we don't like each other very much. We tend to feel that our region is being screwed by some other region. Ontario people, for instance, think Montreal gets too much of Ottawa's attention. Quebec people tend to think Ontario is the cause of Quebec unemployment. Westerners think Toronto is robbing them. Maritimers think that central Canada is ignoring them. People in Northern Ontario think people in Southern Ontario don't care about them.

The Canadian style as expressed in regionalism tends to be suspicious, narrow, nasty, even paranoid.

FOUNDATIONS OF UNITY

The then Communications Minister Jeanne Sauvé made the following statement about the basis of national unity in a speech to the Association of American Editorial Cartoonists in 1976.

. . . National unity is founded on a feeling of belonging to a community of people and on the forces which bind this family together, uniting it with its past and with its future. National unity presupposes loyalty freely given, and the acceptance of a charter to define the scope of freedom reserved for each citizen.

. . .

We are proposing this ideal to all those who in complete good faith recognize that it is still possible to understand one another without coming to blows, to affirm one's own existence without ignoring the other person's, to unite without betrayal and, as Saint-Exupery wrote, to look outward together in the same direction.

REGIONALISM AND NATIONAL UNITY

J. Wreford Watson made the following comment in the Canadian Geographical Journal. *(Vol. 131, Part I (1965))*

. . . Regionalism need not mean disintegration. It may mean diversification. And as long as all the diversities involved recognize their dependence upon each other, they can actually add to the idea of unity.

WHAT WESTERN CANADA WANTS

These comments were made by Owen Anderson in an article which appeared in the book The Unfinished Revolt. *(From* The Unfinished Revolt *by John J. Barr and Owen Anderson, reprinted by permission of The Canadian Publishers, McClelland and Stewart Limited, Toronto.)*

The question of what Western Canada wants is answered by the Rowell-Sirois Report. What Western Canada seeks is what the Report said the provinces must have: a real and not an illusory autonomy; autonomy which comes from the recognition that the governments of Western Canada are elected by their citizens to govern in the best interests of those citizens; recognition that these governments know what is best for their jurisdictions— and if this is not in keeping with what the central government considers to be in the national interest then it will be their electorates who will do something about it, not another government which was the creation of the federating provinces and is at best coordinate with the provinces and not superior. But, being realistic, the West recognizes that autonomy can replace subservience only when the provinces have sufficient financial resources to meet their constitutional obligations. Therefore if the division of taxing power is to remain in its present form the redistributive function of the central government must be on the basis of unconditional grants. How the money is spent must be left to the provinces in accordance with the priorities they have set and their electorates have approved.

ANTI-EASTERNISM . . .
A FLAME THAT RARELY SUBSIDES

On April 17, 1976, the Globe and Mail *printed a letter to the editor from which the following extract is taken.*

The citizens of Calgary are Calgarians first, Albertans second, and related to eastern Canada only when they can't avoid it. Anti-Americanism may occasionally flare up, but anti-easternism is a flame that rarely subsides.

REASSESSMENT OF GOVERNMENT NECESSARY

The following remarks appeared in the Regina Leader-Post *on April 16, 1977.*

Premier Bill Bennett of British Columbia says Canada needs a more flexible form of government to cope with the problems of the '70s.

The Social Credit premier says the existence of five distinct regions in Canada must be recognized in any formula to amend the constitution and these regions must be given a voice in deciding what changes are necessary in the British North America Act.

[From the interview]

. . . We need a redefinition of what level of government can best deliver services and should be given the taxing power to provide these services while maintaining the fabric of the system.

Q: So you are saying that federal powers should be diminished somewhat and regional powers increased?

A: Where they can best deliver services. And not because we're out to seize power for power's sake. It's time to realize that many problems cannot work on a rigid national basis.

TEN GALLON HATS AND KILTS

On February 18, 1976, the Edmonton Journal *raised an interesting point about regional characteristics:*

Sinclair Stevens, a former Toronto financier, has come up with a unique little idea for keeping his name before delegates to this week's Progressive Conservative Leadership convention.

He will dress some of his supporters in costumes representing regions of the country, then turn them loose to circulate through his six hospitality suites.

Western boosters will wear 10-gallon hats, Maritimers will wear kilts and Puritan costumes, Quebecers will be dressed in bon-homme carnival and French peasant outfits.

And those reflecting the spirit of Ontario will wear—you guessed it—business suits.

"FOREIGN" INVESTMENT IN THE MARITIMES

The Atlantic Provinces Economic Council made the following comments regarding industrial development in the Atlantic provinces in a brief presented in 1972.

To be blunt, it seems as if certain segments of opinion in central Canada, having achieved the benefits of industrialization for themselves, now wish the Atlantic Provinces to forego the industrialization they never had, in the interest of maintaining an ill-defined Canadian economic independence. . . .

We tend not to make any distinction between investment that comes from central Canada, the United States or other foreign countries, regarding it all, somehow, as "foreign".

REGIONALISM IS NOT UNIQUE TO QUEBEC

On December 9, 1976, Premier Frank Moores of Newfoundland reminded his Toronto audience that the Parti Québécois election victory of November 1976 had not destroyed regionalism in the rest of Canada.

Regionalism in our country today is not just unique to Quebec. While regionalism, spelled out in terms of separatism, is more identifiable with Quebec today, regionalism as such exists across the nation and challenges the essence of our federation. . . .

The situation is serious. In my opinion, it is the most serious turn of events that has faced our nation in peacetime.

CANADA'S REGIONS: SEVERAL SMALL COUNTRIES

The following excerpt is taken from an article titled "Regionalism and Nationalism", by Gordon Merrill. It appeared in the book, Canada: A Geographical Interpretation. *(John Warkentin, ed., Methuen, 1968.)*

The physical diversity of Canada underlies its regionalism. However, cultural diversity appears to be emerging as a dominant element, surpassing physical attributes in importance. In 1967, an overall look at Canada separates out into six pictures: the Atlantic provinces at one end of the table of Canadian bounty, and seeking a better seat; Quebec, restless, semivolatile, engaged in soul-searching and conscious of her isolation; Ontario, self-satisfied, confident and somewhat disturbed by her neighbour; the Prairies, the first generation of pioneers departed, productive and set apart from the rest of Canada; west coast, expansive, aggressive, frontier-like and beyond the Cordillera; the north, vast, distant, waiting. A sense of isolation is part of the self-portrait in 1967 of all regions of Canada except southern Ontario. In this sense, Canada is not one large country but a number of small ones whose boundaries are defined by regional consciousness.

What do you think?

1. *Is the area in which you live represented in these documents? Do you agree with the views presented here about your region? How would you describe your region's relationship with the rest of Canada?*
2. *What do these documents say about regional problems in Canada?*
3. *What specific issues can you name as a result of reading these documents?*

Regions and Regionalism

2

In broad terms, a region is a part of the world that is different from other parts of the world. For our purposes, we must narrow the scope of the definition and describe a region as a distinct part of a country that has some quality or combination of qualities that make it different from another part of the same country. There are many factors that can create a region: physical geography, climate, concentration of population, language, culture, social structure, form of government, to name a few. When a combination of these qualities exists, giving a particular area a unique identity, we can usually call that area a region.

As we have just stated, every region has its own special identity. Regionalism recognizes and affirms that identity—it is a response *within* people to their surroundings. The region in which you live influences how you see both yourself and the issues that concern you; however, your regional viewpoint only becomes apparent when you compare it to the attitudes and interests of people who live in other areas. Thus, we can define regionalism as the expression of the values, interests and concerns of people living in a particular area to others who do not live in the same region.

Regional attitudes take many forms in Canada, but the most common and perhaps most effective expression of regionalism is political. In order to present their views to others, people from one region may organize protest movements or even political parties. Sometimes local politicians assume the function of communicating regional concerns to national politicians.

In this section, you will be asked to look at maps and statistics in order to determine which qualities make some regions in Canada different from others. What kinds of problems are created by dividing Canada into regions? Does the process of regionalizing help us to better understand the nature of our country?

PHYSIOGRAPHIC REGIONS OF CANADA

Physical geographers have compiled very detailed maps of the physiography of Canada. Here is a simple one which shows only the main features of Canada's physical make-up.

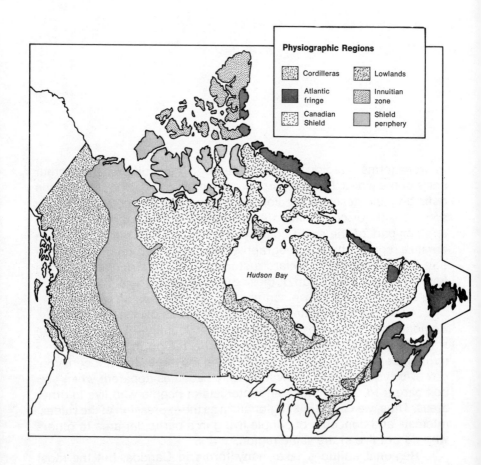

What do you think?

1. What are the main physiographic regions of Canada? What are the main characteristics of each region?
2. How could physical geography affect regional sentiments?

MINERAL PRODUCTION IN CANADA

This map shows the major areas in which mining is carried on in Canada.

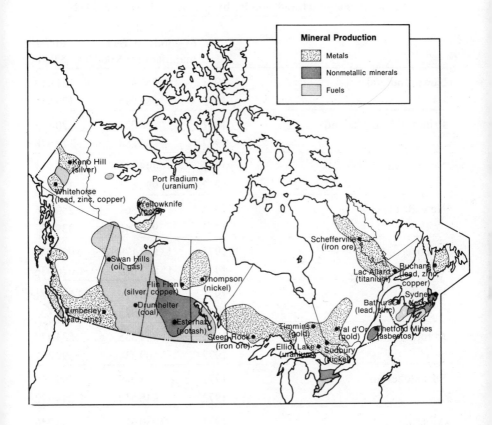

Mineral Production

- Metals
- Nonmetallic minerals
- Fuels

Keno Hill (silver)
Port Radium (uranium)
Whitehorse (lead, zinc, copper)
Yellowknife (gold)
Schefferville (iron ore)
Swan Hills (oil, gas)
Lac Allard (titanium)
Buchans (lead, zinc, copper)
Flin Flon (silver, copper)
Thompson (nickel)
Sydney
Bathurst (lead, zinc)
Kimberley (lead, zinc)
Drumheller (coal)
Esterhazy (potash)
Timmins (gold)
Val d'Or (gold)
Thetford Mines (asbestos)
Steep Rock (iron ore)
Elliot Lake (uranium)
Sudbury (nickel)

What do you think?

1. What are the major areas of mineral production in Canada?
2. What areas probably have the greatest revenue from the mining industry?

MANUFACTURING IN CANADA

The following statistics reveal something about the manufacturing industries in Canada. Canada Year Book 1975. (Reproduced by permission of the Minister of Supply and Services.)

Value of manufactured goods, by province, 1971 and 1972

		Value of shipments of goods of own manufacture $'000	Value added $'000
Newfoundland	1971	261 931	121 019
	1972	284 095	129 558
Prince Edward Island	1971	58 024	20 153
	1972	66 888	22 578
Nova Scotia	1971	798 152	297 754
	1972	993 641	368 833
New Brunswick	1971	806 806	280 416
	1972	965 046	339 037
Quebec	1971	13 833 179	6 054 856
	1972	15 091 616	6 676 036
Ontario	1971	26 270 629	11 596 471
	1972	29 225 025	12 869 823
Manitoba	1971	1 344 855	534 472
	1972	1 509 334	599 867
Saskatchewan	1971	578 039	209 965
	1972	646 510	244 772
Alberta	1971	2 080 617	755 246
	1972	2 425 341	849 515
British Columbia	1971	4 235 968	1 864 409
	1972	5 020 254	2 212 050
Yukon Territory	1971	2 285	1 035
	1972	1 516	795
Northwest Territories	1971	5 432	1 719
	1972	5 395	1 886
Canada	1971	50 275 917	21 737 514
	1972	56 234 663	24 314 751

What do you think?

1. Which areas benefit most from manufacturing? Which seem to be least involved with manufacturing and thus derive the least benefit?

AGRICULTURE

The following statistics should tell you something about the agricultural industry in Canada. Canada Yearbook 1975. (Reproduced by permission of the Minister of Supply and Services.)

Cash receipts from farming operations (excluding supplementary payments), by province, 1970-74 (thousand dollars).

Province	1970	1971	1972	1973	1974
Prince Edward Island	44 613	38 868	44 782	72 002	84 004
Nova Scotia	67 644	65 618	73 919	94 692	104 139
New Brunswick	58 486	52 801	65 117	95 571	104 027
Quebec	667 414	690 125	772 024	962 358	1 108 967
Ontario	1 410 863	1 427 965	1 637 699	1 947 551	2 277 554
Manitoba	335 731	367 841	478 478	611 642	818 305
Saskatchewan	686 057	901 408	1 172 288	1 435 534	2 025 426
Alberta	705 280	776 886	896 023	1 193 241	1 602 176
British Columbia	216 585	223 048	246 038	316 648	402 009
Total	4 192 673	4 544 560	5 386 368	6 729 239	8 526 607

What do you think?

1. What are the primary agricultural areas in Canada? What do you suppose would be the main agricultural products?
2. Which areas are least well off in terms of agricultural income?

EDUCATION

These statistics deal with the level of education in the province. (Reproduced with the permission of the Minister of Supply and Services.)

Highest Level of Schooling

Province	Population over 15 years and not at school	Percent with Elementary	Percent with Secondary	University Some	University Graduated
Canada	13 168 025	37.2	53.0	5.1	4.7
Newfoundland	280 865	48.9	20.2	4.3	2.1
Prince Edward Island	65 135	42.1	49.0	5.9	3.0
Nova Scotia	470 080	35.5	55.8	4.7	4.0
New Brunswick	366 875	49.1	45.2	4.3	3.3
Quebec	3 679 040	47.1	36.8	4.6	4.5
Ontario	4 766 015	32.8	57.1	5.0	5.1
Manitoba	610 345	36.8	53.7	5.1	4.4
Saskatchewan	557 555	41.0	49.9	5.6	3.4
Alberta	958 220	28.4	60.5	5.8	5.3
British Columbia	1 385 400	26.2	61.9	6.5	4.9

What do you think?

1. *What provinces appear to be best off in terms of education level?*
2. *What effect can education (or the lack of it) have on regional sentiments?*

FAMILY INCOME IN CANADA

The following table deals with the average family incomes in Canada by province. (Reproduced by permission of the Minister of Supply and Services.)

Average income of families in current and constant dollars by region, selected years, 1951-73

Region	1951	1957	1961	1967	1971	1973
			Current dollars			
Atlantic provinces	2 515	3 422	4 156	5 767	7 936	9 965
Quebec	3 523	4 517	5 294	7 404	9 919	12 024
Ontario	3 903	4 997	5 773	8 438	11 483	13 912
Prairie provinces	3 261	4 355	4 836	6 908	9 309	11 760
British Columbia	3 669	5 238	5 491	7 829	11 212	13 942
Canada	3 535	4 644	5 317	7 602	10 368	12 716

What do you think?

1. *Based on these statistics, which provinces appear to be "haves" and which "have nots"?*
2. *Are there other factors that might change your assessment of "have" and "have not" provinces?*

EMPLOYMENT AND UNEMPLOYMENT

In this table the employment statistics for the provinces are recorded. (Reproduced by permission of the Minister of Supply and Services.)

Employment and unemployment by province, 1966-74 (thousands)

YEAR	PROVINCE									
	NFLD.		PEI		NS		NB		QUE.	
	Employment	Unemployment	Employment	Unemployment	Employment	Unemployment	Employment	Unemployment	Employment	Unemployment
1966	127	11	34	—	235	13	190	14	2016	100
1967	131	12	34	—	238	14	190	14	2080	116
1968	130	14	34	—	239	15	193	15	2082	145
1969	131	15	36	—	244	14	194	18	2132	158
1970	133	16	34	—	246	15	196	17	2144	183
1971	139	18	36	—	244	20	198	16	2197	197
1972	145	20	36	—	247	20	207	19	2225	201
1973	157	23	39	—	262	19	218	22	2353	189
1974	155	29	41	—	278	20	227	23	2427	190
	ONT.		MAN.		SASK.		ALTA.		BC	
	Employment	Unemployment	Employment	Unemployment	Employment	Unemployment	Employment	Unemployment	Employment	Unemployment
1966	2651	69	348	9	324	5	550	12	678	32
1967	2745	89	348	9	326	6	564	14	723	39
1968	2830	104	360	13	334	8	586	18	750	47
1969	2936	95	363	10	339	11	611	17	795	42
1970	2996	134	363	17	334	15	622	28	810	67
1971	3079	170	371	19	335	13	633	31	847	64
1972	3218	162	378	18	337	15	657	30	879	72
1973	3366	142	392	16	345	13	689	29	937	65
1974	3519	152	411	13	353	10	731	20	996	64

[1]Unemployment figures for Prince Edward Island are not published due to high sampling error.

URBAN AND RURAL POPULATION

This table prepared by Statistics Canada indicates the proportions of population living in rural and urban settings. (Reproduced by permission of the Minister of Supply and Services.)

Number and percentage of the population classified as urban, and rural by non-farm and farm, by province, 1971.

Province or Territory	Urban		Rural Non-farm		Rural Farm		Rural Total		Total Population
	No.	%	No.	%	No.	%	No.	%	No.
Newfoundland	298 800	57.2	218 775	41.9	4 525	0.9	223 305	42.8	522 105
Prince Edward Island	42 780	38.3	47 725	42.7	21 130	18.9	68 860	61.7	111 640
Nova Scotia	447 400	56.7	315 290	40.0	26 270	3.3	341 555	43.3	788 960
New Brunswick	361 145	56.9	247 845	39.1	25 565	4.0	273 410	43.1	634 555
Quebec	4 861 240	80.6	861 215	14.3	305 300	5.1	1 166 520	19.4	6 027 765
Ontario	6 343 630	82.4	995 840	12.9	363 640	4.7	1 359 475	17.6	7 703 105
Manitoba	686 445	69.5	171 390	17.3	130 410	13.2	301 800	30.5	988 245
Saskatchewan	490 630	53.0	202 280	21.8	233 335	25.2	435 610	47.0	926 240
Alberta	1 196 250	73.5	195 590	12.0	236 025	14.5	431 620	26.5	1 627 875
British Columbia	1 654 405	75.7	456 700	20.9	73 520	3.4	530 215	24.3	2 184 620
Yukon Territory	11 215	61.0	7 120	38.7	55	0.3	7 170	39.0	18 390
Northwest Territories	16 830	48.4	17 955	51.6	25	0.1	17 980	51.7	34 805
Canada	16 410 785	76.1	3 737 730	17.3	1 419 795	6.6	5 157 525	23.9	21 568 310

What do you think?

1. What do these statistics indicate about settlement patterns in Canada? What can you learn from statistics such as these regarding possible occupations of people?
2. Which areas have the highest employment rates? Which have the lowest?
3. How do employment rates reflect regional economic differences?

ETHNICITY—AS INDICATED BY MOTHER TONGUE

The following table will indicate something about the ethnicity of the provinces of Canada according to the mother tongue of the head of the family. (Reproduced by permission of the Minister of Supply and Services.)

Families by mother tongue of head, by province, 1971

Province or Territory	Total family heads	Mother tongue of family head					
		English		French		Other	
		No.	%	No.	%	No.	%
Newfoundland	108 135	106 125	98.1	970	0.9	1 040	1.
Prince Edward Island	24 260	22 230	91.6	1 665	6.9	365	1.
Nova Scotia	180 720	165 320	91.5	10 520	5.8	4 880	2.
New Brunswick	140 435	93 355	66.5	44 780	31.9	2 300	1.
Quebec	1 357 185	180 890	13.3	1 070 380	78.9	105 910	7.
Ontario	1 881 835	1 368 260	72.7	120 255	6.4	393 315	20.
Manitoba	235 995	142 665	60.5	14 905	6.3	78 425	33.
Saskatchewan	215 760	139 605	64.7	8 365	3.9	67 785	31.
Alberta	382 115	266 850	69.8	12 340	3.2	102 925	26.
British Columbia	533 630	412 035	77.2	11 500	2.2	110 095	20.
Yukon Territory and Northwest Territories	10 615	5 995	56.5	430	4.0	4 200	39.
Canada	5 070 680	2 903 325	57.3	1 296 105	25.6	871 250	17.

What do you think?

1. What languages do you think are included among the "other" percentages recorded here? Try to determine where the greatest concentrations of these "other" languages occur.
2. How do you think "mother tongue" might influence regional identity?

POPULATION BY PROVINCE

The following charts should tell you something about population distribution and growth patterns in Canada. (Reproduced by permission of the Minister of Supply and Services.) Canada Year Book 1975

Annual estimates of population, by province, as at June 1, 1966-74 (thousands)

Province or territory	Census 1966	Estimates 1967-70				Census 1971	Estimates 1972-74		
	1966	1967	1968	1969	1970	1971	1972	1973	1974
Newfoundland	493	499	506	514	517	522	532	541	542
Prince Edward Island	109	109	110	111	110	112	113	115	117
Nova Scotia	756	760	767	775	782	789	794	805	813
New Brunswick	617	620	625	628	627	635	642	652	662
Quebec	5 781	5 864	5 928	5 985	6 013	6 028	6 059	6 081	6 134
Ontario	6 961	7 127	7 262	7 385	7 551	7 703	7 825	7 939	8 094
Manitoba	963	963	971	979	983	988	992	998	1 011
Saskatchewan	955	957	960	958	941	926	916	908	907
Alberta	1 463	1 490	1 524	1 559	1 595	1 628	1 655	1 683	1 714
British Columbia	1 874	1 945	2 003	2 060	2 128	2 185	2 247	2 315	2 395
Yukon Territories	14	15	15	16	17	18	19	20	19
North West Territories	29	29	30	31	33	35	36	38	38
Canada	20 015	20 378	20 701	21 001	21 297	21 568	21 830	22 095	22 446

Components of population change, by province, 1961-66 and 1966-71

Province or territory	Total population change		Natural increase		Net migration	
	1961-66	1966-71	1961-66	1966-71	1961-66	1966-71
Newfoundland	35 543	28 708	59 577	49 096	−24 034	−20 388
Prince Edward Island	3 906	3 106	8 506	5 207	−4 600	−2 101
Nova Scotia	19 032	32 921	59 526	37 418	−40 494	−4 497
New Brunswick	18 852	17 769	53 229	35 233	−34 377	−17 464
Quebec	521 634	246 919	457 717	288 727	63 917	−41 808
Ontario	724 778	742 236	487 852	373 072	236 926	369 164
Manitoba	41 380	25 181	70 340	49 260	−28 960	−24 079
Saskatchewan	30 163	−29 102	75 691	50 867	−45 528	−79 969
Alberta	131 259	164 671	134 607	105 293	−3 348	59 378
British Columbia	244 592	310 947	104 103	88 494	140 489	222 453
Yukon Territory and Northwest Territories	5 494	10 075	6 745	6 720	−1 251	3 355
Canada	1 776 633	1 553 431	1 517 893	1 089 387	258 740	464 044

What do you think?

1. *Which provinces have the greatest population? Why might population be distributed as it is?*
2. *Look at the figures for net migration in the second chart. Which provinces lost people through migration in 1961-66? in 1966-71? Compare the two periods. Why might there be differences between the two periods?*

What do you think?

1. *What factors would you consider in identifying a region?*
2. *Given the information in these documents, draw a map to show how you would divide Canada into regions. What effect might other factors have on your breakdown?*
3. *Now that you have established your own regional breakdown of Canada, why do you think regionalism exists? What proof do you have to support your contention?*
4. *We have decided to treat British Columbia, the Prairie Provinces, Ontario, Quebec and the Atlantic Provinces as regions in this text. (We have not dealt with the North here at all since an entire volume in the* Canada: Issues and Options *series is dedicated to that region. For a detailed examination, see* The Canadian North: Source of Wealth or Vanishing Heritage?) *How does our breakdown differ from yours? Can you suggest reasons we might have had for ours?*

Case Study:
The Oil Debate
and Regionalism

3

The issue of energy supply and demand is at the heart of one of the most recent displays of regional sentiment in Canada. Since the Arab oil embargo was imposed in 1973, many Canadians have become concerned about the increasing cost and decreasing availability of foreign oil. Canada's own declining supplies and uncertainty about available reserves have led to intense debate over ownership of energy sources, cost and national self-sufficiency. Thus, oil is one of the most explosive issues affecting the Canadian federation today.

The oil debate is a very complex issue. Central to the problem is the fact that almost all of Canada's known oil sources are concentrated in one area. The way that region deals with its resources has an enormous impact on all other regions of Canada. As you read this case study, keep the following questions in mind: Why are provincial governments divided over the oil question? What role does the Federal Government play in the debate? In what ways does the debate reflect some of Canada's regional characteristics? To what extent should regional feelings be allowed to affect such an important issue? How could a national energy policy be a unifying force in Canada?

THE NATIONAL OIL POLICY

In 1961 the Federal Government introduced the National Oil Policy, a set of voluntary guidelines which suggested to the industry that the refinery needs of Quebec and the Atlantic Provinces should be supplied from offshore imports of crude oil and the refinery demand in the rest of Canada should be reserved for Canadian crude. The policy was intended to increase the production of Western Canadian oil. It saw expanding markets in the United States as an avenue for growth which at the same time would ensure the cheaper offshore crude to eastern Canada and maintain traditional supply relationships. The cost of imports in the east were to be largely offset by exports to the midwest and northwestern United States.

CANADA'S OIL SUPPLY: 1962-1972

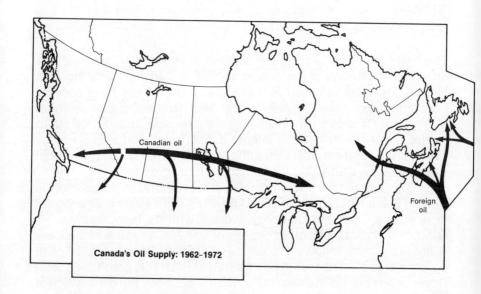

Canadian oil

Foreign oil

Canada's Oil Supply: 1962–1972

What do you think?

1. *Why was the outlined National Oil Policy acceptable in 1961? Who benefited and how?*
2. *Can you suggest any problems that could develop because of the 1961 National Oil Policy?*
3. *If you lived in the Maritimes in 1968, where would your oil and gasoline come from?*

OTTAWA FREEZES OIL PRICES

Maurice Cutler, the Ottawa Bureau Chief of Oilweek, *wrote the following informative article on the Trudeau government's introduction of a new oil policy for Canada for the September 10, 1973 issue of that magazine.*

"The pressure of events has forced me to move a little quicker."

That was how Energy Minister Donald Macdonald explained the Trudeau government's surprise announcement this week of a new oil policy for Canada, a policy that will transform oil marketing patterns in existence for more than a decade.

. . .

In an interview with Macdonald, *Oilweek* learned that the government was thinking of more than the request for a price freeze, the control of export prices and extension of the pipeline to Montreal.

. . .

He called the policy moves "a permanent structural change" in the Canadian oil market. Canada would reduce oil exports to the United States in order to serve Eastern Canadian markets now using offshore crude.

. . .

Outside the Commons, Prime Minister Trudeau said the government was taking the actions on oil because "the entire petroleum industry in the world is experiencing an upheaval."

"Prices of petroleum products, including gasoline and home heating oil, in Canada today, have reached the point at which the government believes immediate measures are required to stabilize the action of the market place in the interest of consumers and the rational development of Canadian industry," he told Parliament.

Macdonald was philosophical about industry reaction to the proposals. He said it would probably be hostile and that he didn't expect "there will be wild enthusiasm in Calgary". The province of Alberta, he added, "will have some rather fixed ideas about this."

He conceded that the re-ordering of Canadian oil marketing will have profound effects on the exploration for new reserves, the construction of new refineries and super ports designed to accommodate tankers carrying offshore crude.

The industry, Macdonald said, "will probably pause, gasp and reflect on the kind of return they are going to get." This will be reflected, he said, in development plans made during the recent upsurge in industry financial health, particularly those relating to tar sands extraction and frontier exploration.

"But we wanted to prevent a situation where the refineries were taking advantage of market uncertainties to increase their margins," Macdonald said.

. . .

"We decided to take this action because Canadian producers have been doing very well in the last year. We wanted to ensure that the Canadian consumer gets some protection. We've asked the industry to exercise this restraint to enable us to take legislative action to deal with the supply of oil from Western Canada."

On the subject of insulating Canadian consumers from the effects of U.S. demand, Macdonald conceded that there was "no way we can insulate Canadian consumers from all international market influences. The intention is to help even out the bumps in international marketing trends."

While Trudeau mentioned an export tax or a national oil marketing board, Macdonald indicated that the latter was the more likely method. The proposed board would buy . . . at Canadian prices and then sell in the world market at the highest possible prices. The difference between the purchase and the selling price would go back to the provinces, producers and consumers, although details on how this is to be accomplished have not yet been worked out.

It would be unlikely that the province of Alberta would be a loser. It would probably get at least as much of a return as it now gets in royalties and taxes. The board would serve as the collector of greater "economic rent", a role proposed in the recent energy analysis for the suggested national petroleum corporation.

. . .

The Canadian domestic price would reflect the international offshore price, apparently on the assumption that the U.S. price would stay higher because of the difficult supply situation facing that country.

What is meant by?

"royalties"

What do you think?

1. *Explain how the new federal oil policy intends to deal with the energy problem.*
2. *Why did the Federal Government introduce this policy?*
3. *How might Albertans respond to this policy? Why?*
4. *How would this policy affect your area? Would the policy be acceptable to you? Why or why not?*

ARE THE DAYS OF ABUNDANT AND CHEAP OIL OVER?

Some of the political aspects of the energy debate were examined by Jack McArthur, a financial analyst for the Toronto Star *on September 18, 1973. (Reprinted with permission—The* Toronto Star.*)*

The Liberal Party's political fencebuilding program in the Prairie West is a shambles. Deep divisions and misunderstandings are abroad in Canada. And national policy concerning the oil, natural gas and refining industry has collapsed into a collection of extremely difficult and unpleasant tangents.

. . .

Reacting to Ottawa's decisions, Alberta Premier Peter Lougheed ominously threatens a response which "some will call un-Canadian".

Alberta Liberal Leader Robert Russell wonders bitterly why radical anti-inflationary federal controls on product marketing have leaned heavily on western-originated products like oil, gasoline, beef, wheat, and bread.

The implication is that Ottawa knows it can win few votes in the West; that it's protecting its image in the 619 product-consuming areas of Ontario and Quebec.

Try to understand the bitterness look at oil.

For the moment—a major, patchwork change is inevitable—this is Ottawa's policy:

Canadian crude oil will be sold more cheaply to Canadian refineries than those in the U.S. Ottawa is thinking about supplying more Canadian refineries with the Canadian product and cutting exports to the U.S., thus widening the area in which western oil must be sold more cheaply.

Meanwhile, the additional revenue received from sales to the U.S. goes as a kind of tax to Ottawa, rather than to the companies (which might spend it to seek more oil and natural gas) or to the provinces, Alberta primarily, which own the natural resources.

Ottawa has arm-twisted the refiners, which have added 5 cents a gallon to gasoline prices in Ontario this year. They have agreed to freeze prices for a while. Presumably the federal government in those few months will try to figure a more workable policy . . .

But several things should be said:

—If you want to keep companies from making excess profits, you generally tax the profits. You don't juggle hamhandedly and hurriedly with markets and prices.

—If you want more of Canada served by a Canadian-produced product, depressing the price of that product does not seem likely to encourage the increased supplies needed.

—If you want special subsidies in order to keep deserving cases from being injured by high prices, you single out the deserving and aim at them. You don't introduce sweeping measures in which subsidies can't be controlled or measured; and which have massive and uncertain side effects.

What do you think?

1. Why should Alberta premier Peter Lougheed "threaten a response 'which some will call un-Canadian'"? Can you suggest what that

response might be? Why might it be considered "un-Canadian"?
2. *According to McArthur, why are Westerners angry at the Liberals?*
3. *Do you feel the Westerners had a right to be upset? Why or why not?*

WHICH WOLF ATTACKING WHICH SHEEP?

Gordon Gibson, then a Liberal Member of Parliament from British Columbia, wrote the following article which appeared in the Ottawa Citizen *on September 21, 1973.*

. . . When we talk of export controls on oil, the question is definitely not one of supply. The requirements of the National Energy Board leave no worry on that score for the time being, especially with the enormous reserves of the oil sands coming on stream.

There are three main points at issue. The first is price, which is dear to the heart of the consumer.

The second is who gets the enormous windfall profits that have been and will be made on oil sitting in the ground, which is dear to the heart of the international oil executive.

The third point is a power struggle for control over petroleum policy between the federal and provincial governments, which can generate more bitterness than the other two together.

If we just exported oil, we would want the price to be as high as possible, and vice versa if we just imported. The trouble is we do both, exporting in the West and importing in the East.

. . .

. . . Even our domestic price has to be high enough to return a reasonable profit to the oil producers, if we want to ensure future supply.

. . .

Now the price world has been turned upside down by the Arabs and shortages in the U.S.

Western oil is now competitive with world prices, and can be economically produced for less than we can get in the U.S. market. We want to charge the highest price there we can, but should the Canadian consumer have to match that? The federal government has decided on a lower price for Canadians, but let's leave the exact mechanism for a minute.

The second issue is windfall profits. Western oil, which was economic to produce in the $3 area a year ago, has gone up by 95 cents since then. Costs have not risen, so that is all profit.

There are around 10 billion barrels of proven reserves in western Canada, without counting the oil sands. Somebody's asset has gone up by almost $10 billion.

It is not your and my profit gentle readers. We Canadians do not own our own oil, and under the present system, even the Alberta government doesn't get much benefit. They take a royalty of around 22 per cent, and the federal government sometimes gets some tax revenue, at best at a $1/_3$ effective rate because of depletion provisions, and at worst nothing at all (or indefinite deferment) because of other tax expense rules.

The oil producers get most of that $10 billion windfall, and while exact figures aren't available, about two thirds of it accrues to foreign owners. Maybe the energy crisis isn't costing the Americans so much after all.

Now comes the fun. Alberta gets a bit twitchy at this situation, and raises royalties somewhat—from around 16 per cent, up to the area of 22 or 23 per cent. But they want to keep exploration going, and particularly they want to keep a favorable climate for the development of the oil sands, the unquestioned key to the next industrial boom in that province.

The federal government gets super twitchy, because they want to keep prices down to fight inflation, and because many in the government and the NDP feel more than slightly nationalistic about all those windfall profits going to foreigners.

The result of the mixture is a collision course. One way to capture the windfall profits is to raise royalties, but the province has already made its move there, taking only a small percentage. And on the other hand, higher royalties mean higher prices to Canadians.

The federal government then stepped in, using its power over exports, to say in effect: "The domestic price stays the same, but we're going to charge 40 cents a barrel extra to foreign buyers, and pocket the difference."

Alberta is outraged. First of all, they are not getting the extra 40 cents in the Canadian market they might have received if Ottawa hadn't stepped in. And worse, they aren't getting the extra foreign revenues.

. . .

. . . The benefits, as matters now stand, go to the Canadian public as a whole. Ottawa now has to make explicit the mechanism it is going to use if it wishes to maintain the two price system. That in itself is a subject for debate, but assuming it for now, Ottawa has two basic choices.

The first is to impose an "export tax" on oil exports. . . .

With the export tax, the benefit goes to the general consumer, because the tax holds the domestic price of the commodity below world prices by the amount of the tax. The cost goes to the producer.

What is causing so much trouble here is that the producers are largely concentrated in one province, and virtually completely in the west. Is it fair to ask the west to subsidize the national consumer in this way?

Some say "yes", because Alberta has had a protected market—in fact a subsidy from eastern Canada for the last dozen years—and should show some appreciation for that.

The west says that that is very nice, but how about the subsidy we've been paying in the form of high price tariff protected goods to look after the central Canada manufacturer since Confederation.

Half of the answer is relatively easy. Surely the province is entitled to the royalties they would otherwise have collected on the export differential. They are also entitled to some share—how much is arguable—of the windfall profits which would otherwise have gone to the producing companies as a result of the higher export price.

. . .

The other half of Alberta's "loss"—the lower price paid by Canadians on domestic consumption—is more complicated. If that were to be fully compensated, out of federal revenues collected from the same consumer who is supposed to be saving the same amount of money on the oil, it becomes economic nonsense.

The answer may be that in effect the producing companies will see little if any future windfall profits, and that instead they will be divided between the consumer and governments.

The companies deserve a fair profit, quite apart from our interest in seeing continued exploration. But at some stage, the increase in the value of the resources has to belong to the people.

What do you think?

1. *What does Mr. Gibson claim are the three main points at issue in the controversy about oil exports?*
2. *How do the profits of oil companies influence future supplies of energy?*
3. *Do you agree with Mr. Gibson's conclusions? Why or why not?*
4. *What, if anything, in this article indicates that energy might be a regional issue?*

ALBERTA PLAYS A TRUMP CARD

The Ottawa Citizen *on October 5, 1973 tried editorially to propose how the Federal Government should approach the oil-producing provinces.*

Mr. Lougheed can be expected, with his proposed tax, to pick up the difference between the price of Alberta oil delivered in Ontario and the now high-priced offshore crude east of here. In the U.S., where offshore oil prices are shooting still higher, he can expect Alberta oil to remain competitive even with the new Alberta royalties tacked on to the new federal surtax.

Yet Ottawa, already on extremely weak ground in its dealing with Alberta, can't afford to let Mr. Lougheed get away with it. Not now—while a promised freeze on oil and gas prices is one of the few anti-inflation weapons the federal government has managed to offer Canadian consumers.

The federal government landed in this mess because it got greedy. It tried to give Canadians a buffer against rising prices and at the same time, without a by-your-leave to Alberta, to cream off for its own coffers the windfall tax profits from the province's chief resource.

It's time now to pull back from that unhappy position. Ottawa owes it to Canadian consumers, just as it owes it to Alberta, to get back to the bargaining table—with an offer to return to Alberta the major portion of the revenue from its new oil tax. In return it would be entitled to ask Alberta to defer its threatened legislation.

What do you think?

1. *In what way did the proposed Alberta royalty create problems with the Federal Government's oil policy?*
2. *Who should benefit from the windfall profits created by rising world oil prices? Why?*
3. *Is Alberta's policy justifiable? Explain your response.*
4. *Do you feel the solution suggested in this editorial is realistic? Why or why not?*

MIDDLE EAST ANNOUNCES OIL LIMITATIONS

The October 22, 1973 issue of Oilweek *carried the following story:*

Although the federal government has been talking about the security of Canada's energy supplies for some months now, that phrase suddenly gained a new urgency last week in light of the dizzying pace of events in the Middle East.

Coming in rapid succession, three announcements from the Arab States added yet another element of uncertainty to the world's precarious energy equation.

They were:
The Arab states would drastically raise the price of crude exports; Exports to Countries "Friendly to Israel" in the current conflict would be subject to progressive monthly cuts of 5 per cent; Saudi Arabia, the world's largest oil producing nation, would immediately cut back production by 10 per cent and threatened to completely cut off supplies to the United States.

While the impact of these developments on Canada is uncertain, it appears likely that these developments could have the following results: Petroleum products east of the Ottawa Valley, where supply consists entirely of imported crude, will be subject to price increases of as much as 4 cents per gallon. The latest round of crude price increases by the 11 Arab States is expected to raise the price of crude imported to Montreal by about $1.25 per barrel. In line with the terms of the price freeze on petroleum prices laid down earlier by the federal government, producers would be allowed to pass on the extra costs of imported crude to consumers subject to approval by Energy Minister Macdonald.

The federal government will be under increased pressure to ensure the security of oil supplies to areas east of the Ottawa Valley line. Extending the Interprovincial Pipeline to Montreal has suddenly become a much more attractive proposition, although Quebec politicians in the midst of a provincial election campaign are unhappy with the prospect. Ottawa can also be expected to begin looking in earnest for a new long-term arrangement for supplies from countries such as Venezuela.

The arguments for new incentives for exploration and the construction of new energy projects such as the Mackenzie Valley pipeline have also been enhanced by the current difficulties.

What do you think?

1. *If you lived in Quebec in the late months of 1973 how would you have reacted to the increase in the price for crude petroleum? Why?*
2. *How will "the psychological effects" of this situation influence relations between the provinces and the Federal Government?*

WHERE CANADIAN OIL GOES

The information for this map comes from Oilweek *magazine February 16, 1976.*

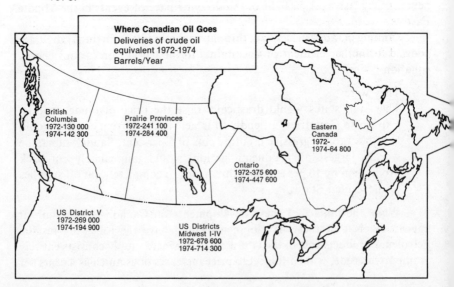

Where Canadian Oil Goes
Deliveries of crude oil equivalent 1972-1974 Barrels/Year

British Columbia
1972-130 000
1974-142 300

Prairie Provinces
1972-241 100
1974-284 400

Eastern Canada
1972-
1974-64 800

Ontario
1972-375 600
1974-447 600

US District V
1972-269 000
1974-194 900

US Districts
Midwest I-IV
1972-678 600
1974-714 300

What do you think?

1. *How will the changes in distribution of Canadian oil and the lack of cheap foreign imports affect the relationship between oil-producing and oil-consuming provinces?*

THE GREATEST DANGER: PROVINCIAL REGIONALISM

W. A. Wilson, an Ottawa-based columnist for the Montreal Star *cautioned in an article on December 17, 1973 against a too-vigorous regional reaction to the energy question.*

The divisiveness of the oil problem in this country is basic and it does not arise from the peripheral aspects of the issue.

It comes from the fact that, on one hand, the governments of Alberta and Saskatchewan have conveyed the clear impression that they see the period of shortage as a form of leverage to use for at least long-term and perhaps even short-term political and economic gain. Much of the rest of the country inevitably sees the same period in terms of serious inconvenience and entertains increasing fears of real economic danger.

These two outlooks are almost as far apart as those of the Arab governments and the American administration. They are bridgeable, but only with effort. That is the nub of the problem.

There is obviously some willingness to spread price increases—"phase them in" is the current term—but it seems quite clear that both Alberta and Saskatchewan want to secure world prices for their oil within, say, the next year or so. The world price is a reflection both of economic factors and of oil's role as a weapon used to secure certain political advantages. The two Western governments argue that world prices prevail for other commodities and should for oil. A basic flaw mars this analogy.

There is a great deal of difference between letting scarcity establish price levels for a commodity where supply can be expected to respond before long to high prices and doing the same thing where there are absolute limits on supply, or where artificial ones can be successfully imposed. . . . To whatever extent normal market forces are allowed to operate, improved supply will moderate the high prices that drew it forth.

This is not the case, however, where there are either natural or effective, artificial limits on supply, as in the case of oil. Then, charging all that the traffic will bear goes beyond the justifiable operation of market forces and earns a different label. We were quite familiar with it during the Second World War. The label is profiteering. The higher price in these cases cannot draw forth increased supplies. . . .

Premier Blakeney finds it "a little remarkable" that the federal government wants the price of oil to bear some relationship to the cost of producing it. What on earth does he think the argument about food costs in supermarkets has been all about? The supermarkets suffer serious unpopularity because the conviction is so widespread that some of them have tried to charge all the traffic will bear and failed to relate prices to costs.

. . .

The Western provinces feel that they have some grievances and, because this is deeply and sincerely felt, it demands the attention of the rest of the country. But they have, in the first place, already driven this message home in the right way; by refusing to elect members of the governing party, the clearest of all ways to signal dissatisfaction. In the second place, an effort to come to grips with their grievances has already started. Freight rates rank high on the Western list of dissatisfactions and a mass of individual rates already is under intensive study to give Messrs. Blakeney and Lougheed a chance to prove their case.

. . . Finally, it would come as a relief if someday a Western spokesman, complaining about freight rates, would at least nod in the direction of all the decades during which the below-cost Crowsnest Pass rates have subsidized Prairie grain shipments.

The Lougheed-Blakeney proposition that the oil shortage can be used as an occasion to wrest "concessions" from the rest of Canada may be correct as a power equation. There is, however, another part of the equation: the bitterness that would accompany the effort.

What do you think?

1. *According to Mr. Wilson, what are "legitimate" Western claims?*
2. *Which are not legitimate?*
3. *How has the Alberta-Saskatchewan policy affected the rest of Canada? Why?*
4. *What differences can you find between Mr. Wilson's arguments and those of Western writers which have appeared in this section? How would you account for the different approaches?*
5. *Can you find any similarities between the arguments of Western leaders and the leaders of Quebec?*

THE DANGER BECOMES A REALITY

This article by Hartley Steward appeared in the Toronto Star *on December 15, 1973.*

John Poyen received a copy of [a] bumper sticker at his Calgary office. There was no accompanying letter, no signature, only a big sticker, in bold capital letters: Let the Eastern bastards freeze in the dark!

Poyen does not, he will tell you, quickly, subscribe to the hyperbolic sticker message, but he wasn't surprised to receive one.

"Oh, there have always been rednecks in Calgary," he says. "And I have no doubt there are those who believe exactly the sentiments expressed in that silly sticker. But to think it reflects a widespread Western view? That's Eastern conceit coming out. Only the tiniest minority here believes that.

And Calgarians in the street and in the pubs and shops were reacting to the publicity given the stickers with either a chuckle at Eastern naiveté (Do they really think we feel like that?) or with genuine disgust that such a thing as cutting off Eastern supplies would be suggested.

The mood in Alberta seems to be not so much one of strong anti-Eastern feelings, but merely strong pro-Western sentiment.

"Let's not be silly," says Doug Thompson, a Gulf Oil employee. "Nobody out here wants to let anyone in the East freeze. What we want, and what we expect our government to get for us, is a price that will keep the industry active and growing. So we'll all have jobs.

Charles Dunkley, senior vice-president of Dome Petroleum had this to say. "It's not a matter of resentment or getting back at the East on our part. It's a matter of getting a price for oil that will keep the companies here and exploring for more oil so the industry will grow and there will be jobs.

That's what Albertans are worried about."

The Canadian Petroleum Association's John Poyen puts the average Albertan's mood this way:

"Well, we've been discriminated against because of geography for a long time—paying prices for most goods made in the East. That's the way it is. We haven't asked to be subsidized. Now, we've got something the East wants and needs and we're going to get everything that's coming to us.

"It's not resentment. Hell, it's business."

What do you think?

1. *How do you account for the extreme Western resentment expressed in the bumper sticker?*
2. *How do you react to the point of view expressed by John Poyen? Why?*

WILL TALKING SOLVE THE PROBLEM?

After the Dominion-Provincial Energy Conference was held in January 1974, Joan Fraser provided the following analysis for the Financial Times of Canada *on January 28, 1974.*

It will be a major miracle if Canada's 11 governments reach sane solutions to all the problems left unresolved by last week's energy conference in time for their self-imposed March 31 deadline.

The basic questions are all interrelated, and all relate ultimately to money and therefore to political power.

They are complicated by regional disparity and—to a remarkable degree—by ideology.

The immediate problem, of course, is the price of oil in Canada after April 1. Following inevitably from that are the division of revenues between Ottawa, the provinces and industry; the course of Canada's economy, decisions on pipelines running both north-south and east-west; arguments about how to achieve self-sufficiency in energy (and indeed, whether that is possible before the 1990s); whether Canada's political philosophy will take a lurch to the left, and whether the reins of power will slip from Toronto's, Montreal's and even Ottawa's hands. . . .

Oil policy and pricing also have implications for other energy sources. A natural gas policy, for example, should logically resemble oil policy in a good many aspects. And the development of coal and nuclear power will be influenced by the price of rival energy forms.

Then there is the whole question of quid pro quos—what will central Canada give the West in the way of industrial and transport concessions to compensate for keeping the domestic price of oil down? Will the concessions be enough to change the country's basic economic patterns, as the West hopes? And what about marketing boards for oil and gas?

It has been a long time since such fundamental parts of the Canadian fabric were at stake.

What is meant by?

"ideology"
"quid pro quos"

What do you think?

1. *What does "It has been a long time since such fundamental parts of the Canadian fabric were at stake" imply?*
2. *Do you feel the situation has proven as serious as Joan Fraser thought it would be? Why or why not?*
3. *Why are energy questions "complicated by regional disparity"?*

WANTED—LONG TERM STABILITY

The Kingston Whig-Standard, *in an editorial entitled "Oil and Canadian disunity" March 27, 1974, summed up the mood of many Canadians about the whole question of energy policy.*

The situation in oil illustrates the outstanding Canadian dilemma—the failure of the country to act nationally because of the determination of the provinces to insist on every scrap of constitutional power to which they are entitled. Wealth in this country has traditionally been concentrated in the East. Now the Western provinces are finding themselves with bonanzas of petroleum and other natural resources in a time of acute shortage. With long memories of freight-rate injustices and a general disposition on the part of the East to discriminate against the West, the Prairie provinces are intent on getting some of their own back.

In the meantime, this country, impaired by other internal troubles such as the nationalism of Quebec, and by the increasing restiveness caused by unsatisfatory economic relations with the United States, staggers on from crisis to crisis. Canadian national unity has never been so necessary—nor so apparently remote.

What do you think?

1. What is the "outstanding Canadian dilemma"?
2. Do you feel more a part of Canada than a part of your province? Why?

IT'S NOT OVER YET

Another aspect of the natural resources question is discussed in this Canadian Press article which appeared in newspapers on May 17, 1974.

Alberta has served notice it will vigorously fight a massive petro-chemical development planned for Sarnia, Ontario, that Premier Peter Lougheed says will damage his province's attempt to set up its own petro-chemical industry.

In a policy statement delivered in the legislature Thursday, Lougheed opposed the proposed $250 million Petrosar Ltd. plant in Sarnia on the grounds that it will hurt Alberta.

"It will jeopardize the possibility of new jobs in Alberta from petro-chemical development as it will absorb a significant portion of the limited available Canadian market and render Alberta-based plans less feasible."

Alberta's position might set off another round of federal-provincial feuding since the Petrosar consortium is controlled by Polysar Ltd., a federal Crown Corporation.

The petrochemical industry, using Alberta natural resources, has been centred in Sarnia and Montreal but Lougheed said he doesn't want to cripple existing plants in the east that are dependent on Alberta for raw resources.

"Our policies contemplate a continued viable Ontario petrochemical industry based on maintaining existing facilities and normal growth using Alberta resources."

But Alberta wants to make a start on getting the thousands of jobs possible through processing petrochemicals and using them to make numerous plastic-based products ranging from garbage bags to toys. The premier emphasized that Alberta must seize the opportunity to diversify its economy.

Otherwise, "we accept the risk that creation of new jobs will decline as the conventional petroleum industry headquartered in Alberta and its related services begin to level off.

"The area of petrochemicals offers a promising opportunity for Alberta now. There is a need for new facilities in Canada to serve Canadian markets now and Canadian markets are the key because of the high tariff barriers facing exporters." . . .

Ottawa thinks the market can support three plants, while Alberta feels there will be demand for only two.

What do you think?

1. *Who made the decision about where the Petrosar plant should be located? Why?*
2. *Why was Premier Lougheed so concerned about this decision?*
3. *Where do you think the major petrochemical plant should have been built? Why?*

A NEW TEST OF NATIONAL UNITY

Charles Lynch, a senior journalist for the Southam Newspapers outlined, in December 1973, the recent developments and their consequences for the nation, especially for those residents who lived east of the Ottawa Valley.

After all our government has done to ensure equal opportunity for all Canadians, along come the Arabs and the Venezuelans with decrees that make second-class citizens of every Canadian living east of the Ottawa Valley line.

What it means, as things stand is that people who live in Eastern Ontario, Quebec and the Atlantic Provinces will be paying 20 cents a gallon more for gasoline and fuel oil than Canadians who live in the rest of the country.

Energy Minister Donald Macdonald . . . says "it is almost impossible to operate a market with this kind of differential". What he means is that it is almost impossible to operate a country under such conditions, with Canadians in one section paying 50 per cent more to heat their homes than other Canadians pay. It's another case of the "haves" getting richer and the "have nots" getting poorer.

The problem is one of equalization, a question to which assorted federal governments have addressed themselves over the years, redistributing billions of dollars in the process. We have gone so far down the equalization road that the principle has become a central fact of Canadian nationhood, more deeply entrenched than anything in our constitution.

Mr. Macdonald makes clear . . . that some formula must be found to subsidize eastern consumers.

Yet such a subsidy would be so costly that even the federal government, which deals in boxcar figures, is aghast at the prospect. To bring eastern gasoline and fuel oil prices down to the levels set for the balance of the winter in the rest of the country would involve payments on a scale never contemplated before, in the long history of equalization transfers, from the "haves" to the "have nots".

[Mr. Macdonald] feels a price differential of, say, 10 cents a gallon is tolerable—not pleasant but tolerable. Beyond that, it becomes intolerable—a burden that the people of Quebec and the Atlantic provinces should not be asked to carry, while their brethren elsewhere are paying so much less. What it may add up to is frozen prices west of the Ottawa Valley, and frozen people east of there.

What do you think?

1. *Why does it cost Maritimers so much more for their petroleum products?*
2. *Should there be such a difference in price between East and West? Why?*
3. *What effect, if any, does such a price difference have on national unity?*

ALBERTA HAS FORGOTTEN THAT WE INVENTED HER

Harry Bruce, once a Halifax-based journalist, wrote the following article, "Alberta has forgotten that we invented her" (November 22, 1974) which offers an important Maritime perspective. (Reprinted with permission— The Toronto Star.)

The oil is there in Alberta by reason of what insurance people call an act of God. Albertans did not put it there. Albertans, when they settled their countryside, did not even know about it. Albertans, by themselves, did not even bring it out of the ground. The Americans did most of that.

"Oil parasites" is too strong a label to paste on Albertans. Nor can we call them camp followers, for it was the oil camp that followed them. Let us just say they're lucky to live where they live and that, judging by their premier, their luck has not made them foolishly generous.

They used to be just about as poor as us Maritimers, you know. Before the oil boom Alberta was just another one of your average have-not provinces and remember, the boom began a mere 27 years ago.

The oil gave Alberta sudden wealth and a convenient memory. Maybe people who win million-dollar lotteries also find parts of their past easy to forget.

Alberta, of course, hasn't much past anyway. Not as a province of Canada. We invented her, really, and helped people her, too. By "we" I mean Ontario and Quebec and the old Maritime provinces who got together to form Canada in 1867.

It was our Parliament, the Canadian Parliament, that created the province of Alberta in 1905. That was little more than a generation before the oil boom. The romance of European immigration rightly dominates prairie history these days but it was our people, eastern Canadian people, who provided the bulk of Alberta's first settlers.

Like Premier Peter Lougheed's Nova Scotia forebears, they left family behind in the East—and therefore I like to think they would not have approved bumper stickers urging, "Let the eastern bastards freeze in the dark". The stickers are products of the new Alberta, and so is the oil.

The old Alberta (or, at least, the somewhat older Alberta) faced general bankruptcy in the '30s, and, of course, you know who bailed her out, don't you? Yes, it was the federal government with tax revenue from people across the country including eastern bastards.

And that was only a dozen-odd years before the great days of Alberta oil. Now, however, Albertans often talk about their oil the way British Columbians talk about their weather, as though its existence were somehow proof of their own excellence.

"We've got oil," they seem to say, "because we deserve oil. Perhaps the rest of you are simply not worthy of its marvellous, economy-fattening, account-swelling, larder-filling and life-giving benefits."

This attitude may be part of the reason why Premier Lougheed reacted as he did to the federal government's budget news that it intends to tax the oil industry to benefit all Canadians.

With a truly Texan mastery of the art of hyperbole, Lougheed said Alberta was now the victim of "the biggest rip-off of any province that ever occurred in the history of Confederation". (Some Nova Scotians still insist the biggest rip-off in the history of Confederation was Confederation itself but even they might concede that Lougheed, for a young prairie pup, demon-strates a flair for Ottawa-knocking.)

Alberta insists the British North America Act gives it exclusive rights to tax the petroleum industry. Alberta oil, in other words, is Alberta's oil. It is not Canada's, nor partly Canada's. It is all Alberta's.

A few naive questions:

What's happening to that shining northern experiment in happy, side-by-side survival that we used to insist was so wonderfully Canadian?

What does "Canada" mean if Canadians in one spot exploit provincial rights and an accident of nature to grow ever more rich at the expense of Canadians who are already much poorer than they are?

What does "Canadian nationalism" mean if the real threat is not the gargantuan outside influence of the U.S., but, rather, the sour inside influence of provincial meanness?

Are we now on the road to becoming just a bunch of nasty, squabbling, little half-countries? Will P.E.I. apply for entry to the United Nations?

Consider the sovereign states of Alberta, British Columbia, Quebec and, if they strike it rich offshore, of Nova Scotia and Newfoundland, too. Maybe even Ontario will want to go it alone.

For a rich personage, Ontario has always been awfully keen on Confed-eration but, what the heck, Canada's only okay if you're poor. Once you're well-to-do who needs it? It's a drag.

What do you think?

1. According to Mr. Bruce what is "provincial meanness"?
2. How do you account for Mr. Bruce's attitude to Alberta?
3. How do you respond to this article? Why?

NOVA SCOTIA'S "LOVE-AFFAIR WITH ALBERTA"

In October 1976 the editor of the Halifax Chronicle-Herald *declared:*

. . .The best place for Atlantic Canada to line up is four-square with Alberta and force a new deal within Confederation . . . if Ontario wants Atlantic Canada to line up on her team then Ontario should be committed to a new and more equal deal for all partners within Confederation.

When Alberta was dirt poor not long ago she looked in vain to Ottawa and Toronto for assistance. Far from help what Alberta got was the same thing the Atlantic provinces now get—lots of advice, lots of surveys and lots of condescending pity as the better folks wondered why those shiftless Albertans didn't get off their rear ends and do something.

What do you think?

1. According to the Chronicle-Herald, *what does Alberta have in common with Nova Scotia?*
2. Do you agree with this editorial? Why?
3. How can you account for the difference between the points of view expressed in Mr. Bruce's article (p.37.) and this editorial?

GAS PRICE HIKES—ARE THEY FAIR?

The Toronto Star *editorialized on July 3, 1973 on the Alberta government's decision to raise natural gas prices that June. (Reprinted with permission—The* Toronto Star.)

Natural gas prices went up by as much as $5 a year for the average residential consumer in Ontario last week, and he may not have heard the last of it by any means.

A hearing that could foreshadow further bad news for Ontario users starts tomorrow when the province of Alberta asks its own Energy Conservation Board to increase the price of gas now flowing—under a two-year old contract—to Ontario.

The gas, produced by Consolidated Natural Gas Co., was originally destined for United States markets until the National Energy Board decided there were not enough surplus reserves in Alberta to justify such exports. It was then diverted to eastern Canada through a contract with TransCanada PipeLines Ltd.

Alberta is challenging the validity of the contract switch and, as a first shot in its battle to win higher prices for its gas resources, will attempt to have the price increased or the deal nullified.

Ontario, in its turn, will argue tomorrow that the Alberta Energy Conservation Board has no right to rule on the disposition of gas once it has been given the okay for removal out of the province.

Whatever the outcome of these hearings, the case likely will go on to the Supreme Court of Alberta. And whatever the outcome of that, the unalterable fact will remain: In the absence of federal government leadership, in the absence of a national energy policy designed to ensure the owners of natural resources a fair return and the Canadian consumers of those resources a fair price, Canadians in the West and East can expect to be at each other's throats for some time to come.

There's no doubt that Albertans deserve a far better return for their natural gas. At the same time, Ontario users should not be expected to pay exorbitantly high prices based on critical shortages in the United States.

Overall, it's ludicrous that two provinces should find themselves court-room adversaries on a matter of domestic trade. The arbiter of such a disagreement should be the federal government.

What do you think?

1. *Who should decide where Alberta gas is sent? Why?*
2. *How do you think the case of gas pricing might have affected Alberta's attitude towards Confederation? Why?*
3. *Why are Alberta and Ontario at odds over the energy question?*

GASOLINE PRICES 1972-1976

Regular Gasoline Prices 1972-1976

	Tank Wagon Price		Federal Sales & Excise Taxes		Dealer Mark-up		Pump Price	
	1976	1972	1976	1972	1976	1972	1976	1972
St. John's	43.0	23.7	13.9	2.7	10.3	10.5	92.2	61.9
Saint John	41.5	22.4	13.9	2.5	7.8	10.0	80.4	54.9
Charlottetown	43.6	24.3	13.9	2.7	10.5	8.5	89.0	56.5
Halifax	41.7	22.4	13.9	2.5	11.5	8.5	86.2	54.5
Montreal	59.8	22.6	13.9	2.5	7.5	8.8	79.9	50.9
Toronto	42.2	22.0	13.9	2.4	8.1	10.5	80.9	53.9
Winnipeg	41.0	23.0	13.9	2.6	7.8	10.3	78.3	52.9
Regina	40.1	23.0	13.9	2.6	13.0	8.3	79.9	54.9
Edmonton	40.1	22.2	13.9	2.5	13.9	11.2	77.9	49.9
Vancouver	40.7	22.8	13.9	2.5	8.5	11.6	76.9	51.9

What do you think?

1. *Based on gasoline prices, where is the best place to live in Canada? Why?*
2. *What regions might be more likely to complain about gasoline prices? How might Alberta's stand on oil affect them?*

What do you think?

1. Why are the federal and provincial governments divided over the energy question? What argument does each side give to justify its position?
2. How does the oil debate reflect regional differences? Explain your point of view.
3. How much influence should regional demands have on important issues like energy supply?
4. Could the government's energy policy be a force for unity in Canada? What problems would it solve? not solve?
5. What effect might the oil debate have on regional perceptions of Confederation? Does this debate suggest it may be necessary to reconsider the present day Confederation arrangement? How might a reconsidered Confederation deal with problems like energy?

The Contemporary Problem

4

The issue of Quebec separatism has attracted a great deal of attention in Canada throughout the 1960s and the 1970s. In the 1970s particularly, as this problem has become more acute, other regions of Canada have become more vocal in voicing their concern about regional problems. In this section, we will examine aspects of contemporary regional dissatisfaction in Canada and see how some federalists have tried to deal with regional protest.

Regionalism is a real issue in Canada partly because of the widely divergent views and attitudes specific regions hold about their roles in federal Canada. What are these different points of view? What demands and grievances grow out of these points of view? To what extent do these demands and grievances accurately reflect the problems that affect each region? Why are some regions and provinces more aggressive in making their concerns known? What kinds of alternatives and options are proposed to improve the situation?

BRITISH COLUMBIA

Geographically, British Columbia is separated from the rest of Canada by the Rocky Mountains. This geographical isolation combined with the great wealth of the area, has resulted in a distinct identity and way of life for British Columbians. This section will examine B.C.'s response to its place within Confederation, its perception of itself and other regions, and the nature of its demands and grievances as a "have" province.

SEPARATION IS OLD STUFF IN B.C.

British Columbia, like other parts of Canada, responded to the "Quebec Question" during the 1960s and early 1970s. Donald Stainsby, writing for Saturday Night (April 1964), made the following comments.

While Canada as a whole stands mesmerized by the upsurge of separatism in the province of Quebec, what is in many ways the most separatist unit of all, the province of British Columbia, continues to be ignored.

British Columbia has never really been a part of Canada at all, in the sense of belonging. It has stood outside the Canadian story from the beginning, and its attempts to join the Canadian mainstream—such as it is—have been steadfastly rebuffed, perhaps unconsciously.

This has been ably demonstrated in the last two issues of *Saturday Night*. An exchange of letters in the February issue between a Quebecker, Roger Lemelin, and "another" Canadian gained considerable impact from the apparent differences in locales and backgrounds of the correspondents. . . . The implication was that these two men, writing each other from the two "most different" parts of Canada, would have the greatest possible gulf between them.

Yet the deeper truth is that while these two parts are very different from the rest of Canada, *they are different in the same way*. Quebec and British Columbia could, as a matter of fact, understand one another very well if they ever set about doing it. . . .

British Columbia is a motherland. The reason is simple. It got its own start, had its own history, and developed its own way of life before it— somewhat reluctantly—joined Confederation. The superficial differences of language obscure the similarity of outlook that British Columbia shares with Quebec; and that very difference of language is a complicating factor which makes Quebec perhaps not the best comparison for the British Columbia condition. . . .

The differences between B.C. and Canada will remain so vast that I sometimes doubt whether they will ever be bridged. They result partly from B.C.'s youth. This province in many ways is still frontier country. The differences are also partly a result of geography. The Rocky Mountains remain at least a psychological barrier between B.C. and Canada, while, at the same time B.C.'s pride in empire has restricted its intercourse with the neighbouring American states of Oregon and Washington.

But overriding the geographical causes is the fact of history. . . . To Canada, B.C. is just something tacked on to the end of the country. But B.C. was created in a different era under different conditions, and in a different way by different men. These differences still have their effect. They are to a large extent, what makes a British Columbian.

The Canadians arrived in B.C. en masse only after the Americans had plundered B.C.'s gold, after Victorian British had set up B.C.'s laws and mores, and after the Chinese had built a railway for the Canadians to travel in comfort across the mountains on. This, of course, explains why even those British Columbians who would like to get rid of the province's ridiculous name will never accept the "Canadian Columbia" so kindly proposed in Quebec. Surely our French-speaking compatriots will understand our reluctance to substitute for British, which at least has a colour of historical right, the word Canadian which has none!

The Canadians who stayed on did so on one basis only—they became British Columbians. If they could not adapt, they fled, as they still flee. What choice is there? They find here a new, different and exciting way of life. And once here, they find themselves cut off by their Canadian homeland.

This has always been so and it is demonstrably true. The most immediately evident symptom of it is the appalling lack of B.C. news in eastern papers, so little that a British Columbian visiting or living in Toronto, say, could wish he had come from Djakarta.

But more important are the woeful gaps of education. Canadian history books written in the east spurn B.C., which undoubtedly explains the proliferation of local history associations, the preoccupation with its own past which is so marked in B.C. Toronto book publishers are consistently—and happily—astonished at the extent to which books about B.C. are bought by British Columbians. . . .

So we sit smugly upon our beauty spots, express our confidence that this is the best of all possible lands and that in it we live the best of all possible ways of life, not awfully caring whether Quebec secedes or not, but understanding their feelings and being quietly interested in its mechanics. We can't help thinking that geography would make a parallel operation at the western end of Canada a very logical, neat and tidy affair.

What do you think?

1. What does Mr. Stainsby mean when he says that Quebec and British Columbia are "different in the same way"? Do you agree? Why or why not?

2. Do you think that the rest of Canada ignores B.C. as Mr. Stainsby suggests? In what ways? If you do not agree, how does the rest of Canada treat B.C.?

BRITISH COLUMBIANS
NOT NECESSARILY SEPARATISTS

Martin Robin, a British Columbia historian, commented on the then recently created B.C. Separatist Association for Canadian Dimension *(April-May 1969).*

Mr. Bob Reeds, a Vancouver cabaret owner, has caused a stir. He has announced the creation of the British Columbia Separatist Association. Some people say, "Who's Bob Reeds?" Other people, mostly outside of British Columbia, are worried. René Lévesque is bad enough, but with Bob Reeds joining in, Canada is in real trouble. They don't really care who Bob Reeds is, or what kind of food, tasty or lousy, kosher or otherwise, he serves in his cabaret. They only care that he is making trouble for Canada. If Quebec leaves, they feel, Canada will endure notwithstanding the drop in the consumption of pea soup and Pepsi Cola within its shrunken borders. But with British Columbia gone, with all those nice mountains and lovely girls taken away, what will be left? Canada will become an international joke.

I would say that we need not worry—about British Columbia's departure that is. Quebec is another matter. Separatism is not an active part of the British Columbia political scene. There is no political party which advocates separation, no prominent (or even obscure) political leaders who talk secession, no interest groups who bandy the banner of independence.

This is not to deny British Columbia's distance, cultural as well as geographical, from the faintly beating Canadian heart. British Columbians like to dote on their uniqueness; they bask in narcissistic idolatry. Their more exuberant bards speak of the Rocky Mountains as a great barrier, a shelter which nurtures the growth of a special race of men who have wrestled an ample living from the cruel and beautiful wilderness.

Now poets are prone to exaggeration. In fact exaggeration is their occupation. But British Columbians *are* different. The West Coast of Canada is full of pagans and promoters. People there avoid the dusty Church like the plague and instead prance naked in the outdoors. They delight in the mountains, the oceans, the longlimbed women and trees. They slurp juicy peaches, dripping with sweet nectar. When they are not slurping, they are promoting. They wheel and deal. They try to make a fast buck from a little gesheft so that they may retire early to nibble cherries.

British Columbians may be different, but that doesn't make them separatists. Quebec nationalism is based upon the assertion of communal values. The great majority of Quebecers share a common ethnic and religious heritage. They consider themselves a conquered nation. Quebecers are rightly concerned with the preservation of their language and culture as well as with bread and butter questions. The folk yearnings of the Quebec masses have been articulated and preserved by the Church and intelligentsia. British Columbia is not a community. It is a province. Sentiments against the federal government are regional rather than communitarian. They are not sentiments against the English. British Columbia is an ethnic and religious conglomeration. More than half of the contemporary population were born elsewhere. British Columbia is a divided society, split into distinct and separate geographical and cultural entities, and fractured by class divisions, between worker and capitalist, more severe than in all other parts of the country. Quebec nationalists speak of becoming masters of their own house, a self-determination which includes cultural and religious in addition to economic values. British Columbia's claims against the federal authorities have always been couched in material rather than cultural or nationalist terms. British Columbians want "better terms", a fair tax deal, rather than an opportunity to develop their cultural personality.

Lacking a community base, provincialist sentiments in British Columbia are only mildly felt, although they have been effectively exploited by politicians in the past. British Columbians may not feel very close to Canada, but they don't really dream of living alone. Quebec separatism is psychologically moored to the great umbilical cord stretching across the Atlantic, at the end of which stands a tall Frenchman with a long nose and drooping beady eyes. Intimations of loneliness following separation are mollified by the pleasing thought of returning to the cultural womb of France. But if Bob Reeds has his way, British Columbia will become a political orphan. It may be absorbed into the great maw of popcorn, Hershey bars, and neon lights to the south or, cast adrift from the Canadian mainland, British Columbia may float across the Pacific and attach itself as a suburb to Hong Kong. These are not cheering prospects to most British Columbians.

What do you think?

1. How do British Columbians see themselves, according to Mr. Stainsby and Professor Robin?
2. Stainsby maintains that British Columbia is a "motherland", Robin that B.C. lacks a "community base". Explain what each author means. Which point of view seems more valid to you? Why?

B.C. OPPOSES EQUALIZATION PAYMENTS

In early 1972 the Social Credit government of British Columbia led by W.A. Bennett attacked the Federal Government's system of equalization payments. This system, simply put, took money from the richer provinces (like B.C.) and gave it to the poorer ones (like P.E.I. or Newfoundland). B.C.'s response is described from an eastern point of view in the following article taken from the Toronto Star, *February 16, 1972.*

There is a theory that at some time Canada was tipped and everything loose rattled into British Columbia. But who really knows what goes on out there beyond the mountains? Travellers tell of cabinet ministers sent to jail for taking bribes, the premier being held liable for slandering one of his own civil servants, the people busily digging up the province and selling it to the Japanese. It may be true. What we do know of Premier W.A.C. Bennett and the Social Credit government is largely derived from their occasional meeting with other prominent Canadians.

At such times, the premier has been known to call the Liberal government in Ottawa "stupid" and its policies "criminal". He has insulted Quebec by shouting that it "always has its hand in the trough" for federal handouts. In return, Prime Minister Trudeau has called Premier Bennett "a bigot". Nice round political abuse, but nothing to trouble ordinary Canadians who have more important worries these days.

Now, however, Premier Bennett proposes to put us all to the trouble of a Supreme Court case in which he proposes to stop Ottawa paying equalization grants. These are payments, from the wealthy "have" provinces—Ontario, Alberta and British Columbia—to the poorer "have not" provinces—all the rest. They are designed to establish a minimum level of public services across the country. Over $1 billion is expected to be distributed this way for 1971-72, nearly half of it to Quebec.

This is Premier Bennett's "trough". It is, in fact, the very essence of a federal system: The equitable collection and distribution of resources from areas of plenty to areas of scarcity. Such provincial grants permit individual governments to decide on spending based on community need, rather than individual choice, as, say, a guaranteed annual income program would do. Equalization payments may not be a perfect instrument for equitable distribution of the national income, but they are better than any other system yet devised.

What do you think?

1. *What are B.C.'s objections to the equalization program?*
2. *In what ways can the province put forward its grievances?*
3. *Do you think the province would be successful in its application to the Supreme Court? Why or why not?*
4. *Would other regions and provinces support the Federal Government or B.C. during such a court action? Which ones would support Ottawa? Why? Which would support B.C.? Why?*

EAST RUNS COLONIAL EMPIRE

L. V. Goodwin of British Columbia expressed a widely held point of view in this letter to the editor of the Toronto Globe and Mail *June 18, 1974.*

Well here we are with another federal election, and in the West it's a laugh. You may not believe this but Pierre Trudeau is promising us a better deal on freight rates—one of the things old John A. Macdonald promised us in his election speeches almost 100 years ago. We are still waiting. How's that for progress?

We don't have representative government in Canada. The only provinces that are represented adequately are Ontario and Quebec. Their members make the Government and everyone elected outside those two provinces is "farm" and obviously carries no weight whatever.

Prime Minister Trudeau and Opposition Leader Robert Stanfield, from a hardworking westerner's point of view, certainly leave a lot to be desired. They have no idea how the average man lives. They have never suffered from deprivation such as crop failures, strikes or recessions. What they want is power—God knows they have everything else.

Mr. Trudeau, in fact, won't even speak to the average man or woman by way of radio phone-in shows. He made a very disparaging remark about such people.

The East (Ontario and Quebec) want our wheat and our oil and gas and our lumber and all the other things we have, and let the poor sod pay through the nose for it. Talk about a colonial empire!

Will you please keep your Trudeaus and Stanfields and all their ilk in Ontario and Quebec. We not only don't like them, we don't need them.

What is meant by?

"colonial empire"

What do you think?

1. *What are B.C.'s objections to the equalization program?*
2. *Why do some British Columbians feel exploited by central Canada? Do you think their grievances are justified?*
3. *What kinds of solutions would you propose to the issues raised in these documents? How would your solutions affect the rest of Canada?*

THE PRAIRIE PROVINCES

Since the late 1960s many residents of Alberta, Saskatchewan and Manitoba have grown increasingly critical of their status within Confederation. Many Westerners believe that Central Canada and the Federal Government disregard their regional concerns. Although the electoral victory of the Parti Québécois in November 1976 has focused national attention on the issue of Quebec separatism, it may be argued that prairie alienation and the resulting regional protest pose a no less significant threat to Canadian unity.

This section presents various aspects of prairie alienation and protest. What are the regional issues which affect the Prairie provinces? Why are these regional attitudes and demands important to all Canadians? How can such regional concerns be accommodated within the federal structure?

WESTERN ALIENATION REMAINS AND GROWS

I. H. Asper is a well-known tax expert and former leader of the Liberal Party of Manitoba. In a speech to the Canadian Club of Toronto, January 25, 1971, he outlined the discontent of the West.

My concern is that the rest of Canada is not fully aware of the dimensions of the Western Fact and is liable to be unprepared in the Nineteen Seventies for the pressing of the case for Western Canada, as it was shocked and unprepared for the French Fact during the Sixties.

. . .

What should be clear is that the West is different in structure from the East—and this difference is significant enough to create continually distinct problems, as well as special disadvantages and opportunities for the people of the region. Distinct problems and opportunities lead to demands for distinct policies at the national level.

The fact is that the economic and political power of Canada—and thus the power to develop national policies—remains concentrated in Ontario and Quebec. Nineteen out of 20 of Canada's largest corporations have their head offices in these central provinces, drawing earnings from across the country to be spent within the golden triangle.

Real legislative power—in terms of both provincial political power and political representation in Ottawa—lies in Ontario and Quebec. These two eastern regions, huddled around our capital of Ottawa, together elect 51 per cent of Canada's members of Parliament. Some 76 per cent of Canada's senators come from Eastern Canada, including the Maritimes.

Western Canada was not part of the negotiations leading to Confederation. The net result is that Canada's distinctive Western half has been forced to live within a political structure which was never designed to provide effective regional security or power for underpopulated regions. . . .

Western alienation remains and grows, and should be taken seriously, for the critical fact is that, during the first 100 years of Confederation, Western Canada's position in Confederation has changed more than that of any other Canadian region.

It is the new West, not the old West, which demands a new relationship within the political and economic decision-making structure of Canada.

Since the Second World War, the West has permanently changed. In effect, for the first time since Confederation, the West no longer feels the need to be an economic colony of the East. The West is a maturing region, in the sense that it is settled, has a potential for growth and prosperity, and is now predominantly urban. . . .

In many senses, current Western discontent begins in fear: fear that our people will somehow be at a disadvantage in a bilingual Canada; fear that our own multicultural society will be submerged by strident Eastern biculturalism; fear that Prairie industry and towns will be forced to undergo severe change to meet new economic conditions, while less efficient industry will remain protected behind a tariff wall; fear that federal policy, and changes in the constitution, will ultimately serve to harm us, given the supreme power of Canada's central provinces.

There is more than fear, however, in current discontent. There is also the conviction that the West has distinct opportunities for the future, and a distinct contribution to make to the world, but that we are denied our rightful destiny because Canada is not changing its economic structure to accommodate Western emergence.

. . .

The problem, from the viewpoint of the West, is that Canada today does not have an adequate form of federalism. In fact, Canada still suffers from the blueprint stamped out by the fathers of Confederation—a blueprint designed in the spirit of centralization, with the image of an imperial rather than a federal form of government.

We in Manitoba, in the Prairies, in the West, are the strongest federalists possible. But we must have redress. We must have the attention and assistance of other Canadians if our people are to meet and overcome the challenges of the Seventies. We must have new freight rate structures which will allow the West to develop its industrial potential, we must have new international free trade zones so that the West can compete in international markets.

We must have more meaningful and selective federal regional development incentives. We must have tax reform of a far more imaginative kind than has yet been offered or is contemplated in the federal white paper. We must have new immigration policies which will deflect population to our underdeveloped areas. We must establish a new banking structure for Canada which will guarantee availability of capital not only in Eastern Canada but uniformly across this nation. We must have constitutional change which will guarantee a true federalism in Canada—a partnership of 10 equal provinces rather than the current structure which guarantees that the West in general, and the Prairies in particular, will have little or no political effect in the decision-making process of Canada.

What do you think?

1. According to this document, what are the differences between the new West and the old West?

2. According to Mr. Asper, what are the West's grievances? What are the reasons for the grievances?

3. How does Mr. Asper propose to solve the problem?

4. Do you think Mr. Asper is arguing primarily for regional independence or for regional security within the federal system? Why?

THE PRAIRIE PERSPECTIVE

Dr. John Archer is a distinguished Saskatchewan historian. The following excerpt, originally published in 1971 in One Country or Two?, *is still a relevant presentation of Western attitudes towards Canada. (Ed. R.M. Burns, McGill-Queen's University Press, 1971.)*

Westerners as a whole have little understanding of the emotional roots of Quebec nationalism. Western opposition to anything resembling special status and the extremely antagonistic attitude towards Separatism is an indication that Prairie opinion would not be inclined towards economic or political co-operation with an independent Quebec. In the Westerner's view, a separate Quebec would probably mean that, for a period at least, Ontario would dominate the Canada remaining—a bad thing for the West. Some sort of counterpoise to Ontario would have to be built, perhaps one government for the Prairie region. The Lethbridge Conference (May 1970) on "One Prairie Province" showed that there was little enthusiasm for any such step short of some drastic realignment in the federal structure. . . .

The West feels alienated, snubbed, and ill-used. The feeling is much more widespread than in 1919 or during the thirties. Farmers are angry—angry that Easterners have clearly bungled the marketing of wheat. A few years ago cabinet ministers urged them to grow wheat promising that it would be sold. The Toronto *Globe and Mail* stated editorially on 18 July 1969: "In 1966 they (the Prairie farmers) were assured by the annual meeting of federal and provincial agriculture ministers and their officials that Canadian wheat exports would stay at a high level until at least 1970. . . . These were assurances that were being reiterated—while they were also, in some quarters being contradicted—as late as last year." . . . Western oilmen feel that they are deliberately excluded from rich Eastern Canadian markets—the victims of an arrangement made by Eastern distributors with American producers. Western financiers have felt the rebuke of so-called colleagues in banking circles in Eastern Canada. There is a general, widespread belief that what Montreal or Toronto, Quebec or Ontario wants Ottawa will grant—be it subsidy to dairymen, maintenance for Air Canada, or aid for Expo. Back of it all is the maddening, frightening knowledge that in terms of political weight the Prairies no longer qualify even for the welter division. Mistress in her own house, the West would be a power to be blandished.

. . .

Quebec, to the degree that it is Separatist, is Separatist on emotional grounds. Economically, Quebec is bound closely to a united Canada. The West, where separatist at all, is separatist on economic grounds. Emotionally the region is deeply Canadian. There is, then, no real understanding or appreciation of the dynamic forces boiling up under the surface in either area. The West sees Quebec as a gainer economically from Confederation and either misjudges or refuses to believe the mounting evidence of Separatism. Faced with an actual separation, the West would not act in haste, for sound economic policies are not formed of snap judgements made in times of stress. If a separate Quebec meant little disturbance and the door were left open for a return, the West would probably opt for a continued Canada without Quebec. But the bargaining over national policies of the new Canada would be hard and sharp, unless the West were sure of some means of countering Ontario's economic, financial, and political power, it would consider going its own way. . . .

What, then, is the Prairie perspective? Westerners still opt for a federal Canada. Anger, exasperation, and the feeling of alienation have not yet broken down the traditional expectations that governments can and will respond to regional arguments boldly argued. When economic justice has been done, then there will be a more acceptable time to pursue such necessary and proper goals as biculturalism. But biculturalism in the West will be ordained, legislated, and practised in the light of the history and traditions of the Westerners. It cannot be imposed by the action of a political majority representing regions other than the West. While most Westerners are ready to widen the avenues open to those whose language is French, or those who would become proficient in French, the same Westerners will remind the listener that land was indeed free to all who would come to the prairies, and if those who came from Quebec were few in number, Quebec leaders today cannot fairly condemn Western leaders for carrying out the expressed wishes of their constituents. Yet there is little of such fruitless argument. The West hopes Quebec will find a satisfactory role in the Canadian federation. While Westerners do not always appreciate the roots of Quebec nationalism or Separatism, their instinct is to compromise for the sake of a whole Canada. Should Quebec leave Canada, however, Westerners may very well decide that separation for them is also an option to be considered. If that decision is made in the present mood, there is a very real possibility that the West would shun Ontario, seek some accommodation with British Columbia, and strike out independently.

What do you think?

1. *Why does the West feel alienated from Central Canada, according to Dr. Archer?*
2. *How do his views differ from Mr. Asper's?*
3. *How is Western alienation different from Quebec alienation?*
4. *What kinds of policies could you suggest to improve the situation?*

PERCENTAGES OF VOTE BY PROVINCE

The following is a table of distribution by province of party vote in the general election of July 8, 1974 and is prepared by The Canadian Press.

	Lib	PC	NDP	Other
Nfld	46.9	43.4	9.4	.30
PEI	46.3	49.0	4.6	.10
NS	41.4	48.0	10.2	.40
NB	47.6	33.6	8.0	2.7
Que	54.0	21.0	6.6	18.4
Ont	45.1	34.9	19.4	.60
Man	26.8	46.8	24.8	1.6
Alta	24.8	61.3	9.1	4.8
Sask	30.8	36.3	31.5	1.4
BC	33.1	42.0	23.0	1.9
Y-NWT	28.8	39.3	31.9	—

What do you think?

1. *What parties might be included in the category "other"?*
2. *Where in Canada is Liberal support strongest? Conservative support? NDP support? What factors might explain these differences?*

BILINGUALISM TRUDEAU'S DOWNFALL IN THE WEST

The federal election of July 8, 1974 returned a majority Liberal government under Pierre Elliott Trudeau. Frances Russell in the Winnipeg Free Press wrote an analysis July 12, 1974 from which the following comments are extracts.

Election results, Monday, July 8. The Trudeau tide hitting the impregnable, the obdurate, the staunchly Tory, prairie provinces.

The 1974 mandate was not to unite the country.

The three prairie provinces held against the national consensus of the people of the Maritimes, Quebec and, strangely enough B.C. It is B.C. that everyone thinks is cut off from the rest of Canada. But Monday night showed B.C. mildly in time with the national beat. And the Prairies keeping time to their own drummer, oblivious to anyone else.

Why?

A dislike and distrust of the Liberals that has become a tradition on the Prairies since the magical image of John Diefenbaker arrived on the western scene nearly 20 years ago.

An extreme antagonism to Prime Minister Trudeau because of his arrogant image, his sophistication—and above all, his French Canadian heritage.

A feeling of separateness, of rejection of and by Central Canada, of grievance sufficient to maintain the prairie side of Canada's sectionalism even against a national trend manifest in seven other provinces.

. . .

In 1972, when the West also turned its back on the Liberals, commentators were at pains to explain that the western decision had nothing to do with bilingualism, the Official Languages Act and French Canada.

It would, indeed be nice to think that.

Unfortunately, however, that was a decisive issue in 1972, just as it was again Monday night.

More than inflation, more than neglect, more than any other single issue, bilingualism has raised the wrath of westerners against the Liberal party.

. . .

Bilingualism is a virulent issue in Western Canada because, . . . western Canadians have a discernible target for all their historic frustrations and grievances against Central Canada.

These frustrations and grievances are, in reality, against Ontario or, at most, Ontario and Montreal. They are not against Quebec, with whom the West has much in common economically.

Unfortunately, it is easier to dislike a different language, a different culture, than to dislike a person like yourself, who just happens to be more wealthy and powerful.

Quebec is reaping the harvest of resentment sown in the West by Ontario. And the Conservatives, after the campaign they ran here, now have the answer to why they can't break through in French Canada.

What do you think?

1. *Why do you think bilingualism is an important issue in Western Canada?*
2. *What is meant by "Quebec is reaping the harvest of resentment sown in the West by Ontario"?*

FREIGHT RATE DISPARITIES DISCRIMINATE AGAINST THE WEST

The Grain Handling and Transportation Commission, commonly known as the Hall Commission, was appointed on April 18, 1975. Its investigations were "primarily concerned with an evaluation of rail requirements, the response of grain producers, elevator companies and the communities to changing circumstances, and the socioeconomic impact of an evolving network." After sitting for two years, the committee submitted a report and recommendations to the Federal Government. The following article responding to the Commission's proposals on transportation was written by James Rush and appeared in the May 17, 1977 issue of the Globe and Mail. *(Reprinted with the permission of the* Globe and Mail, *Toronto.)*

The commission suggests that a reversal of policy be made wherein all unnecessary transportation of goods be avoided and the most efficient mode of transportation be used for each commodity.

In principle, the first item that should be attended to "would be a freight structure in which the processed product in its concentrated form should cost no more to transport on a per ton basis than the same product in its raw state."

The commission made a study of the economics of location of agricultural processing plants and found a number of cases in which apparent inequities in the transportation system discriminated against Western Canada.

For example, the area's share of the flour milling industry has fallen from 48 per cent in the 1950's to 31 per cent in the 1974-75 period.

"The commission found that the application of certain government programs, of Canadian Wheat Board selling practices and of ancillary rail charges offset the natural geographic advantages that western mills should enjoy."

. . .

In the case of the western rapeseed crushing industry, a number of freight rates discriminate against it. The products crushed—meal and oil—face higher freight rates than the seed moving east, which places the western Canadian crusher at a disadvantage. The cost of moving 100 pounds of rapeseed from Lethbridge to Montreal is 70.5 cents while moving an equivalent amount of oil and meal is 90.2 cents according to one study.

This disparity moving east is 19.7 cents a hundred pounds but moving west to Vancouver it is 40.4 cents.

Another example is the allowance that rapeseed crushers get for the use of their own tank cars to move rapeseed oil. "The railways allow the rapeseed crushed 9.5 cents per loaded mile, although other shippers are allowed 12 cents per loaded mile for the use and provision of these cars."

With livestock, the feed freight assistance program—that only recently was scaled down—encourages shipment of feed grains rather than livestock or livestock products from the Prairies to Eastern Canada or British Columbia.

. . .

In the case of hogs, it is cheaper to ship the equivalent amount of barley east to produce the hog in Eastern Canada than it is to ship the pork east. . . .

What is meant by?

"socioeconomic impact"

What do you think?

1. From these statistics, do you believe Western farmers have a legitimate grievance? Why or why not?

DRASTIC RAIL CUTBACKS URGED IN WEST

The following extracts deal with another aspect of the grain handling and transportation inquiries of the Hall Commission. Again the article by

James Rush appeared in the Globe and Mail *on May 17, 1977. (Reprinted with the permission of the* Globe and Mail, *Toronto.)*

Almost 2,200 miles of railway track in Western Canada should be abandoned in the next 5 years and the railways should turn more than 2,300 miles of track over to a new government agency that would determine its fate by 1990, according to the report of the Grain Handling and Transportation Commission.

. . .

The commission which spent two years studying the grain handling and transportation system, found that, despite some changes over the years, the system is essentially unchanged from when it was set up 50 years ago.

"To date, no one has come to grips with some of the more fundamental problems in the grain handling and transportation system. One of the more basic of these is the deterioration of the branch rail lines in the Prairie Provinces and the aging of primary elevators built half a century ago."

. . .

. . . The issue around which the report coalesces is the abandonment of railway lines of which there are 18,736 miles in Western Canada.

Since the early 1960s the railways have wanted to abandon thousands of miles of track in the area and while Ottawa has allowed a small amount of track to be let go, abandonment has been prohibited over most of the system.

While prohibition took the pressure off the federal government through the 1960s, the 1970s brought a new kind of pressure. Canada was called upon to export record quantities of grain and the system was found wanting.

While the system just coped, governments, grain elevator companies, railways and customers came to realize that if Canada were called upon in the late 1970s or early 1980s to move the massive amounts of grain that the world might hunger for, it probably could not handle them.

Despite massive government subsidies to support uneconomic branch lines, some rejigging of the system and Ottawa's purchase of thousands of hopper cars for grain hauling, the system needs heavy investments to bring it to performance standards that could carry it into the next century. But the railways claim they cannot spend money to improve tracks that carry uneconomic volumes of grain and the companies claim they cannot invest in facilities on a line that might be abandoned.

What do you think?

1. *What are the various points of view involved in this question?*
2. *How does the Hall Commission recommend dealing with the problem?*
3. *What problems might be encountered in putting the recommendations of the Hall Commission into effect?*

4. How might the acceptance of the recommendations affect regional sentiment?

IT'S TIME THE WEST PROTECTED ITS OWN INTEREST

In a letter to the editor of the Edmonton Journal *on April 22, 1976, Dr. J. Donovan Ross proposed the following solution for Western alienation. Dr. Ross was Minister of Health in Alberta from 1957-69 and Minister of Lands and Forests from 1969-71.*

. . . Why not a Commonwealth of Western Canada?

This question has recurred in my thoughts time and time again over the past decade, during part of which time, as a member of the Alberta cabinet, I had been engaged in discussions and battles with the federal government in Ottawa. . . .

. . . No doubt the ministers in our present provincial governments are finding out the same sorry truths we did—that as far as the Liberal government in Ottawa and the government in Ontario is concerned, the Western provinces with all their wealth in food, mineral and energy production are only here to serve the needs of the central provinces of Ontario and Quebec, and maintain their industrial empires.

The gradual but continuing erosion of provincial rights under the BNA Act by the federal government through health and social welfare programs should have been enough to give us concern. . . .

The recent suggestions by Prime Minister Trudeau that he might unilaterally repatriate the Canadian constitution whether the provinces agree or not, should alert us to the very real dangers that may be ahead of us as provincial residents when the mother of Parliaments or Privy Council is no longer in a position to prevent the demagogues of Ottawa from completing the takeover of our natural resources and the erosion of the freedom of our people. . . . Let me make it quite clear that I am not proposing any revolutionary solutions, as a small minority faction did a few years ago in Quebec, but that by the democratic processes of free choice the peoples of western Canada should be permitted to decide for or against secession from the eastern part of Canada. It may well be that the people of the Yukon and western part of the North West Territories would also prefer to be included in the new nation rather than continue as serfs of Central Canada.

There is no question that the present four western provinces and the territories are as viable an economic area as any on this continent with all the necessary attributes of a self-sufficient nation capable of producing its vast natural resources for its own use, as well as for export to other nations (of which Eastern Canada might be one).

There are sea ports on the Pacific and the Atlantic (through Hudson Bay) from which exports of those products from our forests, mines, farms and ranches, in excess of our own needs and which are wanted and needed by other nations, could be shipped . . .

The educational system in the proposed new nation is alike enough that no problem would be encountered in developing an overall national program that should still leave freedom for private institutions, if they are desired, that might receive more adequate financial assistance from the public purse than has been provided in the past. This educational system should incorporate and encourage multi-lingualism for our children rather than enforce the bilingualism we are now struggling with, but the national language should be Anglo-Canadian . . .

If such a new nation were to be considered for establishment it could be simply and economically done through a plebiscite put to the people in the areas under consideration, by present provincial governments—on the same day—after a 30 day program of advertising through all media in many languages including that of our native people.

. . .

To bring government back into proper accountability to the people as a whole there should be only two levels of government set out under the new constitution—federal and municipal. . . .

I . . . hope that this article may stimulate thinking, planning and action before we in the West become a permanently enslaved colony of Central Canada.

FOR ONE NATION

A few days later a Mr. Joachim Nuttack of Edmonton replied to Dr. Ross, (Edmonton Journal, *May 3, 1976).*

I feel obliged to challenge [Dr. J. Donovan Ross] on several points.

It is my firm conviction that no national crisis of any kind can be solved by chopping the country into pieces. History has proven this as far back as Alexander the Great and as recently as Vietnam.

The idea to unite the Western provinces seems to spring from the basic idea of exploitation by other provinces, particularly Quebec and Ontario. Dr. Ross seems to forget, in my opinion, that our immediate neighbours to the east and west are asking for a share of Alberta's resources but we are stubbornly clinging to them. Will we be willing to give them up freely after the creation of a Western Commonwealth?

We must remember that the use of the port of Churchill or any future port on Hudson Bay is not governed by willingness to use it but by the Canadian winter. . . .

The concept of a two level government would only put into practice what Dr. Ross criticized at the beginning of his letter, namely an overall, single powerful central government. Even smaller (in area) countries in Europe have found it necessary to govern on three levels. . . .

What do you think?

1. *What arguments does Dr. Ross present in favour of the formation of a Western Commonwealth?*
2. *How does Mr. Nuttack respond to Dr. Ross's arguments?*
3. *What problems in terms of education, trade and government might Westerners face if a Western Commonwealth came into being?*
4. *Do you think a Western Commonwealth would be a viable solution to the West's regional demands? Why or why not?*

THREE DAYS TO CON(QUOR) THE WEST

The Ottawa Journal, *July 20, 1973, responded to Western alienation in the following manner.*

"The Western Canadian Economic Opportunities Conference." Three days in July to make all well in the West, to soothe the western psyche, to show that the Liberals really care. What a massive pretentious public relations job!

The West has its problems. So have the Maritimes, much greater problems; so has the North. So has Quebec. Yes, so has Ontario. Ask them about alienation and lack of secondary industry in North Bay. Give the Atlantic region the chance to trade its unemployment rate of 9.3 per cent for the Prairies 3.5. Things are not at all black, disaffected and alienated as the West is supposed to feel. The grousing in fact becomes tedious.

The real reason why Prime Minister Trudeau and his key ministers are making still another pilgrimage westward next week is the Liberal Party's problem in the West; not the West's problems, real or imagined.
. . .
The West will consider the Calgary conference a failure unless the federal government comes forward with precise, detailed and acceptable propositions, and not patent bribery; that would be insulting. There will be no patience with another prime ministerial show of penitence, no time for more studies and analysis and promises.

However great the West's expectations, the meeting was wrong in concept, wrong as a political ploy. The political mistake is the Liberals' business; the dangerous implications for the country are everyone's.

Canada is not governed by regional conferences, not by decisions taken by the Prime Minister and a group of premiers. The conference is essentially a downgrading and a by-passing of Parliament, of provincial legislatures, of cabinets. Full federal-provincial conferences pose their own dangers to the role of Parliament and the legislatures in taking on the trappings of a super decision-making body. But at least all provinces are represented and the issues are national.

Next week's conference is a glorification and consecration of regionalism. It enables the West to feed on its own mythology that it has been victimized and oppressed by those slickers from Central Canada.

Saying this will seem to some westerners as a perfect example of Ontario Chauvinism. But said it has to be: the problems of the West are at least as much psychological as economic.

The old cry that the banks serve the interests of Central Canada and not the West's, that freight rates are a major hindrance to the development of western economy are chronic complaints which no longer stand up to scrutiny.

For example, the four western provinces receive 33.6 per cent of the loans made by the chartered banks of Canada while the population of these provinces comprises 26.6 per cent of the country. Despite some undoubted anomalies in some rates, the whole freight-rate structure is not so prejudicial to the West that it is holding back development of secondary industry.

. . .

The West does feel that it is out of the main stream and that it does not have enough say in the country's decision-making processes. But that feeling is a long way from western separatism which is largely a creation of sensation-seekers. The last three western premiers who did adopt anti-Ottawa rhetoric (Bennett, Thatcher and Weir) were defeated and replaced by men with 20/20 national vision.

The West's dissatisfaction is with the Liberal government, with the Prime Minister's old indifference and his style. One conference is not going to end that. The Prime Minister's conversion has come too late in the day to seem to be anything more than desperate political salvage.

What do you think?

1. What was the Western Economic Opportunities Conference? What kinds of issues were discussed there?
2. How do the West's economic problems differ from those in the rest of Canada?

TWO-WAY STREET

The following document which appeared as an editorial in the Edmonton Journal *on February 5, 1977, deals with the West's concerns that it may be ignored now that Quebec has elected a separatist government.*

Premier Peter Lougheed has reiterated his not unreasonable warning that Ottawa must not allow itself to become so preoccupied with Quebec that it forgets the West.

Regardless of some Eastern attitudes that the traditional complaints of the West constitute only so much belly-aching, the problems of transportation, freight rates, and tariffs remain a constant and real concern; they have not disappeared since the election of a separatist government in Quebec.

The premier has said that "if, just when the West is on the verge of finally being able to get close to its potential, an election in Quebec becomes an excuse for the Ottawa bureaucracy and the Toronto establishment to say 'Oh, we can now forget about those Western provinces and their problems because they are minor and concentrate on Quebec,' that I think would be a very tragic decision."

Unfortunately, he is right. For better or for worse, and largely on Mr. Lougheed's efforts, the impatience among Westerners, certainly among Albertans, to see some long-standing grievances redressed has been heightened to the point where we will no longer be willing to accept a return to Ottawa's former lack of interest.

However, this is a two-way street. Alberta has to accept that there has been a fundamental change in the makeup of Canadian life since the election of the *Parti Québécois* on November 15. The premier suggests Alberta should not get involved in the Quebec debate, but it is difficult to see how Alberta can avoid it. The problem of Quebec independence is the most immediate concern facing Canada, and that fact is going to color any relationship from now on between the federal government and the provinces.

In the same way that the federal government must realize Alberta's impatience to progress despite the issues of Quebec, Albertans must guard against a tendency to brood over no longer being the centre of Ottawa's attention.

The election of a separatist government in Quebec has made it necessary for all of Canada to examine and reassess the terms of Confederation, and this is not an exercise that Alberta can opt out of.

What do you think?

1. According to this article, what effect will the Parti Québécois victory have on Alberta? Why?

THE EAST MUST SHIFT POWER WEST

The following remarks were made by Alberta's Premier, Peter Lougheed, at the Progressive Conservative Conference in Edmonton on April 14, 1977. (The Globe and Mail, *Toronto, "Just What Was Said")*

I want to finalize my comments today by spelling out Alberta's position in Confederation. To reach our goal of a strong and diversified Alberta by 1985—to attain that fundamental change in Canada's economy—major changes must occur nationally.

First, there must be a shift of decision-making westward from Toronto.

Second, there must be a reduction, to a marked degree, of the interference and obstacles to our objectives by the federal Government in four important ways: our natural resources must be sold for value at international prices; there must be a completely new deal on freight rates in this country; the livestock producer in this province must be involved in a North American market with North American cooperation and good will; and we must have, finally, export markets for our grain that are stable—markets that we can rely upon.

These are fundamental changes, affecting business, labour, communication, and governmental aspects of Canadian life. They are not parochial for just Alberta for they will benefit the entire West. But more important, as you've heard me say—and as I think you believe—a stronger West will create a stronger Canada.

. . .

. . . I have a point of view that I believe we will all share in this room. I said, "Alberta is no less a province than Ontario or Quebec." And I was attacked vigorously the next few days in the Toronto area—and elsewhere— for being narrow, arrogant, parochial, and non-Canadian.

Well, I thought, my friends, I was doing my job—standing up for Alberta. That's what I was elected to do.

And I know that mood that we had here . . . in October on the Constitutional issues—and in the Legislature afterward. Don't accept the view that this issue has gone away. Mr. Trudeau wants that Constitution under his thumb in Ottawa—he may even be prepared to bring in an amending formula and override the objections of any province to patriate the Constitution.

Since that time there's been a critical new development in this nation. A new Government in Quebec elected and committed not to strong provincial rights—but to independence. This requires a mature response from us.

First of all, it requires (and let us make this absolutely clear—and I haven't the slightest concern about it, nor do I think this convention has the slightest concern about it—because they understand) we are Canadians before we're Albertan. We think that being strong for Alberta is good for a unified Canada.

. . . This country is without a doubt a richer, greater, united country with Quebec a full partner, and this province and our citizens will work together to maintain a united Canada.

We want, as well, to have normal working relations with all the ministries in the new Government in Quebec and we will. We also want to do something else as Canadians—because I'm sure these tensions are difficult for other parts of Canada whose economies are not as strong as ours today. So we want to indicate to our friends in the Atlantic provinces not to believe a lot of this nonsense that is written about the West and about Alberta—we've got confidence in a united Canada.

Make no mistake about it, if Alberta does not make significant progress in transportation, in trade policies, in energy pricing, in the next few years, we'll never secure them for the rest of the century and we'll not have a strong Alberta a decade from now. This is the one time in Confederation for Alberta to help create a new economic arrangement in Canada.

. . .

. . . Common sense tells me one thing: Just as Albertans want more control over their own destiny, primarily for economic reasons, Quebeckers, I sense, want also more control over their destiny—essentially for cultural and linguistic reasons.

Hence, just as Albertans want more government decisions made in Edmonton than in Ottawa, I think Quebeckers, for different reasons, but somewhat similar motives, want more government decisions made in Quebec City, and fewer in Ottawa. Thus, the objective of both provinces is to want less centralization—and hence less suffocation by Ottawa.

What do you think?

1. *What is the issue according to Mr. Lougheed?*
2. *How does he propose to change the situation?*
3. *What common ground does he feel there is between Quebec and Alberta?*
4. *What effects would Mr. Lougheed's solution have on Canada?*

ONTARIO

Peter C. Newman, an influential author and editor of *Maclean's* magazine, once described Canada as being composed of three regions: Upper Canada, Lower Canada and Outer Canada. Upper and Lower Canada (Ontario and Quebec, respectively) are commonly referred to as Central Canada and contain most of the nation's industrial base, as well as almost two-thirds of Canada's total population. These advantages are partly responsible for the resentment that Outer Canada (B.C., the West and the Atlantic provinces) feels towards the central core region and Ontario in particular. Despite these perceived advantages, Ontario too has its share of problems within Confederation and regional issues number among them.

The next section looks at Ontario's view of its role in Confederation and deals with the issue of tax-sharing agreements, long a major source of tension between the governments of Canada and Ontario.

The question of whether or not a distinct regional identity exists in Ontario is also raised, as well as the extent to which external factors, such as the perceptions of other provinces, have contributed to this identity or lack of it.

DOES ONTARIO REALLY EXIST?

The following extracts are taken from Ontario: The Linchpin *by Fraser Kelley and John Marshall. (Reprinted by permission of The Canadian Publishers, McClelland and Stewart Limited, Toronto.)*

Ontario is many things to many people. Ontario is usually at the centre of any controversy which involves economic, cultural, regional, or federal arguments. The Atlantic fisherman is depressed when he compares his lot as a Canadian with that of his fellows enjoying the good life of Ontario. And the Western wheat-farmer, whose income has almost vanished because of a ruined crop and world oversupply, whose debts pile up as costly machinery comes from the tariff-protected manufacturing plants of Ontario, questions the high price he pays for Confederation. And the xenophobia of the young Quebec separatist, picketing his own politicians, feeds dangerously and negatively on the wealth and power of Ontario which symbolize the success of the English founding partner of Confederation. Ontario is a multi-faceted place, both to those who view it from a distance and to those who live within its borders.

One scholar, A.R.M. Lower, Professor Emeritus at Queen's University . . . even questions half-facetiously whether Ontario actually exists. In the June, 1968 issue of the Ontario Historical Society magazine Dr. Lower writes:

Ontario is a space on the map, it is a legal entity administered from Toronto, it is a section of Canada, but has it any of its own flesh and blood on its bones? Does Ontario exist?

First, place this name Ontario on the map. A vast space indeed: one thousand miles from north to south, still more from east to west. Two hundred and thirty million acres all told, full of lakes big and small, rivers long and short, with a sea coast, and down at the southern edge, some good agricultural land! Can you have a body made up of odds and ends that do not fit together—an assortment of unmatched arms and legs stuck on to a mostly empty body—the "legs" of the interlake peninsula, the "arm" of the Ottawa Valley and so on, stuck on to the great northern expanse of forest, lake and muskeg. Does that composite creation make an animal?

In human terms, the resulting piece of work is even more bizarre, a museum specimen rather than a living being. The Ottawa Valley counties are mixed French and English, the North is mixed everything, and Toronto is polyglot. A young woman who went to school in Sudbury once told me that in one of her classes, there had been representatives of seventeen national groups. In the old days when the West was being settled, they used to say that one could hear seventy languages on the streets of Winnipeg: today, there must be almost as many to be heard on the streets of Toronto.

Professor Lower wonders whether anyone ever thinks of himself as an Ontarian. He maintains people did about the time of Confederation when Ontario consisted of scattered communities along the southern portion of the province from Montreal to Windsor. He says the settlers of the previous eighty years, the Loyalists, Highlanders, Lowlanders, Catholic Irish, Protestant Irish, English, Americans, Pennsylvania Dutch, Lutheran Germans, were starting to get some sense of community.

But the gradual opening of the province's hinterland and the arrival of settlers from many lands have confused that sense of community. This will change as assimilation takes place, just as English, Irish and Scots have been more or less rolled together.

Dr. Lower says the sense of origin of these older groups is fading; and instead of thinking of themselves as, say, Scottish, people tend to think of themselves as Canadians of Scottish ancestry, or, if of mixed origin, as just Canadians . . .

What do you think?

1. Professor Lower suggests that Ontario lacks a cohesive identity. Do you agree with him? Why or why not?

2. According to this article, why might people from other regions of Canada resent Ontario?

THE ROLE AND PLACE OF ONTARIO IN THE CANADIAN CONFEDERATION

The following extracts were taken from a publication of the Ontario Economic Council prepared by Joe Martin and deal with Ontario's perception of its role in the Canadian Confederation (January 1974). The views expressed are those of the author. One of the major points of contention between Ontario and the Federal Government has always been taxation and the revenues derived therefrom.

In spite of (the) political leadership changes the basic theme of the period was unchanged from 1966, i.e., there was simply a continuation of confrontation federalism. Uncertainty was added to the debate by those political factors but tax-sharing and shared cost programs continued to be the issues of the period.

An analysis of the federal and Ontario budgets shows a startling contrast in attitudes. In Ottawa the issues were basically ignored. In Ontario they were hammered at with an increasing ferocity reaching a fever pitch in 1971 and then subsiding somewhat in 1972 and still more in 1973.

In his 1967 budget Mr. Sharp made two references to the Tax Structure Committee. In the first reference Mr. Sharp stated that on the basis of the Report he had sought "through our fiscal arrangements to define more clearly the respective responsibilities of the two levels of government". He later referred to the fact that data had been presented by the Committee which showed a "common need for increased revenues". It is obvious that the provinces needed massive amounts of revenue to avoid deficits while the federal government needed money only for new programs and/or surpluses.

Ontario's Treasurer, Mr. MacNaughton, took a tone of assertive confrontation. In his 1968 budget address he said: "Nothing short of comprehensive tax reform and a major redistribution of taxation fields will provide an intelligent solution to this problem."

He emphasized that whereas "the inexorable pressures for government expenditure today" lie with "the burgeoning urban communities, it is the federal government which has access to the growth fields of taxation while the provinces have only the regressive fields." He stressed that this put the federal government in a position to "invent new programs, largely within provincial jurisdiction" and that "through the shared-cost mechanism, the provincial government must then resort further to regressive tax fields to finance programs which may not conform to their priorities".

"Total tax-sharing reform among the three levels of government" was required, he said. And he concluded, " . . . What is needed to meet these problems is co-ordinated action by all governments. We must establish priorities for government spending as a whole. We must reform the entire spectrum of taxation. Above all, we must agree on a division of tax fields which will enable each government to finance its responsibilities and commitments effectively."

On the federal side lines hardened even further with the coming to power of Mr. Trudeau and his new Finance Minister, Mr. Benson. In his budget address Mr. Benson prefaced his remarks on all the federal government had done for the provinces by saying, "This government and this House recognize the financial problems being faced by the provinces—*even the wealthiest of them, which is the most outspoken on the subject*".

The general attitude expressed by the federal government and Mr. Benson's specific suggestion to the provinces that they go out and raise taxes, just before the Ministers of Finance meeting in late '68, caused Mr. MacNaughton (and other provincial Treasurers) to react strongly. In his 1969 budget address Mr. MacNaughton referred to the need for a "fair-minded review of federal-provincial expenditure requirements and financial capacities . . . along the lines *promised* in the original terms of references of the Tax Structure Committee in 1964."

. . .

The 1970 budget address of the Honorable Charles MacNaughton continued his confrontation with the Federal Government based, particularly, on the federal government reaction to the 1970 report of the Tax Structure Committee:

> Notwithstanding the widespread recognition of the totally unsatisfactory distribution of revenue sources, I must report, with regret, that the recent tax structure committee exercise has left us no closer to resolution of the problem of federal-provincial fiscal imbalance . . . In recent weeks, we have asserted our fundamental disagreement with the federal approach to tax reform. We will continue to make proposals for a more acceptable tax system and to suggest means of achieving that goal.

In the section of the address entitled "Federal/Provincial Fiscal Imbalance" Mr. MacNaughton made a number of points. He stated:

> In 1969, the Tax Structure Committee was reactivated to examine again the balance of fiscal responsibilities and resources of each level of government. Its 1970 report confirms the findings of the original 1966 study, which documented the chronic underfinancing at the provincial/ municipal level and the potential fiscal surpluses at the federal level.

In the next paragraph he noted that "the federal government virtually ignored the 1966 findings and told the provinces 'to go out and raise taxes'." He concluded this section by stating "The failure to obtain a sensible resolution of federal/provincial tax sharing problems will inevitably limit the government's ability to increase aid to municipalities and to maintain essential provincial services."

The 1971 budget address delivered by the Honourable W. Darcy McKeough, who has a more abrasive personality than Mr. MacNaughton, was more assertive in tone. His opening remarks in his "Report on Confederation" were as follows:

> Over the past several years, two things have become clearly evident. First, the federal government is firmly bent on a course of greater centralization and concentration of power in its own hands. Second, Ontario has been singled out for a reduced role in the building of our nation.

From the record it appears that the Canadian Confederation is impaled on the horns of a dilemma. On the one hand, Ottawa has revenues disproportionate to its responsibilities and on the other hand, the provincial governments are faced with responsibilities disproportionate to their revenue base.

A simple resolution of the dilemma would appear to be to assign more responsibilities to Ottawa. But this is not possible for a number of reasons. The most important reason is that the government of Quebec does not wish to lose any social programs and they are the programs that are costly. Much of the postwar era has been characterized by the struggle of Quebec for preeminence in the social policy areas, first quietly under Duplessis and since Lesage, more loudly.

The government of Quebec has been joined in this struggle by the government of Ontario. Indeed in more recent years Ontario has sometimes taken initiatives rather than Quebec. However, while their ends may be the same, the two provincial governments have distinct concerns.

Ontario, becoming increasingly assertive, is returning in a sense, to the historical position of Oliver Mowat with his compact theory of Confederation. It is useful to refer to Mowat in order to realize that, in Ontario, Ottawa confrontation is as old as Confederation itself. At the same time, it would be a mistake to view the current stand off as simply an inevitable historical re-occurrence. As was noted earlier a gap was created between the federal government and the Ontario government (indeed all provincial governments) in 1966 which has not been bridged. The federal government does not even admit that such a gap exists. It was caused partially by the false expectations created by Prime Minister Pearson's co-operative federalism approach. And there was a sense of relief after the shock of the Quebec City Conference in the Spring of 1964.

At that Conference the Federal-Provincial Tax Structure Committee was created. The Committee which was to prepare detailed projections of revenues and expenditures by level of government reported in September 1966.

The report showed that the federal government would be in a surplus position while the provinces and their municipalities would be faced with large deficits. Rather than coming forward with proposals to alleviate the situation, the federal government threw down a gauntlet. Mr. Sharp stated:

> The conclusion seems clear: The problem is not lack of access to revenue sources, but rather the difficulties the Provinces face—in company with the Federal Government—in raising taxes that are already high.

To others, a very different conclusion "seems clear" from reading the Report of the Tax Structure Committee.

This immediate federal response plus subsequent actions has created a credibility gap between the federal government and the Ontario government. But that was not the only error in 1966.

Another major error was the announcement by the federal government of its intention to introduce Medicare. Probably no provincial government opposed Medicare but most provincial governments did oppose the universality aspect and the timing of its introduction. At a time when provincial governments were struggling to find money for education they could not see the point of introducing a new costly program. Ontario was one of the leading critics of this federal initiative.

Subsequent events have done little to reconcile the governments of Canada and Ontario. Federal announcements and programs, the withdrawal from shared-cost programs, the social development tax and tax reform, all seem designed to irritate rather than soothe.

What is meant by?

"tax sharing"
"shared-cost programs"

What do you think?

1. *What is the main problem in dealing with the Federal Government in the eyes of Ontario's politicians? Why is it a problem?*
2. *What proposals have Ontario's finance ministers made to counter the problem as they see it? What are the advantages and disadvantages of their proposals?*
3. *What implications do Ontario's demands on the Federal Government have for the other regions of Canada?*
4. *In his 1971 budget address, Darcy McKeough stated that "Ontario has been singled out for a reduced role in the building of our nation." What factors discussed in the article may have led him to come to this conclusion? Does his statement in any way reflect regional concerns? Why or why not?*

ONTARIO SUFFERS AS PORK BARREL OF CANADA

Certain groups in Ontario, particularly primary producers, have long claimed that Federal Government policies discriminate against them. The Ontario Federation of Agriculture argues the case for some changes in those policies in an article in the Globe and Mail *on June 12, 1969. (Reprinted with the permission of the* Globe and Mail, *Toronto.)*

Ontario cannot go on being the pork barrel of Canada if it has to compete with government subsidies to other regions, the Ontario Federation of Agriculture said in a brief presented last night in London, Ont., to the Commons agricultural committee.

Ontario producers look "with concern on federal policies which assist the Maritime Provinces to move their vegetable and garden products into this province in competition with Ontario products."

Referring to treatment of Ontario as a "have" province in the recent federal budget, the federation says "it is fine for the federal Government to view Ontario as one big fat pork barrel which is bottomless.

"But Ottawa had better take some steps to secure the bottom of the barrel against leaks which may be created by open borders, subsidized imports, and reduced tax concessions."

Main focus in the brief was the cost of inputs, the goods and services the farmer buys for the production of his crop. It said research in 1968 showed "Ontario farmers were paying up to twice as much for some inputs as a number of agricultural producers with whom we compete in global trade."

What do you think?

1. *Why do you suppose the Federation feels that the Federal Government regards Ontario as the pork barrel of Canada? Do you think they have a case?*
2. *Compare the regional concerns of Ontario food producers with those of the Prairie provinces. How are they alike? How are they different?*

NORTHERN ONTARIO ALIENATION

Even Ontario has to face its own special brand of regional protest—Northern Ontario alienation. Douglas Fisher, a well-known journalist, describes this phenomenon in the following article from W. Kilbourn (ed) A Guide to the Peaceable Kingdom (Macmillan, Toronto, 1970).

In this century the region has staged from frontier to development to stability and, in much of it, to stagnation. The chambers of commerce and the politicians keep the style and cliches of the past—'inexhaustible resources', 'the treasure-house of the continent'. Northern Ontario has been 'next year' and 'next generation' country. But now there's a shrillness. The demands, claims, and plaints no longer have the swagger. There has never been, of course, a coherent regional movement of any kind. Just a similarity in hopes and grieving of each of its towns and subsections!

This is the striking paradox of Northern Ontario: the climate and landscape, the people and their work, are so much alike but there is no entity, merely a scatter of locales. . . .

Each community has had its colourful characters, especially its strong men, but there have been few regional spokesmen and no concerted political action from the whole. Every once in a while a secession movement pops up—e.g. Cochrane or the Lakehead or Kenora—but it never has more than a few wild disciples. C. D. Howe, Sir James Dunn, and Roy Thomson started on the road to power and wealth in Northern Ontario. Each came as an adult, attained a certain scale, and then moved on to bigger leagues.

The lack of a past, the separateness, the distance, the boom and bust of mining and logging, and the mixed ethnicity of the people have made for open local societies, and intense community life, and a frenetic liveliness. The Moose, the Masons, the Elks, the Royal Order of the Purple, the Eastern Star, the Lions, the Kinsmen, the Foresters, the Dante Clubs, the Prosvita Societies, the Legion, and a clutch of sporting clubs preoccupy the communities. They make for vociferousness, not brooding. It was symbolic that the imposter professor, MacDonald, not only held a university post at the Lakehead for two and a half years but was treasured for a host of community works.

Movement, boom, depletion, completion and change! These are intrinsic to railroading, road, hydro, and rail construction, mining, logging, and lumbering. At first strong backs were more essential than skills. Thus the Finns, Swedes, Balts, Italians, and Ukrainians found places in the flood years of immigration. Most of the merchandising and professional people came from old Ontario. The engineering and techniques were drawn from the U.K. and U.S.

Such diversity allied with the isolation, the rawness, and the dreams to make communities which bridged their people without a set class structure or a strong administrative grouping to control them. Any tendency to company dominance, always likely—especially in the Sault with Algoma Steel and in Sudbury with INCO—tended to dissipate with the flow and variety of folk. One doesn't regiment or keep down railroaders or loggers or miners very easily.

What do you think?

1. *Why has Northern Ontario felt alienated from the rest of the province? Do you see any common ground between this region's alienation and that expressed by other areas, for example the Maritimes, the Prairie Provinces?*
2. *Do you think that there are significant enough differences between Northern Ontario and the rest of the province to encourage the further growth of the existing separatist movement in the north? What kind of alternatives would such a movement propose or offer to the residents of the region?*

QUEBEC

Relations between Quebec and the rest of Canada have been an important part of our national life since before Confederation. The Quebec situation has been examined in great detail in a separate volume of this series, *Canadiens, Canadians and Québécois.*

However, in light of the election of a provincial government committed to separation, certain aspects of Quebec's relationship to Canada should be re-examined.

The following section looks at separatist sentiment in Quebec. Is Quebec separatism a form of regional protest? What distinguishes it from other regional protests? What effects has the PQ victory had on regional discontent in the rest of Canada? What options are available to the Federal Government in dealing with the Quebec situation?

WE ARE QUEBECOIS

In his book, Option for Quebec, *René Lévesque, Quebec Premier and leader of the Parti Québécois, talked about the significance of the term Québécois. (Reprinted by permission of The Canadian Publishers, McClelland and Stewart Limited, Toronto.)*

What that means first and foremost—and if need be, all that it means—is that we are attached to this one corner of the earth where we can be completely ourselves: this Quebec, the only place where we have the unmistakable feeling that "here we can be really at home."

Being ourselves is essentially a matter of keeping and developing a personality that has survived for three and a half centuries.

At the core of this personality is the fact that we speak French. Everything else depends on this one essential element and follows from it or leads us infallibly back to it.

. . .

Until recently in this difficult process of survival we enjoyed the protection of a certain degree of isolation. We lived a relatively sheltered life in a rural society in which a great measure of unanimity reigned, and in which poverty set its limits on change and aspiration alike.

We are children of that society, in which the *habitant*, our father or grandfather, was still the key citizen. We are also heirs to that fantastic adventure—that early America was almost entirely French. We are, even more intimately, heirs to the group obstinacy which has kept alive that portion of French America we call *Québec*.

All these things lie at the core of this personality of ours. Anyone who does not feel it, at least occasionally, is not—is no longer—one of us.

What do you think?

1. *How does Lévesque define the term, "Québécois"? What does he claim lies at the root of the Quebec identity?*
2. *Does any other region in Canada have a similar basis for claiming a separate identity? Explain your answer.*

DEAR ENEMIES

The following excerpt is taken from a letter written by the French Canadian journalist Solange Chaput Rolland to an English Canadian, Gwethalyn Graham. The women published their letters in the form of a book entitled Dear Enemies. *(Reprinted by permission of The Canadian Publishers, McClelland and Stewart Limited, Toronto.)*

Because I live in a democracy, I want above all a freedom of being. But if, in order to live in freedom in a Canada entirely dominated by English thinking and an English way of life, I must constantly do battle to keep my language and its spirit intact, then both what I have to say and my happiness in being alive will always be clouded. I shall shut myself up again in my French solitude, and my bitterness will snuff out the dynamism that is indispensable to creative work and to economic or social success. We Canadians don't recognize the love which is within us; this country of snow and desolation, this icy tundra, this people closed in on themselves and their problems, creates in our souls a hunger for love from which will flow one day, perhaps, a stream of moral richness. But life demands love, and we don't know how to live with it.

True bilingualism, the kind I believe in, wouldn't oblige every Canadian from the Atlantic to the Pacific to speak two languages, but it would bring about a greater understanding between our two realities, our two mentalities, our two histories.

What do you think?

1. *In the previous excerpt René Lévesque says "At the core of this personality is the fact that we speak French." Does Chaput Rolland agree or disagree with this view? What possibilities does she see for resolution of the issue?*
2. *To what extent does Chaput Rolland's portrait of the country as a whole contribute to your understanding of the Quebec issue?*

THE BOTTOM OF OUR DIFFICULTIES

Claude Ryan, the provincial leader of the Liberal Party and former editor-in-chief of the famous Montreal French-language newspaper, Le Devoir, *is one of the most respected voices in French Canada. In an editorial on July 11, 1972, he analyzed the relationships between economic and social problems and those concerning culture and language in Quebec. (Reprinted by permission of* Le Devoir.*)*

If the questions of culture and language are to be approached in an atmosphere of complete calm and impartiality, people must be able to feel themselves economic and social equals; they must have the impression that everybody has an equal opportunity in life.

Now under existing economic conditions, anglophones start off with undisputed advantages. Until economic power is distributed on a more uniform basis—and this means a good deal more than government programs for the redistribution of income—we shall be begging the question.

Actually, the sharing of power also goes further than what is called the working-language question. It covers all structures issuing economic decisions. Whatever the cost may be, francophones must make their way into these structures. There is no doubt that they control the promotion, duration, and vitality of their language.

What do you think?

1. *According to Ryan, how can French Canadians obtain economic and social equality? What problems will they face in trying to achieve this goal?*
2. *What are the differences between Lévesque's and Ryan's view of the basis of regional protest?*

WHY ACUTE NOW?

The following excerpt from an article in Canada and the World *in April 1972 analyzes the reasons for the recent prominence of the separatist ideology. ("The History of Quebec Separatism 1760 to 1972", by Charles White)*

Why has the separatist problem become acute only since 1960, when history shows so many examples of friction between Quebec and the rest of Canada? We should consider these points:

1. The population shift to the cities has been going on for many years in Quebec. One effect of this has been to weaken the hold of the church, which was usually conservative and on the side of authority. Another has been to strengthen the influence of trade unions which are more and more involved in radical politics. These results of urbanization have only recently come into focus.

2. Immigration to Quebec, while it has slowed in the past year or two, is threatening the language and culture of the province. Most immigrants, no matter what their nationality, show a preference for learning English which they see as more useful for a future career in Canada. Quebeckers are reacting to this threat.

3. The birth rate in Quebec has historically been above the Canadian average. In 1951 it was still 23 per cent higher than in the rest of the country. But after that it started to decline so that by 1965 it was 5 per cent below the mean. Pessimists in Quebec predict that this trend combined with immigration will reduce the French-speaking people in Quebec to 72 per cent by 1991. Alarm over this puts separatism in a "now-or-never" mood.

4. For the past ten years minority revolt has been sweeping across the world. Terror in Algeria, race riots in the U.S., separatist struggles in Spain and Yugoslavia, civil rights everywhere. The impact of television and the other news media is instant and has furnished activists in Quebec with ideas and methods.

5. The reform of education in Quebec during the Quiet Revolution, while not too successful, has produced a new breed of young people who are questioning federalism. Many of them become teachers themselves and pass on their radical opinions to their students.

6. For the first time, after the death of Maurice Duplessis, Quebeckers began to see their own provincial government as a possible instrument to bring about national independence. The Parti Québécois now has a foothold in the National Assembly and may become the vehicle the separatists are looking for.

What is meant by?

"the Quiet Revolution"

What do you think?

1. What other reasons can you suggest for the increasing popularity of the separatist movement in Quebec?

2. How has the introduction of Quebec's language bill, Bill 101, affected the situation in Quebec?

HOMELAND FOR QUEBECKERS

Following the victory of the Parti Québécois on November 15, 1976, René Lévesque addressed his supporters. These are excerpts from his remarks.

. . . and I renew in the name of everyone tonight the promises we made, and we will do our best to keep each and every one of them. I will not repeat them tonight but we will not forget a single one.

And I repeat in particular the one, the principal promise, a fact which will not change, that from the bottom of my heart, from the bottom of all your hearts, we hope, in friendship with our fellow-citizens in Canada, to make of Québec a sovereign state; but Québec would only become a state when an adult society, with confidence in itself, will have so decided in a referendum by a clear and democratic majority, as we have promised.

. . .

. . . and I would like to say in a very calm and sincere way, I would like to tell our opponents in Québec, and to those here and elsewhere, who may have feared the results of a Parti Québecois victory, that we intend to make of Québec, and we intend to work with all our might to make of Québec, a place which will be more than ever the home-land of all Québecers who live here and who love Québec.

What do you think?

1. What is your reaction to these remarks? Why?

2. How would you expect Canadians outside Quebec to react to Lévesque's remarks? Inside Quebec?

OLD QUEBEC IS DEAD AND BURIED

The following analysis of the changes occurring in Quebec was written by Michel Brunet, a well-known historian from Quebec. It appeared in the Toronto Star on November 20, 1976, under the title "A New Party for a New Québec". (Reprinted with the permission of Michel Brunet.)

The Parti Québécois' victory is merely another milestone in the three hundred and fifty years old history of the French-speaking inhabitants of the St. Lawrence valley. Since the beginning of the seventeenth century, they are in search of a fatherland.

When Québec was part of the French North American empire, it was called Canada. Its French-speaking settlers were known as the *Canadiens*.

In 1763, after the conquest of New France, they became British subjects in a colony known as the Province of Quebec. However, they continued to call themselves *Canadiens* and the British administration used the same name to identify his majesty's new subjects. The English-speaking settlers who established themselves in the St. Lawrence valley were named British Americans.

Under Louis-Joseph Papineau's leadership, the *Canadiens* claimed that they did form the *nation canadienne*. Their program of nation-building came to naught in 1837-38.

After the foundation of United Canada in 1841, the British Americans began to call themselves Canadians. The *Canadiens*, who had become a minority, were now known as French Canadians. Even after the creation of the *Province de Québec* with Confederation in 1867, they continued to be identified as such.

Inside Québec, the French Canadians did form the majority of the population. However, they still behaved as a minority. In fact, they accepted without contest—except in time of war—the political leadership of English Canada, and they were told by their traditional leaders that their living depended on the economic initiative of the English-speaking bourgeoisie.

This alliance between the earthen pot and the iron pot, known as the great compromise of Canadian history, lasted from 1854 to the 1950s. During this century, the French Canadians of Québec were politically naïve and wanted to believe that Canada was their fatherland.

During the Great Depression and World War II, many French Canadians began to ask themselves if it would not be more realistic to promote the economic and cultural progress of their community inside the borders of Québec instead of waging exhausting and fruitless fights to establish bilingualism throughout Canada and to secure the collaboration of their English-speaking fellow citizens in building an hypothetical Canadian nation.

The Québécois were born. Maurice Duplessis' struggle to consolidate Québec's autonomy in fiscal matters and his choice of a national flag received the voters' enthusiastic support. Louis Saint-Laurent himself, when he tried to influence his Québec compatriots in provincial matters, learned that he was not the leader of the Québécois.

The Quiet Revolution, initiated by Jean Lesage, René Lévesque, Paul Gérin-Lajoie and Georges-Emile Lapalme in 1960, accelerated the historical evolution begun in the 1930s. The new educational, social and labor policy adopted by the Lesage government was supposed to enable the Québécois to be "masters in our own house", according to the Liberal slogan in the general election of 1962.

When the Union Nationale, under the leadership of Daniel Johnson and Jean-Jacques Bertrand, came back to power in 1966, it had no choice but to continue and complete the reform policies first adopted by the Liberals. During the '60s, the provincial government was being nationalized by the Québécois who demanded the establishment of a positive state with policies that would take into account their national ends. They were engaged in the exalting process of building a fatherland for a new nation.

The Parti Québécois, founded in 1968, democratically proposed its program to achieve this goal at the general election of 1970. Six hundred thousand voters supported the new party.

At the general election of 1973 the Parti Québécois got the votes of 30 per cent of the electorate and became the official opposition in the National Assembly. It counted only six members in the Assembly but this fact mattered little. Being the official opposition, it could normally expect to take power at the next general election. Is it not the normal way that democracy works?

Monday's election has shown once more how democracy operates in a free country.

The Québec voters who went to the polls knew that a grave decision had to be taken.

A majority among them (66 per cent) refused to yield to the blackmail organized by the Québec and Ottawa Liberals.

People voted for a change, and were ready to face the consequences of their choice.

The Parti Québécois has become the government of all Québec citizens.

Under its leadership, the new Québec, which has been in the making for two generations, will pursue its march towards the future. A living and dynamic collectivity never goes backward.

Will English-speaking Canadians realize that the former Canada they were used to exists no more, because the old Québec itself is dead and buried?

Will the Québécois meet a new English Canada with which they will be able to negotiate a new partnership?

The answer belongs to the English-speaking Canadians as a nation—not to Ottawa alone.

What do you think?

1. *What is meant by the phrase "old Québec is dead and buried"? What implications does such a statement have for English Canadians? Do you believe Professor Brunet's claim? Why or why not?*

2. What role does Professor Brunet feel that English Canadians will play in the Quebec question? How reasonable do you think Professor Brunet's expectations are?
3. Brunet maintains there is a New Quebec, while in a previous article, I. H. Asper heralded the birth of the New West. What similarities exist between the New Quebec and the New West? What differences?

THE TAKE-OVER STRATEGY

These documents appeared in the Toronto Star *following the election of the Parti Québécois on November 15, 1976. The first outlines the step-by-step procedure which would be followed in the attempt to gain independence for the province. The second, an analysis of the plan, was written by John Brehl, and is reprinted with permission—The* Toronto Star.

a) The Parti Québécois approved plans at a conference of delegates last year to make immediate moves on Quebec's independence once the party was elected.

The delegates approved making proposals to the National Assembly to:

—Demand from Ottawa the handing over to Quebec of all powers, apart from those that the two governments wish, for the purposes of economic association, to control jointly;

—Undertake, with a view to attaining this objective, technical discussions with Ottawa on the orderly transfer of power;

—Work out, with Canada, understandings dealing notably with the division of possessions and debts, and also with the ownership of the public works, in conformity with rules of international law;

—In the event that it must proceed unilaterally, take over methodically the exercise of all powers of a sovereign state, assuring itself beforehand of the support of Quebeckers by referendum;

—Submit to the people a national constitution worked out by citizens at the constituency level and adopted by the delegates of the people gathered in a constituent assembly;

—Request the admission of Quebec to the United Nations and obtain the recognition of other states;

—Respect, among the treaties binding Canada, those which are favorable to Quebec, and follow in the denunciation of other treaties, the rules of international law;

—Reaffirm and defend the inalienable rights of Quebec over all its territory, including Labrador and its coastal island and claim possession of the Arctic Islands and lands now Canadian that are due to it by the same right as to other northern countries;

—Failing agreement on this question, take measures of legal occupation (such as granting of concessions, establishing institutions and take the case before the international courts of justice).

b) If they get independence on their terms, here's the way they see the future of a French-Canadian nation:

An independent Quebec would have a president and a social democratic system somewhat resembling the Scandinavian countries.

It would want to take its share of Canada's present assets—and be prepared to take on its share of the national debt.

It would operate in a customs union with Canada, providing free trade between the two countries and identical tariffs with the rest of the world.

It would run its own internal air services, nationalize some industries like Bell Telephone and the railway system, buy back some foreign-controlled industries.

It would spell out clearly which economic fields would have to be under domestic ownership, which industries could be under mixed control and which would be open relatively freely to foreign ownership.

It wouldn't have an army; it would handle most of its own social security schemes like old age pensions, but would expect Ottawa to continue paying some, such as war pensions.

The St. Lawrence Seaway would be owned and run by three nations instead of two and the customs union would allow free movement of goods and people between the two parts of Canada—the Atlantic provinces and the rest—which are severed by Quebec.

And Lévesque claims it can all be done amicably and we'd stay friends.

Business, being business, would adjust and accept the situation because it's in its interest to do so.

Ontario would be hurt more than Quebec if Canada boycotted Quebec, because, Lévesque guessed several years ago, Ontario sells twice as much to Quebec as vice versa.

Language problems in Quebec would disappear because Quebec would, quite simply, be French-speaking.

. . .

There Quebec sits, geographically the largest province, 15 per cent of our land mass, containing more than 26 per cent of our population. It's tightly entwined in the national economy, with 30 per cent of our manufacturing, much of our pulp and paper and mineral resources, its share of federal installations and assets and programs.

It lies along the St. Lawrence Seaway, and it sits right across the passage from the Atlantic provinces to Ontario and the west.

Even with Canada relatively prosperous in the world, Quebec has economic problems already: more of its people are jobless than the national average; capital investment decreased last year; provincial debt rose by almost 16 per cent a year over the last four years.

Much of its economy is owned either in other parts of Canada or in foreign countries.

Yet the PQ wants to go it alone and believes it can succeed.

What do you think?

1. *What problems might be encountered in any attempt to grant Quebec independence?*
2. *How do you think Mr. Brehl feels about the Parti Québécois proposals? What caused you to draw this conclusion?*
3. *How realistic are the proposals of the Parti Québécois conference delegates?*
4. *To what extent do you think the demands of the Parti Québécois are legitimate?*
5. *Can the demands of the Québécois be met without separation? How?*

NEWSPAPER COMMENT

The following comments appeared in newspapers from coast to coast in Canada on November 16 and 17, 1976, following the election of the Parti Québécois in Quebec.

VANCOUVER *PROVINCE:*   René Lévesque managed to convince the voters in Quebec that he was not the bogeyman depicted by Robert Bourassa and the frightened money men of Montreal. Once that referendum (on separation) is held—and if the election polls accurately represented the attitudes of Quebec voters—they will vote for staying in Canada. He will then, have no more power than, say, the premier of British Columbia.

EDMONTON JOURNAL: If the Quebec election result meant anything, it was a repudiation of the notion that anything could be tolerated, in Quebec City or Ottawa, in the name of keeping the separatists out of power. Compared with Robert Bourassa's economic and cultural excesses and bungling, the prospect of flirting with separation obviously lost much of its terror in Quebec.

PRINCE ALBERT *DAILY HERALD:*   The separatist Parti Québécois victory will bring one of the nation's lingering problems front and centre. . . . The Parti Québécois was obviously the beneficiary of a large vote of protest against the governing Liberals, whose arrogance and indifference to some of the vital issues cost them dearly.

WINNIPEG *TRIBUNE:*   We implore Prime Minister Trudeau to keep his cool. There is no room here for outbursts. There is room for discussion, for rational argument. We implore Western Canadians not to act the fool but to say simply that Canada can survive if enough Canadians want it to.

The future? We can't predict. In Quebec, scare tactics failed. They will fail in Canada, too. Let us meet the future with confidence, not with fear.

MONTREAL *STAR:*   The Parti Québécois ran in the Quebec election campaign as a party like any other. It was elected as a party like the others and it has won a mandate to tackle Quebec's social and economic problems as a party like the others. . . . The split in the popular vote, however, should . . . temper the new government's enthusiasm to push for Quebec's independence, the fundamental plank in its platform which remained hidden for most of the campaign.

QUEBEC—*LE SOLEIL:* Quebec after this election . . . is not the same, for it has undertaken the greatest risk and the greatest challenge in its existence. The challenge is a double one because the government chosen by Quebec voters is dedicated to two major objectives: Political sovereignty for Quebec and social democratization.

What do you think?

1. *Most of the newspaper excerpts indicate the belief that Quebec elected a government not on the basis of independence but on that of good government. To what extent do you think this is true and why?*

YOU CAN'T GET THERE FROM HERE

This cartoon appeared in the Toronto Star *on November 19, 1976. (Reprinted with permission—The* Toronto Star.*)*

·HALIFAX? YOU CAN'T GET THERE FROM HERE." FRI., NOV. 19. 1976

What do you think?

1. *Do you think the cartoon makes a valid statement? Why or why not?*
2. *How do you think a Quebecker would react to this cartoon? Explain your answer.*

ALBERTA WILL TRY TO WORK WITH QUEBEC

In the following excerpt from an article entitled "We'll work at pact with Lévesque on economy" Gerald Utting describes the feeling of the government of Alberta about the election of the Parti Québécois. (Toronto Star, November 17, 1976. Reprinted with permission—The Toronto Star.)

Alberta will try to work with the new Quebec government of separatist René Lévesque to help provinces achieve greater control of their own economies, Premier Peter Lougheed said yesterday.

Alberta has had a good working relationship with Quebec for the last five years on constitutional issues. The Quebec election isn't going to make Alberta change its constitutional position—that all provinces should be equal, regardless of region or population, he said.

"The common position [with Quebec] is that this country would be better off if we had less centralization in Ottawa and Toronto," Lougheed said. "Certainly, western Canada would be stronger if it were not being suffocated by the bureaucrats in Ottawa."

What do you think?

1. *How might the election in Quebec pave the way to changes in Canada's constitution?*
2. *Do you agree with Premier Lougheed about the role of Central Canada in Confederation? How would you propose to change it if you do?*

GRAVE DANGERS FACE CANADA OVER QUEBEC

This extract is taken from an article written by Professor Frank Scott which appeared in the Toronto Star *on November 16, 1976. (Reprinted with the permission of F. R. Scott.)*

Today, political forces are pushing for the dismemberment of Canada not only openly in Quebec but subtly and by implication in other provinces. By implication in Quebec too, for M. Robert Bourassa has been as much a separatist as any recent Quebec premier—more effective, in fact, because he has the steady support of Prime Minister Pierre Trudeau. No statute in Quebec has ever been so separatist as Bill 22. At least yesterday's elections in the province made that clear. Trudeau did not oppose it or help the school boards who alone were fighting it, while our federal official language commissioner, Keith Spicer, actually spoke favourably of it in Montreal.

What I fear almost as much as Quebec's pressures at this time are the mounting forces in other provinces aiming to reduce, further than Trudeau has already reduced, the federal government's authority to govern this country in those matters of common interest which were entrusted to it in 1867.

What do you think?

1. *What is Professor Scott's main concern? Do you agree? Explain your point of view.*

ATLANTIC PROVINCES
THE MARITIMES AND NEWFOUNDLAND

In the 1860s and 1880s some of the angriest opponents of Confederation and defenders of regional interests were to be found in the three Maritime Provinces and in Newfoundland. In recent years, however, national attention has been focused on developments in Quebec and the phenomenon of Western alienation. As a result, the particular regional concerns of the four Atlantic provinces have not been examined in any great detail in the national media. This does not mean, however, that the Atlantic Provinces do not have grievances and do not question their status in confederation.

As this section will attempt to illustrate, regional protest is an active force in the Atlantic Region.

Even though it may seem that this regional concern is not as vocal as are others, it nevertheless exists and must be reckoned with.

JUST SIT THERE QUIETLY—YOU'LL GET YOUR SHARE

The following cartoon appeared on February 19, 1968 in the Halifax Chronicle-Herald, *and illustrates a view of Confederation widely held in the Atlantic Provinces.*

"Just sit there quietly — you'll get your share."

February 19th, 1968

What do you think?

1. Who is speaking? How do you interpret this cartoon?

New Brunswick

PROMOTE NEW BRUNSWICK'S PORT

The following document appeared in the Saint John Telegraph-Journal *on January 16, 1976.*

. . . Saint John is struggling to pay loose Ottawa funds for the forest products terminal everyone here understood was to be provided. It's battling proposed increases in pilotage fees that imperil traffic, and faces planned removal of federal rail subsidies for export grain and flour that could cost the port millions of dollars in lost cargoes and earnings. . . . So just what the port needs is word that Montreal is embarking on a campaign to regain shipping business lost in recent years to ports in the Maritimes and the eastern U.S. . . . And Montreal . . . is now open year round thanks to an elaborate system of ice control, radio, radar, beacons, lights and other winter navigational aids—so long camouflaged as "flood control measures"—that Maritimers are taxed to help support in the 1000 mile St. Lawrence channel to Montreal. . . .

Montreal's battle plans demand extra effort on our part to hang onto the gains and find more.

What do you think?

1. Why is the Saint John newspaper so angry with Montreal?
2. If you were a resident of New Brunswick would you be a supporter of the St. Lawrence Seaway? Why?
3. How does this document indicate a regional concern? What is it?

VANISHING TRAINS

(Saint John Telegraph-Journal, January 31, 1976)

. . . Transport Minister (Otto) Lang says he is going to improve railway passenger service. . . . The improvements he has in mind will be in the heavily-populated strip between Quebec City and Windsor, Ontario, and cuts will be, of course, in the Maritimes and Western Canada. . . .

Saint John has a particular stake; it is the eastern terminus of C.P. Rail and also served by C.N. Both provide some passenger service . . . There is a great deal of point in asking whether this is the time Canada should be demanding rail passenger service. The energy crisis may even threaten highway travel in the foreseeable future. Trains have the capability of hauling the most people at the least cost using the least fuel and creating the least pollution ... And if there is to be a cutback somewhere, why must the first to get it in the neck again be the Maritime Provinces—which were lured into Confederation on promises to weld the country together with a transcontinental transportation system? . . .

What do you think?

1. *Were Maritimers "lured into Confederation?" Defend your point of view.*
2. *According to the* Saint John Telegraph-Journal, *what area of Canada makes sacrifices first for the so-called national good? Why?*
3. *What proposal does the author of this article oppose? How does his attitude relate to regionalism?*

THE NATIONAL DREAM

The Saint John Telegraph-Journal *carried the following cartoon on its editorial page on February 10, 1976. (London Free Press. Reprinted with the permission of Charles Tingley.)*

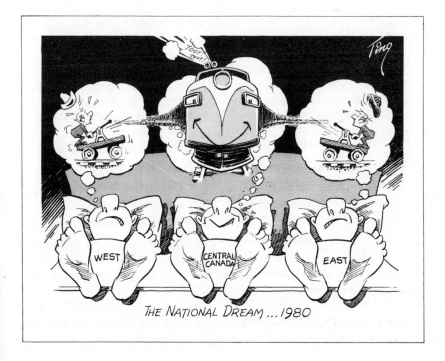

THE NATIONAL DREAM ... 1980

What do you think?

1. *What is the point of this cartoon?*
2. *Who is in a better position in 1980? Why?*
3. *Why is the cartoon's title ironic?*

Nova Scotia

KARSDALE MURAL TO NATIONAL GALLERY

On June 10, 1976, the editor of the influential Halifax Chronicle-Herald *declared:*

Canada's national art gallery has purchased the Karsdale mural at Granville Ferry for an unknown price, reportedly in the range of $50,000 with a view to moving it to Ottawa.

There can, perhaps, be no quarrel with the action of the gallery in purchasing the mural for the purpose of its preservation as a national work of art of superior value.

But the nation of Canada does not exist for the purpose of turning Ottawa into a modern version of Imperial Rome.

Nova Scotia is still part of Canada, or so we are told from time to time. . . .

The only reason of substance that has been publicly given for taking the Karsdale mural to Ottawa is so that more people will see it. That argument is, at least, open to question. . . .

We have reached a remarkable stage in national development if the National Gallery of Canada is, in essence, to purchase and preserve works of art that are the national heritage only if they can be moved to Ottawa. . . .

Canada extends—to a minor degree perhaps—some distance beyond the line of a triangle drawn around Ottawa, Montreal and Toronto. . . .

What do you think?

1. *Should the Karsdale Mural remain in Nova Scotia or should it be moved to Ottawa? Why?*
2. *What is the view of Central Canada which is expressed in this editorial? How is it expressed?*
3. *What kind of regional concern is being voiced in this editorial?*

THE LAST STRAW

The Halifax Chronicle-Herald *on October 30, 1967, printed the following cartoon drawn by the famous Robert Chambers.*

October 30th, 1967

What do you think?

1. Why is the Maritime region depicted as a camel? Who is throwing the "straw" on the camel's back?
2. Why would freight rates be a regional problem in the Maritimes?
3. Freight rates have also been a problem in the Prairie provinces. Compare the grievances there with those in the Maritimes. How are they alike? How do they differ?

TACKLING DISPARITY

The following document dealing with regional disparity appeared in the Halifax Chronicle-Herald *of April 23, 1977.*

One of the matters which has plagued Canada for far too long is that of regional disparity. Perhaps even more than problems associated with language, this has contributed to disunity in the nation. It fosters jealousies, encourages parochialism, and greatly strains the relations which ought to characterize the people of one country.

Regional disparity evidences itself in many ways. It is reflected in pay scales which are not consistent across the nation. It is to be seen in policies, such as those governing transportation, which work to the advantage of some provinces and the disadvantage of others.

It is obvious in employment statistics when, in some regions, large numbers are jobless while, elsewhere, the proportion of unemployed is comparatively low.

Unfortunately, regional disparity, like the weather, is a subject oft discussed but one which, considering its importance, engenders very little action of a remedial nature. Unlike the weather, it is a matter about which something could be done.

Just now, it appears, might be a very good time to begin doing that something. The Economic Council of Canada, in a lengthy report issued a few days ago, asserts that regional economic disparities remain intolerably large but new government measures could help significantly to reduce the dimension of the differences.

An encouraging feature of the findings of the Council is the observation that the disparities could be reduced without an increase in taxes. That is a matter of universal appeal. Perhaps governments have been slow to inaugurate policies aimed at reducing disparities for fear of the tax increases which would not be popular and which would further burden a public already bearing an intolerable tax load.

If, however, the goal can be realized without hiking taxes then it should be pursued without delay. It will require imaginative work on the part of governments, federal and provincial, to redesign policies and programs but the end result will more than justify the effort.

Certain it is that disparity must be seriously tackled. Some progress, to be sure, has been made. That is especially true of the Atlantic provinces but the total impact has been far short of the need. A determined effort to erase the inequalities could greatly strengthen the nation, would encourage new unity and would restore economic stability.

If the Economic Council of Canada is correct in its assessment and in its forecast, no time should be lost in taking the steps which, once and for all, will rid Canada of the categories of "have" and "have not" provinces.

What do you think?

1. What kinds of economic disparities are evident in Canada? How could they be lessened according to this editorial?
2. What effect will lessening disparity have on national unity according to this article? Would you agree?
3. Why do you think the editorial argues that "now might be a very good time to begin doing that something"?

TRANSCONTINENTAL

The following editorial appeared in the Halifax Chronicle-Herald *of May 6, 1977.*

One could be forgiven for assuming that trans-continental means across the continent. Within the Canadian context, however, that is not necessarily so although, admittedly, some allowances must be made for definition.

CP Air, for example, refers to its service between Montreal and Vancouver as trans-continental. Both of Canada's major railway systems use the term, trans-continental, in references to their connections between Vancouver and both Toronto and Montreal.

Insofar as Montreal has access to the Atlantic and Vancouver to the Pacific, it may be argued that there is some justification for use of the term trans-continental to describe these services.

However, it must be admitted that such usage is somewhat less than accurate. Probably it does not matter or, at least, it has not mattered very much until now.

Recent developments, however, suggest that it may be time to reassert the conviction that trans-continental does not end at Montreal or, for that matter, at Vancouver. One is still crossing Canada when his train rolls through Moncton or his aircraft touches down at Gander.

The matter has acquired a fresh relevance in the light of an announcement from the Canadian transport commission concerning what has been called a new trans-continental passenger train system. It has been designed to share $35 million annually from current operating costs and it will link Montreal/Toronto with Vancouver.

Very shortly, the Canadian transport commission is to be in the Atlantic provinces to review rail passenger services in this part of the country. In preparation for their coming, it has been disclosed that the conveying of travellers by train in the Maritimes has been a money losing proposition. Against such a background, it could very well happen that rail passenger links, already operating at a bare minimum, could be further curtailed.

Such an action is made all the easier for the transport commission when the route between Montreal and Halifax is viewed, not as a part of the trans-continental system, which it really is, but as an appendage, a sort of branch line stuck on the end of a national railway system.

What do you think?

1. *What is the point of this editorial? Do you think the grievance is valid?*
2. *How might this transportation question contribute to the problem of regionalism in Canada?*

Prince Edward Island

Prince Edward Island's growing dependence on the Federal Government has prompted some outspoken Islanders to criticize the gradual undermining of Island values. These people do not blame Upper Canada and Ottawa for all their problems, but feel that something unique to Prince Edward Island is being destroyed in the name of progress. The articles in this section describe the efforts being made to improve PEI's economic situation, but also demonstrate that Islanders have not lost that fighting spirit and fierce independence which made them initially resist the notion of union with Canada.

DEVELOPMENT IN PEI

Since 1969, the Federal Government has been operating an extensive program of social and economic development in Prince Edward Island. Peter Desbarats, a noted Canadian journalist, describes this program as well as the reactions of Islanders to it, in the following selection. (Toronto Star, May 18, 1972. Reprinted with permission—The Toronto Star.)

When Prince Edward Island was trying to make up its mind about joining Confederation in 1873, the big question of course had to do with building a railway on the island.

Next year, when the smallest province celebrates its centennial, the question will be whether Confederation in the second half of the 20th century is enabling Prince Edward Island to build a new society.

Since the spring of 1969, this province of 2,200 square miles and 110,000 people has been the site of a unique, comprehensive and expensive program of economic and social development. "The plan"—as it is always called here—is projected over a 15-year period; both federal and provincial governments have committed themselves to spending up to $243 million during the first six-year phase. That amounts to more than $2,200 for every man, woman and child on the island; and by the centennial year, it should be possible to see if this kind of massive investment, handled in this way, can solve the problems which beset Prince Edward Island and many other regions of Canada east of Ontario.

BENEFITS FOR ALL. All Canadians have a stake in the plan—an involvement in its outcome as well as a financial investment, through the federal government, of $125 million in the first six years. If this province can interrupt the cycle of poverty which has robbed it of people and initiative for decades, other governments will have to pay attention, and the lessons learned here through trial and error will be a textbook for regional development in other parts of the nation.

In many ways, Prince Edward Island is an ideal laboratory for the experiment now in progress.

In addition to possessing a classic set of economic and social problems, Prince Edward Island also has a small and homogeneous population under the jurisdiction of a single provincial government. This has made it possible, for the first time in Canada, to plan on a provincial scale with total integration of all federal and provincial government departments.

Prince Edward Island is also one of the most political places in Canada. Politics on the Island are inbred and personal. In the minds of some planners, this was an important negative qualification for the experiment now in progress. They felt that if the plan could win the confidence and support of the islanders, and survive the pressures of local politics, it could probably work anywhere in Canada.

A lot of money has been devoted initially to this aspect. The development plan is currently spending almost $4 per capita per year on the island to encourage "public participation" in its programs, particularly by farmers. The intensity of this effort can be appreciated if you realize that spending on a similar scale in Toronto or Montreal would mean, in each city, a "citizen activation" program costing $8 million a year.

This order of priorities indicates the essential nature of the plan. In its original financial projections, "social development" accounted for about half the total budget; and last year even this generous allocation was revised upward, at the expense of more traditional types of investment in resource and industrial development, to envisage the spending of $154 million on "social development" in the first six years.

The target of the plan, stated in its simplest form, is a revolution in decision-making at every level in the province. The objective is to give every decision-maker in Prince Edward Island, from the provincial cabinet to the individual farmer or businessman, the knowledge, apparatus and skill to function productively.

A NEW SOCIETY. This is a much more difficult endeavour than simply pumping funds into public works, and industrial subsidies in a depressed area. It means building a new society on the assumption that eventually it will be able to provide for itself.

The development plan still encounters hostility and scepticism on the island. There is continuing resentment of outside experts who try to impose textbook solutions on problems which farmers and fishermen have endured for decades. Critics claim that the heavy investment of the plan itself in capital works and high-cost personnel has created a kind of false prosperity in the province.

One of the four Conservative MPs on the island, David MacDonald, maintains that the plan has failed in the industry where improvement was most essential, agriculture; that there is no effective evaluation procedure; and that public participation has been inadequate despite the amounts of money poured into it under the plan.

. . .

"A plan will only be as good as the degree to which people get involved. From start to finish, there has been a feeling in Prince Edward Island that the plan was being imposed on the people."

MacDonald and other local critics already talk about the plan as if it symbolizes yet another lost opportunity for the province—a brief, optimistic chapter of history that is already being forgotten.

Partisans of the plan, among the Liberal supporters of Premier Alex Campbell and the technocracy, give a completely different reading. They claim that the development plan is just beginning to gain public acceptance and show statistical results.

They claim that income figures eventually will show that Prince Edward Island has boomed in the past 18 months while the rest of Canada has been in a period of economic recession. An early indication of this came when the provincial government discovered to its surprise that it had underestimated revenues last year, particularly from the sales tax. Evident signs of a healthy commercial and residential construction industry have been confirmed by the Central Mortgage and Housing Corporation, which has seen its funding increase from about $1.5 million three years ago to a 1972-73 budget allocation of $8 million for the province.

Education on the island has been thoroughly overhauled, the showpiece institution being a progressive college of applied arts and technology in Charlottetown with 600 students.

Even the controversial Land Development Corporation—a state program for purchase and leasing of farm land—has started to grow after two years of relative stagnation. Only about 15,000 acres of land were acquired by the corporation in the first two years. The annual acquisition rate is now said to be double that figure, with corporation offices "totally inundated" by farmers wanting to sell or acquire land.

THE EVALUATION STARTS. After a great deal of discussion with Ottawa about criteria for evaluation, the planners here are now ready to start on an 18-month evaluation process which should provide some measure of the plan's success, as well as guidelines for the second phase.

Not surprisingly, Premier Campbell has already made his intuitive assessment.

In an interview this week, he said it was fortunate for the province that after the agreement for the plan was signed with Ottawa in 1969 and ratified by the provincial legislature, an election in 1970 gave the government a firm mandate to proceed with the program.

"Many programs like this never reach that stage," he said, "and I would suggest that we are fortunate, in my judgment, in that we are one of the very few areas in Canada where you can point your finger and say, 'Now there's a development plan working.'"

What do you think?

1. *Why does Desbarats feel that the PEI plan "will be a textbook for regional development in other parts of the nation"? Do you agree with his assessment? Explain.*
2. *What kinds of problems did the plan have to overcome in order to be accepted by the Islanders?*
3. *What facets of the program are attacked by critics? Why?*
4. *To what extent can such development programs be a positive force in solving regional problems in Canada? Discuss.*

PEI RESENTS BEING 'OTTAWA'S WARD'

Despite the positive results expected from the Ottawa government's development program, many PEI residents are very vocal about their dissatisfaction with Confederation. The next document is an article by Lyndon Watkins, a Halifax reporter for the Toronto Globe and Mail. *It shows that regional protest is still very much a force to be reckoned with in PEI. (The* Globe and Mail, *December 30, 1972)*

Prince Edward Island begins its centennial celebrations on New Year's Eve, but not everyone will be cheering.

The 30 Brothers and Sisters of Cornelius Howatt are among the restrained. They are members of a group formed recently to perpetuate the memory and ideals of one of the island legislators who had to decide 100 years ago whether PEI should become part of Canada or go it alone.

It is not that the bus driver, the newspaper editor, the teachers, students and farmers who make up this organization find it hard to raise any enthusiasm for the centennial . . .

It's simply that they don't think joining Canada was a good idea for PEI in the first place. They are not separatists, not trying to reverse history. But they feel the island lost much more than it gained by becoming the seventh province of Canada, having waited six years to join after the original four united.

Confederation, they say, has reduced PEI to the status of being a welfare ward of Ottawa. Changes being imposed on the province under a federal-provincial development plan make prospects for the next 100 years depressing they add.

. . .

The Brothers and Sisters feel PEI was forced unwillingly into Confederation by the pressure of debts involved in construction of a railway. The British were threatening to get nasty about extending further credit if the colony didn't join Canada.

Having overwhelmingly opposed the earlier blandishments of the Confederationists, 27 of the 29 island legislators eventually endorsed the idea. The holdouts were Cornelius Howatt and A.E.C. Holland . . .

Howatt was a tenant farmer. He believed that farming was the basis of the island's prosperity and the reason for the colony's proud record of self-sufficiency going back 100 years. In his day the per capita debt was only $2. Now the overall debt is $650 million. Many of the fine large homes still standing in PEI were built on fortunes made during the 1860s, the period of trade reciprocity with the United States.

To join Canada would be to lose this independence and to sink into a dependent status. "We will be the next thing to nothing. It is just a question of self, or no-self," Howatt said. They are words which 30-year-old David Weale of Cornwall, PEI, a PhD history student at Queen's University in Kingston, feels are extremely prophetic.

With another history student, Harry Bagole of Charlottetown, who is studying at Memorial University in St. John's, Mr. Weale founded the Brothers and Sisters movement. It grew out of research they were doing on a proposed history of the island. They feel that many of the things that Howatt warned about are coming to pass.

They say the province is threatened by the inroads of corporate farming, tourism, the sale of land to non-residents and the increasing economic dependence of the island on financial support from Ottawa.

"We are in the midst of massive economic development and enormous change. But much of the impetus for it and the rationale behind it does not come from the island itself. These are imported solutions. And they are not always good solutions," Mr. Weale says.

"Our primary source of alarm is the destruction of the family farm. For 200 years the island has been a family farm society. The island is a farm. Independence and pride have characterized the family farm and have been the island's strength. But this way of life is threatened by the corporate farm and the destruction of small rural communities."

Mr. Weale admits that what is going on in island agriculture is no different from trends seen elsewhere in the country.

. . .

He feels strongly, however, that the value of the traditional island way of life cannot be measured in dollar terms alone. Neither can the cost of centralization being carried out under the plan be measured in economic terms only. There are grave sociological implications as well.

The promotion of tourism and the sale of land to non-residents are equally threatening. "This could lead to the spoilation of the whole social fabric." The same forces are at work in other "backwater" regions of the continent. But in resisting North American homogenization, PEI has one great advantage—"We are an island".

It may be futile to try to resist the tide of change engulfing Prince Edward Island, but Mr. Weale says if something isn't done the place will cease to have the attractions and society will lose the values they now possess.

"We want to make island people aware of their own history and their own strength. A great deal of the poverty here (PEI has the lowest per capita income level in Canada) is psychologically induced. Lots of my friends are living a very decent, dignified life on $5,000 a year. But because they are told they are subsisting below the poverty line, they have an inferiority complex."

What do you think?

1. Why do the Brothers and Sisters of Cornelius Howatt feel PEI made a mistake in joining Confederation?
2. What fears does Mr. Weale express about the future of Prince Edward Island?
3. Why does he object to the Federal Government's plan for economic development in PEI?

THE 'NATIONAL STANDARDS' HANG UP

Taking his cue from Cornelius Howatt, the PEI patriot who ardently opposed Confederation, the author of the next article questions whether it is a good idea for PEI to emulate other regions in Canada. (Source: H. Bagole and D. Weale Cornelius Howatt: Superstar *(1973))*

There are, unfortunately, many Islanders who seem to subscribe to the philosophy that "if it's good for the rest of North America, then it must be good for Prince Edward Island", and it is alarming to note how many decisions in this Province are justified with the statement that "this brings us into line with national standards". Whether the issue is the carrying of guns by policemen, the type of education we should have for our children, or the question of what constitutes a "decent" wage, this line of reasoning is invariably trotted out and Islanders are assured that what is happening is all for the best because we are more "in step" with current trends.

Perhaps the most glaring example of this type of mentality is to be found in the script of the Development Plan brochure. In the section on agriculture, the following statement appears: "The historical pattern of land ownership in Prince Edward Island is badly adapted to the needs of modern technology". Notice that the historic pattern of land usage on the Island is under fire here—not because it is badly suited to the needs of Islanders—but because it is badly suited to the needs of "modern technology." The statement simply assumes that what is good for "modern technology" must be good for Islanders.

Again, it has been argued by some educationists and politicians that we must decrease the number of teachers in the Province in order to come into line with the national teacher-student ratio. Thus, although decreasing the number of teachers clearly involves a lowering of our standard of education, we are informed that this is a justifiable step to take because it will achieve conformity with national standards.

Recently, moreover, the concept of the Summerside Waterfront Development plan was justified by the Premier by comparing downtown Summerside to the "dying core" of such cities as Halifax and Moncton. For good measure, he even tossed a somewhat mystifying reference to the ghettos of big American cities. Again, then, we see the tendency to simply assume that life on Prince Edward Island is and must be patterned after developments in the rest of North America.

At the crux of this "national standards" mentality is the issue of per capita income. Many Islanders believe—and many other Islanders encourage us to believe—that because the average citizen living on the Island is not earning as much as the average Canadian citizen living in Toronto, or even Halifax, that we are underprivileged and underdeveloped—a have-not Province.

It's true that Islanders do lag behind most other Canadians with respect to yearly wages. But if we are going to wave the banner of national standards we cannot, unfortunately, stop at wages. Consider, for instance, the matter of air pollution. Unless drastic steps are taken, the people of the Island will continue for many years to breathe air with a much lower pollution count than the majority of their fellow-Canadians. Do we desire parity here?

And what about the services that Islanders are missing out on because of the near-absence of organized crime. Surely we realize that this greatly limits the ready accessibility of such things as drugs, hardcore pornography, prostitutes, and gambling outlets. It's not that the determined Islander is completely denied such diversions, but their availability does fall somewhat short of the national standard.

Then there is the matter of traffic congestion. We have come a long way in this field in recent years, but it will be some time before we can match the situation as it now exists in many other parts of the country.

Those who covet national standards in wages are naïve if they think they can plug the Island society into national income standards without encouraging national standards in many of these other related areas as well. It is extremely difficult to have urban-industrial wages apart from an urban-industrialized society and apart from the serious social problems which invariably follow in the wake of such a way of life. It would be nice to be able to enjoy both an Island life-style and a Torontonian's pay-cheque, but that is not the way the world turns.

We in Prince Edward Island are living on the out-skirts of the technological society. Our Province has, of course, already been profoundly affected by technology in many ways, and yet, as a non-industrialized, agrarian community, and as an Island, we have not yet become so totally and irrevocably committed to this way of life as many other portions of North America. In other words, if we are awake enough to realize it, we still have a few options open.

What do you think?

1. *What regional attitudes does the author express about PEI?*
2. *How does he view "economic change"?*
3. *How does he view Central Canada? Why?*
4. *Is there a place for his Island in the Canada and in the world of the 1970s? Why or why not?*

Newfoundland

DARK DAYS FOR NEWFOUNDLAND

The cost of living is a matter of deep concern to all Canadians, but particularly to Newfoundlanders, as this article from the Toronto Star, *January 5, 1976, indicates. (Reprinted with permission—The* Toronto Star.*)*

Ten per cent of this city's [St. John's] homeowners failed to pay their property taxes last year because, says Mayor Dorothy Wyatt, they couldn't find the money.

"Most people don't realize how close to the line most Newfoundlanders live," she said. "Eighty per cent of our city homeowners maintain basement apartments. That is the only way they can afford their homes."

Despite a decade of relative boom, Newfoundland remains Canada's poorest province. Today the annual per capita income is just $3643, slightly more than half the Ontario figure.

And in a province with 10 per cent retail sales tax, 42 per cent provincial income tax (it's 30.5 per cent in Ontario) and 20 per cent unemployment (almost three times the national figure) and where beer cost $4.83 for a 12-bottle case, 25 cigarettes are $1.10 and regular gasoline is 94 cents a gallon (compared with $3.80, 85 cents and 81 cents respectively in Metro) it seems that 1976 will be anything but a happy new year. . . .

Newfoundland . . . has been forced to give up dreaming. After 25 years of trying desperately to attract industry and create economic growth through massive transfusions of federal money and resource giveaways to American promoters, the province has finally conceded that it cannot be like Canada's wealthy provinces.

Ottawa, moving to slow the growth in federal government spending, will have less to give Newfoundland in future; the small provincial market and the distance from North America's major population centres combine to make many industries uneconomic in Newfoundland; and the near-bankruptcy of New York city has led wary investors to steer clear of overextended junior governments.

What do you think?

1. Why do things cost so much more in Newfoundland?
2. How would you describe the standard of living in Newfoundland?
3. Why has Newfoundland "finally conceded that it cannot be like Canada's wealthy provinces"?

QUEBEC AND NEWFOUNDLAND IN SAME BOAT, INQUIRY TOLD

This article by Globe and Mail *reporter Hugh Winsor appeared October 31, 1977. (Reprinted with the permission of the* Globe and Mail, *Toronto.)*

The imperial muskets were beaten into welfare cheques for the victory on the plains of Newfoundland but Newfoundlanders as a conquered people struggling to maintain their culture and identity have more in common with Quebeckers than the rest of Canada.

That was the angry message delivered in trenchant if metaphorical terms to the Pepin-Robarts Task Force on Canadian Unity in the two days of meetings just concluded here.

Far from being shocked or alarmed at the prospect of Quebec separation, Newfoundlanders made it clear they shared Quebec's disenchantment with the Canadian Confederation.

The question in the national unity issue, they said, is not how to keep Quebec in Confederation but whether Confederation can be recast so that both Newfoundlanders and Quebeckers can feel at home.

The members of the task force may have come to Newfoundland expecting support for the federal Government position and to find Quebec Premier René Lévesque and his Parti Québécois painted as the enemies.

Instead, it heard that Newfoundlanders not only understand the PQ's objectives but they have an admiration mixed with envy for the Péquistes' success, especially their success in attracting the attention of the rest of Canada.

"Thank God for Quebec . . . Quebeckers know what they want and they are determined," community organizer Cathy Pennell told the hearings.

"May Quebec be the instrument that awakens the rest of us to the realization that only together and with concern for all Canadians, will we have a true unity. . . . The only people talking about unity are those who don't have to sweat it out day after day to keep body and soul together."

Quebec is less threatening to national unity than regional disparity and the lack of economic opportunity in places like Newfoundland, ran the common theme throughout the hearings. Newfoundland was painted as the colony "of the empire of the St. Lawrence" composed of the Quebec City-to-Windsor corridor by David Alexander, professor of history at Memorial University.

Like colonized people everywhere the natives have become restless and angry. They are frustrated by their lack of power over their own affairs and moreover they are humiliated by their lack of dignity and self-respect as they, in the words of another brief to the task force, "revel in the sweet death of welfare, unemployment insurance and mothers' allowance."

Much of the blame for Newfoundland's unhappiness was placed at the feet of the central Government and the concentration of power and influence in the "empire of the St. Lawrence." Professor Alexander compared Newfoundlanders to "Maritimers in the 1920s who saw their industrial revolution dismantled by the transfer to Montreal of regional control over the Intercolonial Railway, and Westerners who still find it impossible to mill grain, dress beef and manufacture petrochemicals for national markets.

"So Newfoundlanders were to see their ocean resources frittered away to national indifference, and the economic benefits of the disputed Labrador frontier safely ensconced in the empire of the St. Lawrence.

"In times past, injustices like this were defended in the name of unity of the British Empire; today it is offered to us as a necessity of national unity. It is imperialism, plain and simple. In its Canadian transmogrification, fiscal transfers have replaced the imperial garrison at least in Newfoundland, where presumably we are too beaten to require guarding.

What do you think?

1. *According to these two articles, what parallels exist between New-foundlanders and Quebeckers? Where do the two differ?*
2. *Why do Newfoundlanders not feel "at home" in Confederation?*
3. *"Quebec is less threatening to national unity than regional disparity and the lack of economic opportunity in places like Newfoundland . . ." Do you agree with this statement? Do some independent research to support your answer.*

MOORES PONDERS SEPARATION

Confederation has always been an issue in Newfoundland, as this newspaper article which appeared on November 14, 1977, shows. (Reprintd with the permission of CP.)

Premier Frank Moores says he may commission a study to find out whether Newfoundland could profit by leaving Confederation.

The study would be to find "what the cost of Confederation is compared to what the cost would be getting out of it," Moores said in an .nterview at the weekend.

"A lot of people in Newfoundland are damn well fed up with some of the attitudes in Ottawa," he said. "It's degrading when you have to go to Ottawa with cap in hand . . ."

The study would include "what the 200-mile limit would mean if it were ours, what [offshore] oil and gas would mean, what hydro would mean—if all the customs and taxes were our own."

He added: "That's not a threat."

Newfoundland became Canada's newest province in 1949, after 52 per cent of the population voted in favour of Confederation in a plebiscite.

What do you think?

1. *Why would Premier Moores even consider commissioning a study on the feasibility of Newfoundland separating from Canada?*
2. *What might be some of the attitudes of the Federal Government in Ottawa that disturb Newfoundlanders?*

Epilogue

OLD MEN OF THE MARITIMES

The following poem appeared in the Atlantic Advocate *in 1972. Written by Robert Cockburn, it is the poem referred to in the following document by Scott Young.*

You see them often
and wonder where they come from,
where they go.
On corners, in the liquor store,
in supermarkets—there,
fugitive, unsure,
grey-grizzled in used overcoats
that all but sweep the floor,
they fumble with their tiny ladies purses,
grunt,
and scuttle, rubber-booted,
for the door.

OLD MARITIMERS DO NOT ALWAYS CARRY A BOTTLE

Scott Young, a columnist for the Toronto Globe and Mail, *attempted to correct the impression of a regional stereotype he had created about the Maritime character. The article appeared June 9, 1967. (Reprinted with the permission of the* Globe and Mail, *Toronto.)*

When I was writing about Fredericton last week, the tone was largely enthusiastic stressing the youthful atmosphere and the remarkable artistic benefits the city had been given by the infusion of vast sums of money from Lord Beaverbrook and, to a lesser degree, Sir James Dunn.

But as you may recall, I used at the end a poem reprinted from the *Atlantic Advocate* and entitled Old Men of the Maritimes by Robert Cockburn.

Today, the chair recognizes Charles Bruce, the poet and novelist whose own warm feeling for the Atlantic provinces is at the heart of much of what he writes.

Mr. Bruce said he welcomed the feel of the place. "However, with one assumption you make I profoundly disagree," he wrote. "This is the suggestion that Old Men of the Maritimes comes close to being an exact delineation of the facts of the Maritimes today. When Cockburn's page of verse first appeared in the *Advocate* I very nearly wrote Mike Wardell [editor and publisher] to ask him how . . . this particular exhibit got into a selection of such novel and original verse; at least under that title.

"By placing a general title over a piece of verse that describes a particular few, Cockburn caricatures a race of men. Not that they will care much, but I do. If he had given his title a narrower range (applied to Toronto, old men at Queen and Victoria waiting for the wine store to open, would have served) my feeling about it would be less intense."

"But apart from that, the verse is a piece of surface observation."

"I have known a great many old men of the Maritimes and I can assure Cockburn that under the used overcoats, in the Maritimes as elsewhere, there is often something far deeper than he has sensed. Not always, but often."

In the Cockburn poem, there were references to rubber boots and long-used overcoats. One phrase used was "fugitive, unsure, grey-grizzled". Mr. Bruce wrote that he himself once tried to catch the deeper sense-of-being in old men of the Maritimes in a piece called Eastern Shore. This had grown out of long association with his father and their neighbours, particularly one called Alex.

"Alex was grey-grizzled. There were probably times when he was unsure. He certainly wore rubber boots."

"I expect to do so also, if underfoot conditions suggest it, when for the month of August I become an Old Man of the Maritimes, 'fugitive, unsure, grey-grizzled'."

But maybe it is better to let a poet speak through his poetry. In counterpoint to Cockburn's Old Men of the Maritimes, here is

EASTERN SHORE

By Charles Bruce

He stands and walks as if his knees were tensed
to a pitching dory. When he looks far off
You think of trawl-kegs rolling in the trough
Of swaying waves. He wears a cap against
The sun on water, but his face is brown
As an old mainsail, from the eyebrows down.

He has grown old as something used and known
Grows old with custom, each small fading scar
Engrained by use and wear in plant and spar
In weathered wood and iron, and flesh and bone
But youth lurks in the squinting eyes, and
The laughter wrinkles in the tanbark skin.

You know his story when you see him climb
The lookout hill. You know that age can be
A hill for looking, and the swaying sea
A lifetune marching with the waves of time
Listen—the ceaseless cadence, deep and slow
Tomorrow, now, and years and years ago.

What is meant by?

"a caricature"

What do you think?

1. *How do you react to the poem, "Old Men of the Maritimes"? Why did Mr. Bruce react in the way he did?*
2. *What is the role of the stereotype in creating ideas we have about certain regions? How important is stereotyping in creating a sense of regional identity?*
3. *Can you think of other regional stereotypes? What are they? Are they accurate representations?*

THE FEDERALIST POSITION

The Canadian federal system is constitutionally based on strong central government, but it is constantly being challenged by provincial and regional representatives arguing for more local autonomy. Their argument is not against the federal structure as such. What they disagree with is the degree of power, authority and financial resources vested in the Federal Government in Ottawa. These politicians frequently accuse the Ottawa government of failing to formulate policies responsive to particular regional needs. Whatever the issue may be, economic, social or constitutional, the Government of Canada cannot afford to ignore the reality of regionalism.

ROOKIE OF THE YEAR

The following cartoon appeared in the Toronto Star *in February 1968. (Reprinted with permission—The* Toronto Star.*)*

ROOKIE OF THE YEAR

What do you think?

1. *Why would the cartoonist present this particular view of the Trudeau government and regional politics in 1968?*
2. *Was this view accurate in 1968? Is this view accurate now? Explain your answer.*

EQUALIZATION PAYMENTS

The Federal Government's system of equalization payments to the provinces is a complex and confusing financial arrangement for redistributing wealth. Here is a simplified explanation of the program taken from the Financial Times of Canada *on February 28, 1972 and January 21, 1974.*

The formula for calculating the payments has been changed under the [new Fiscal Arrangements Act] and should be simpler. There are 19 sources of revenue in the formula; race track taxes and hospital and Medicare premiums have been added for the first time.

Here is how it works: If a province has 10% of the total population, but only 5% of the country's taxable gasoline sales, then it has less potential to raise revenues from that kind of tax. In the bureaucrat's jargon, it has "fiscal capacity deficiency".

. . . These payments are made to all provinces except Ontario, British Columbia and Alberta. The idea is to help out the poorer provinces so they can provide the same level of services as the rich provinces.

Ottawa then calculates the total revenue produced by gasoline taxes in all provinces. If one province gets less than 10% of the total, it gets a credit for the difference. The same procedure is applied to every revenue base.

When the job is done on all 19 sources, a province's net deficiency or excess is added up. The deficient provinces get a cheque; those with excesses do not.

In the coming fiscal year, equalization payments will cost more than $1 billion. By the end of the current arrangement in 1976-77, the bill will be $1.5 billion a year. . . .

From the earliest of Canada's history as a federation, relations among senior governments have been dominated by disagreements over shares of revenue for provincial purposes. Almost immediately after Confederation, Nova Scotia found it could not live on the financial terms it had accepted.

Per capita revenues 1971-72

Getting grants	Unequalized	Equalized
New Brunswick	$373	$522
Quebec	439	513
Newfoundland	299	509
P.E.I.	279	467
Saskatchewan	399	458
Manitoba	402	453
Nova Scotia	309	432
Average	409	496
Not getting grants		
British Columbia	—	513
Ontario	—	507
Alberta	—	500
Average	—	507

Within two years it petitioned the imperial Parliament in London for release from the dominion. It was bought off with a special 10-year grant. Within six years of Confederation, New Brunswick, Prince Edward Island and British Columbia had joined it as recipients of special grants.

The four days of federal-provincial meetings this week will be bound together by questions of revenue sharing and equalization. The surging revenues that Alberta and Saskatchewan can be expected to receive from rising prices of oil and natural gas, to say nothing of the half share of six months of oil export tax the federal government has promised them are distorting a system that was to remain unchanged until 1977.

Equalization as a distinct programme . . . can be traced back to the 1957-58 fiscal year. Though it has been modified since, the objective remains the same: assisting all provinces to provide their citizens with reasonably comparable levels of basic services, while avoiding unduly harsh taxation.

The share-the-wealth philosophy is publicly accepted, though British Columbia, Alberta and Ontario do complain about their rates of growth being slowed because of what they have to give for the others.

It is a huge program, which this year will pay $1.4 billion to seven provinces. The payments are unconditional.

For some provinces equalization is vital. Sixty-five per cent of Newfoundland's revenue in 1970-71 was from equalization; four of the seven receiving provinces collected more than one-third of their revenues from this source that year.

How the cash is split

	1973-74 Total millions	Per capita	1957-58 Total millions
Newfoundland	$157.2	$311	$11.6
Prince Edward Island	35.3	299	3.0
Nova Scotia	178.3	217	17.4
New Brunswick	151.1	230	8.6
Quebec	664.1	117	43.1
Manitoba	104.8	96	13.9
Saskatchewan	141.7	128	19.2
Alberta	—	—	14.7
British Columbia	—	—	4.5
Totals	$1432.5		$136

What do you think?

1. *Do you think that equalization is necessary in Canada? Why or why not?*
2. *What are the strengths and weaknesses of the equalization scheme?*
3. *How do you think equalization affects federal power?*
4. *To what extent should national policies attempt to ensure cross-country standards of equity?*

FEDERAL PROVINCIAL RIGHTS A PROBLEM FOR CANADA

The problem of provincial rights and the constitutional division of power has long been a divisive force in Canada. In the following article, which appeared May 22, 1971, Jack McArthur, business analyst for the Toronto Star, *outlines how federal-provincial distribution of responsibility endangers national unity and national policy. (Reprinted with permission—The* Toronto Star.)

Canadians have turned a wrecking crew loose on national unity.

It's slowly chopping away at the supports that make Canada a nation rather than a collection of local areas selfishly chasing their own narrow, and economically costly, interests.

The immediate reasons for each swing of the axe may seem persuasive. But the total result may be disastrous—an inability by the federal government to make meaningful national policies of growth, citizen protection, trade, minimum economic and legal rights.

Without the power to do such things, Ottawa can't be held responsible if they are poorly done. Who is responsible? No one. An individual province can't possibly make and enforce a national policy. And broad agreement in so many areas among 10 provinces is a pipedream.

The greatest danger is not that there are developments which may hamstring central power at a time when there are so many things which can only be dealt with effectively by a national government.

It is the fact that Canadians have so little apparent desire to do anything about it. Either they pursue provincialism to advance their narrow interests or they stand paralyzed, wringing their hands in indecision, fearful of doing anything wrong. It might antagonize the French-Canadians, or Ontario Conservatives, or those provinces which have a special interest in advancing their "rights" in a particular field.

Let's look at the long sad list:

1. Offshore minerals: Although Ottawa has had one court ruling in its favor, the subject is not settled, either legally or on the political level. It can be strongly argued that offshore minerals belong to all Canadians, since they are not properly within provincial borders. But the provinces with a possible jackpot in view insist that they should be theirs.

2. Equalization payments: The basic reason for the nation's economic existence involves Ottawa's ability to tax all Canadians and distribute its expenditures to areas of greatest need. This is based partly on the idea that there should be minimum standards for all citizens and partly on the fact that nation-wide corporations headquarters in richer provinces draw money from all areas though it may be taxed as income in just one.

. . .

3. Quebec insists it must control cable television, now within federal jurisdiction. Ontario may be getting similar ideas.

4. Quebec wants Ottawa to shut down national manpower offices in that province. That would create a precedent which could cripple national manpower and employment policies.

5. Quebec continues to try to push Ottawa out of anything to do with income security, whether it's unemployment insurance, welfare or family allowances. . . .

6. A national policy of bilingualism in appropriate areas: The West is angry, Ontario is cautious. Quebec thinks it's fine in largely Anglo areas but

is opposed to encouraging knowledge of English in French-speaking regions.

7. Amending the constitution: This surely should be something in which the federal government—which is the only administration representing ALL Canadians—should be dominant. The provinces have already defeated this idea; and will surely never agree among themselves on a formula which will be anything but over-rigid and useless.

8. Interprovincial trade: It's clearly a federal power. But the provinces already are setting up barriers, the most infamous being in the Ontario-Quebec chicken-and-egg war which is such a fraud on consumers. . . .

There are many other examples of how Canadians and their provinces —often protesting their belief in national unity—are chopping away central government powers.

Yet they insist that Ottawa must be responsible for a stable currency, full employment and prosperous growth without inflation.

What do you think?

1. *What is Mr. McArthur's main concern as expressed in these extracts? Why is he so concerned?*
2. *Do you think Mr. McArthur's assessment of the situation is fair? Why or why not?*
3. *What is the significance of recent federal decisions about off-shore mineral rights in terms of federal-provincial relations?*
4. *Do you think regions or provinces should be granted special rights or privileges by the Federal Government? Why or why not?*

BUSINESS WANTS GREATER POWER RESTING WITH FEDERAL GOVERNMENT

Central Canada is considered the business centre of the nation. The power and control that should accompany this position are part of regional resentment toward the central provinces. The following survey of business opinion by the Financial Times of Canada *published Jan. 21, 1974, reflects a readership that is distributed this way: 41% Ontario; 21% Quebec; 18% Prairie Provinces; 12% British Columbia; 8% Maritimes.*

If business executives surveyed by *Financial Times* were revising Canada's constitution, they would strengthen the federal government at the expense of the provinces.

They would neatly solve the jurisdictional dispute over energy, for example, by giving Ottawa the responsibility, not only for pricing oil and gas, but for production as well.

The latest *Financial Times* survey of Business Opinion shows surprisingly strong support for federal power in disputed areas.

To transfer authority over mining and oil from the provinces to Ottawa would require a change in the British North America Act, the constitution which sets out the powers of each level of government.

—Results in detail—

Here are the detailed results of general questions on federal-provincial relations in the business opinion survey.

1. Do you think the present division of powers between Ottawa and the provinces advances economic efficiency and development, or do you think it holds it back?

    Advances economy 22%
    Holds it back.. 61%
    Has no influence... 6%
    Don't know 11%

2. Do you think there should be constitutional changes to:

    Strengthen provincial powers in relations to Ottawa 30%
    Strengthen federal powers in relation to the provinces 40%
    Distribution of powers should be left as it is 27%
    Don't know 3%

3. Do you think it likely or unlikely that the Canadian constitution, the British North America Act, will be revised in the next 10 years?

    Likely.. 68%
    Unlikely.. 26%
    Don't know 6%

But a majority of the 222 executives who took part in the survey in mid-December did not seem at all disheartened by the numerous attempts—and just as numerous failures—to work out a way of revising the constitution.

What do you think?

1. What conclusions can you draw about the response of business to regionalism from these statistics?

2. Why do you think business responded as they did to these questions?

3. What effect does a strong central government have on national unity? Evaluate your answer from the point of view of Canadian business.

DOMINION-PROVINCIAL CONFERENCES

One of the Federal Government's responses to regional discontent is the calling of Dominion-Provincial conferences, where the first ministers of the provinces and the Prime Minister discuss issues of importance to the nation. In the following excerpt from her memoirs, Judy Lamarsh discusses these conferences, and the role of the media in them. (Memoirs of a Bird in a Gilded Cage, Macmillan, 1969)

At full-scale Dominion-Provincial meetings, the Prime Minister and the premiers were present together with their advisers and their appropriate ministers, who had special responsibility over the matters on the agreed agenda, and their technical and expert advisers. Newsmen, cameramen, radio and T.V. reporters were allowed in before the formal opening, to photograph Canada's political leaders, gathered around the huge, felt-covered oval table, flanked by their ministers, and backed by row upon row of advisers. Such a conference might include two to three hundred people, although it was the Prime Minister and the premiers, and on invitation their ministers, who alone did the speaking. Depending upon the terms agreed to in advance by the provinces for a particular conference, advance statements by the Prime Minister and the premiers would be handed to the press. The photographs over, the press was excluded, the great door to Room 200 of the West Block closed to the world, and the work of the conference began.

These conferences were often dull, but sometimes far from it. The course of our history might have been very different had the unblinking eye of television been watching all the time; reporters with their pencils at the ready to note and emphasize (or miss completely) the most telling points of a presentation or argument. But by tradition, they were closed to the press, and it was only at the last such conference held in the Pearson era that the public could see and hear the participants. The Prime Minister read his statement of the general purpose of the meeting, and each premier in turn read his prepared statement, or said a few words if they had no prepackaged remarks. Louis Robichaud of New Brunswick and Joseph Smallwood of Newfoundland seldom read from carefully worded statements; their comments were mainly off-the-cuff. Premiers were always called upon in the order of the entry of the provinces into Confederation (and their conference seats were arranged in the same order), which meant always that Ontario began, followed by Quebec. Joey Smallwood always had the last word of that first round, as premier of the newest province. His seat was at the far end of the table, where he could watch everyone, and add comments both pungent and pithy. His remarks were often funny, and always welcome after the stilted phrases of the spokesmen for the bigger provinces, more conscious as they were of the relative importance of their position and posture. Except in the rare case where a province had a preconceived, hard position to press, the debate following was usually a leisurely, gentlemanly exposition of points of view, with little blood and thunder. Agreement (or a lack of disagreement) was reached on most points, over the three or four days of the conference's duration. Where this unheated discussion produced no agreement, the contentious point was usually left over for inclusion on the agenda of a later conference.

After three or four days, an innocuous memorandum concentrating on the points of agreement reached was prepared and issued to the press. These memoranda are called communiqués, and derive from international meetings. Because they must cover all shades of opinion and obscure any lack of agreement so that the conference will appear to have been a success, they are pretty bland. All the contentious material is left out. Where no agreement at all is reached, the language of the communiqué usually makes reference to a full, frank, and friendly discussion. They [are] also calculated to leave the press, and thus the public, thinking that all is well. When later, an ugly confrontation on a point of contention surfaces publicly, while the politicians know it has been there all along, souring the relationship between governments and growing steadily more difficult to reconcile, or to conceal, it bursts with unexpected force on the totally unaware public. How much better to have discussions in the open, so that developing quarrels can be seen as they occur. Surely no premier who comes to such a conference with a firm decision to pursue a course adopted by his administration, and in which his ministers have participated, would be afraid to take that same strong position in full view of the public, rather than propounding it only while behind a closed conference door? The presence of the T.V. cameras did not seem to hamper the free discussion of the premiers on the subject of the future of Confederation, that most delicate of political subjects, during the "Conference on Tomorrow." The views they expressed there were much the same as those they had often, over the years, made in the relative privacy of the closed Dominion-Provincial conferences held in Ottawa. It is my recollection (and that of my former colleagues) that nothing new arose during the Toronto conference—although there may have been a softening of the Quebec attitude—and we watched it even more closely than the public. The only really new aspect was that Canadians could see and hear the protagonists and form their own judgments on the views they expressed.

What do you think?

1. *What purposes do Dominion-Provincial Conferences serve?*
2. *Are such conferences useful for coming to decisions on issues facing the country? Support your viewpoint by researching the results of the most recent Dominion-Provincial conference.*
3. *What role did the media play in influencing public opinion and the decision-making process at this conference? Is this role a positive one or a negative one?*

THE NATIONAL LEADERS RESPOND

A considerable measure of the way the Federal Government responds to forces of regionalism lies with the Prime Minister of Canada. The following are statements made by Prime Minister Trudeau, Mr. Joe Clark, the Leader of the Progressive Conservative opposition and by Mr. Ed Broadbent, leader of the New Democratic Party. These statements were made on November 24, 1976 in response to the Parti Québécois victory in Quebec.

TRUDEAU'S CANADA. I do want to issue a caution, particularly for those who think that more decentralization, or a new separation of powers would solve our present worries. I say it is a grave illusion to believe that those who seek the breakup of Canada would suddenly cease to pursue their objective simply because the provincial governments have increased their powers in some areas, say, communications or immigration or fiscal powers, or cultural matters.

The question facing us is much more profound. The stakes for Canadians are much more important and the question is this: can Francophones of Quebec consider Canada as their country, or must they feel at home only in Quebec?

And you know as well as I know that a new sharing of power between Ottawa and the provinces will never give the answer to that particular question, will never make a Franco-phone feel more at home in Toronto or in Vancouver than he does in Quebec.

Quebeckers, like citizens of the other provinces, are proud. They seek personal fulfillment in a free and independent way. The central question, therefore, is whether this growth of freedom and independence is best assured by Canada, or by Quebec alone.

Canadians must think about this brutal question now. Not only think of solving it in words, but by deeds and through their attitudes. In the area of the language problem, of course, but also in the very important areas of regional disparity and social justice.

With the victory of the Parti Québécois we can no longer afford to postpone these questions by one generation, to put the problem aside for the next generation of Canadians, and in this sense, the crisis is real; the crisis is now, and the challenge is immediate. I believe that Canada cannot, indeed, that Canada must not survive by force. The country will only remain united—it should only remain united—if its citizens want to live together in one civil society.

History created this country from the meeting of two realities; the French and the English realities. Then these were enriched by the contribution of people from all parts of the world, but this coming together, this meeting, this encounter of realities, though at times difficult to accept, and hard to practise, this encounter has, itself, become the fabric of our life as a nation, the source of our individuality, the very cornerstone of our identity as a people.

CLARK'S CANADA. It is important to recognize that the erosion of the federal-provincial partnership did not begin on Nov. 15. Nor is it limited to the relationship between Ottawa and any one province.

Rather, what we have witnessed over the past eight years has been a steady disintegration in the spirit of partnership between the federal government and all of the provinces. I am sure that, wherever you are in Canada, you can readily recite a growing list of grievances of your own provincial government in its relations with the central authority.

In some cases, the grievances are linked to the distinct problems of your region or province. In other cases, they are common to all provinces and regions ... from Newfoundland to British Columbia and the Territories.

But underlying all of them is the feeling that Ottawa has ceased to be a partner in Confederation ... that instead the federal government has tried to be a power completely unto itself, almost uncaring about the impact of its unilateral actions on the legitimate needs of the provinces and their people.

My friends, you simply can't govern any federal state on that basis. In particular you can't govern a country like Canada as though there is only one government which counts. Regionalism is part of the reality of Canada. As I have said on many occasions, our diversity sometimes may appear to be at the root of our problems, but it always is at the root of our strength and our richness. . . .

We have a special kind of country. It was formed because the regions wanted to come together. And it has been successful—not just as a country, but as a place to live—because we have given room to individual people, and different levels of government, to make their own decisions.

BROADBENT'S CANADA. As leader of the New Democratic Party of Canada, I reject firmly and unequivocally the separatism of the Parti Québécois. And to pretend the separatist commitment does not exist is to delude oneself. . . .

All Canadians committed to federalism must now show the same tolerance, flexibility and imagination as our forefathers. From this nation's founding, our French and English ancestors have shown—generation after generation—the capacity to create a federalism which appealed to our two principal non-native cultures. It is up to our generation to show how a new union can be forged once again.

We must show that a united Canada is the best means of ensuring not merely the survival but the creative growth of our two principal cultures in this part of North America. We must show that only by working together can we bring about the economic and social change so essential for bringing about genuine equality of opportunity. In all this, we must remember that our federalism has been like friendship. And friendship presupposes equality and freedom.

There can be no agreements based on force between friends. Nor can friends remain indifferent to one another if the relationship is to last. Let us now resolve to remain friends.

In a spirit of optimism, let us remember that in the past we have had our difficulties. But they have been overcome.

What do you think?

1. *What is the central argument in Mr. Trudeau's response to the PQ victory?*
2. *What is the central argument in Mr. Clark's response to the PQ victory?*
3. *What is the central argument in Mr. Broadbent's response to the PQ victory?*
4. *Which position is most sensitive to regionalism? Why?*

A FEDERALIST RESPONDS
TO THE NATION'S LEADERS

On November 29, 1976 in the Financial Times *Mr. George Radwanski presented what may be considered a non-political yet federalist response to the statements made by the leaders.*

The suggestion advanced in some quarters that Mr. Trudeau should step down as prime minister to take up the anti-separatism fight within Quebec as provincial Liberal leader, is just plain silly.

There is nothing Mr. Trudeau can do or say as Opposition leader in Quebec that he cannot do-or say more effectively as prime minister. He would simply be divesting himself of all real powers, to do battle from a vastly diminished position.

A federal referendum—in Quebec or nationwide—would accomplish nothing.

René Lévesque freely admits that there is no majority support for separation. If a federal referendum were held soon and merely confirmed that 20% or fewer of Quebecers favor independence, what would be gained? It would not negate separatist claims that a few years of PQ government will bring majority support, and it would not prevent the PQ from holding its own referendum at a time of its choosing. On the other hand, a stronger than expected pro-independence vote on a federal referendum would only give the separatist cause a major boost.

Similarly, nothing would be accomplished by asking Canadians in other provinces whether they want Quebec to go or stay. There is absolutely no evidence to suggest that there is majority support nationwide for breaking up Confederation.

But French-English tensions are unusually high at the moment, and any substantial "kick-out-Quebec" vote in such a test—however far short of a majority—would be additional fodder for separatist guns.

The final suggestion, moving rapidly toward decentralizing Confederation, superficially looks the most attractive and is the course advocated—without detail—by Mr. Clark. But whatever its long-term pros and cons, it is no answer to the immediate challenge of Quebec separatism.

An important distinction must be drawn between federal-provincial cooperation and decentralization. Of cooperation, within the existing division of powers, we need a great deal more.

There are numerous areas in which the federal government can be more sensitive to the needs and concerns of provincial governments and there will continue to be circumstances in which it will have to be more flexible to avoid creating the impression that Ottawa is the big boss and everything it says must be accepted. The Trudeau government has too often depicted itself as a fortress buttressed against provincial demands, instead of as a senior government eager to cooperate with the provinces in achieving the common good.

Decentralization, however, is another matter.

Among Quebecers who favor separation, the division of powers as such is not a major factor. Some favor independence on primarily emotional grounds: they simply want Quebec to be their own, distinct country. For others, the considerations are more economic: they believe Quebec on its own could have greater prosperity and social justice. In either instance, what is sought is not one or two additional powers, but all the powers necessary for full self-determination.

Consequently, to be a potent antidote to separatism, decentralization would have to be so complete as to make Quebec de facto a separate state. Anything less, given in piecemeal concessions, will only raise expectations that must eventually be frustrated and leave the separatists in a position to say, at the end: "They've kept all the important powers and they've tried to bribe you by tossing you a few bones."

There is also another danger to consider. It is most likely, unless serious mistakes are made by the rest of Canada, that a separatist referendum will be defeated. But if a federal government has meanwhile tried to stave off separatism by bargaining away powers, we may find ourselves with Confederation intact but booby-trapped by a fragmentation of powers that makes it impossible to govern effectively.

Quebec, of course, is not alone among the provinces in clamoring for a redistribution of powers, and there may be some fields in which this is desirable. But it is essential that such change be divorced from short-term separatism concerns. It could become desirable, consequently, for the federal government to take the position that talk of substantial redistribution must wait until we have resolved the fundamental question of whether Quebecers want to remain in Confederation.

Two elements, rather, must be the mainstay of anti-separatism efforts. The first is an intensive nationwide campaign to sell all the benefits of Confederation. The other, even more important is an all-out effort to have maximum positive impact on the lives of all Canadians—in Quebec and outside—through a period of dynamic, ordinary good government.

On their record since the last election, the Liberals will have a hard enough time delivering that, without succumbing to the suggestion of any dramatic anti-separatist gimmicks.

What do you think?

1. *What is Mr. Radwanski's central argument? Do you think his point of view is closer to that of Mr. Trudeau, Mr. Clark or Mr. Broadbent? Why?*
2. *How would more provincial autonomy for Quebec affect national unity? More provincial autonomy for all provinces?*

ON BILINGUALISM

The following articles deal with the subject of bilingualism, specifically with the Official Languages Act, and its role in the Canadian Confederation. The first is an extract from a speech delivered by Laura Sabia, a Montreal-raised broadcaster, to the Empire Club of Canada. This report was made by Margaret Mironowicz in The Globe and Mail, October 20, 1978. (Reprinted with the permission of The Globe and Mail, Toronto.) The second document is from Maclean's, September 4, 1978, and was written by Heather Menzies. (Reprinted by permission of Heather Menzies and Maclean's.)

a) In a biting denunciation of the Trudeau Government that won a standing ovation from a blue-chip audience, feminist and social critic Laura Sabia called yesterday for new leadership and an end to appeasing Quebec.

Mrs. Sabia said Canada's problem is that nobody is a Canadian any more. "We're now divided regionally, linguistically and ethnically—Canadian pitted against Canadian, resentment piled upon resentment."

She spoke to the Empire Club of Canada, an organization begun in 1903 and dedicated to the interests of Canada and the Commonwealth.

In her luncheon speech, she called the club members "the very last bastion of the captains of corporate and professional and intellectual elite." At the end of her address, they stood and gave her thundering applause.

"Who is a Canadian any more?" she asked. "Any Canadians in this house? Not . . . likely. No, sir, we have all become hyphenated . . . Canadians—French-Canadian, English-Canadian, Irish-Canadian, Polish-Canadian, and on and on into the nightmare of divisiveness."

. . .

Mrs. Sabia said the problem of hyphenated Canadians began with the Royal Commission on Bilingualism and Biculturalism in the 1960s. The Official Languages Act, passed in 1969, she said, "sowed the seeds of bigotry and hatred, divided us all and, to add salt to our wounds, cost us a walloping wad of money we couldn't afford."

Mrs. Sabia, who was raised in Montreal, and whose first language is French, said: "You cannot legislate language rights. You can only foster it through the education system slowly and effectively and well." Quebec, she said, doesn't want language rights entrenched in the constitution. It wants to remain unilingual.

She said the time for appeasement is over.

"We appeased Quebec with the flag, with the bilingual and bicultural commission, we appeased Quebec with the Official Languages Act.

"We appeased when we discarded the word 'Dominion,' a perfectly good English word. Few of us looked it up in the dictionary. We thought it smacked of English domination—when in reality it meant 'sovereign or supreme authority, autonomous communities, equal in status, united by a common allegiance to the Crown.'"

She said the country's "economic mess" must be cleaned up first, and the threat to national unity "will fall into place."

b) The Official Languages Act has tried to compensate for old habits and their resultant attitudes. In doing so, it's exposed the anglophones in their hypocrisy.

To a large extent, though, it's been an unconscious hypocrisy—even among those who confess: "I guess I always saw them as a conquered people ... Now, with all this fuss, the press have aroused this deep-seated bigotry that I had but didn't know was there."

Bilingualism is forcing people to realize that their actions and attitudes don't measure up to their self-image as good Canadians. Many anglophones can't see the point of the bilingualism program because the status quo seems to work fine. They take it for granted that speaking English makes no difference to the French because few have experienced the subtle humiliation and outright frustration of being restricted in their self-expression or career advancement by having to speak a borrowed language. Through the bilingualism requirements for the federal civil service, these people are tasting both those formerly exclusive French feelings, being humbled by the process, and realizing that for bilingualism to be always one-sided changes an act of polite accommodation into one of submission.

It's been a slow learning experience, made traumatic by being so long overdue, and aggravated by the federal government's handling of the whole bilingualism program. Rather than ease the havoc of Canadians confronting their mental gap between myth and reality by at least acknowledging the gap's existence, the government exacerbated it. It assumed that everyone would immediately understand and embrace the goals of bilingualism and pounced on examples of default as though the perpetrators were deliberate hypocrites. If nothing else, the success of the book *Bilingual Today, French Tomorrow* stands as a monument to anglophones' misunderstanding and the insecurity they felt in the face of their confusion.

It's also a warning against cloaking a reality of misunderstanding and long-standing unconscious hypocrisy with an illusory expectation. Because when the cloak inevitably rips, the truth of failure comes as such a letdown that nobody can cope with its root causes. The fault doesn't lie in the dirt under our fingernails, but in being too long alienated from the reality of the dirt.

By hiding from the realities of bilingualism now, we could so defeat ourselves by a sense of its failure that we'll have no choice but to cling to empty symbols that augur the final defeatism. On the other hand, by tracing the genesis of the well-publicized anti-bilingualism backlash, we can deal with it. We can see that much of the antipathy for bilingualism in Western Canada translates as antagonism against Ottawa for shoving its will down westerners' throats while continuing to ignore their own deep-seated grievances within confederation. And then we can trust and take more comfort from the high enrolment in French immersion courses not only in the West, but throughout the country.

This is the other reality of bilingualism: that it's working. Despite the personal ordeal of working through past attitudes, despite the grind of French lessons and defensive cries that the program costs too much, the son of that P.E.I. businessman and thousands upon thousands of others are offering a response to the borderline separatist who says: "I'm a conditional Canadian. Unless there is real equality between the French and the English in this country, I will be a Québécois only."

Thus bilingualism offers an alternative to magic formulae, phrases and symbols. It represents the hope that English Canadians can effect what it takes to bring the two-nation myth alive in the here-and-now reality. . . .

What do you think?

1. *According to Sabia, the Official Languages Act "sowed the seeds of bigotry and hatred, divided us all. . . ." Why do you think Sabia feels the Act has had that result? Do you agree? Why or why not?*
2. *According to Menzies, what has the Official Languages Act revealed about Anglophone Canada? Do you agree? Why or why not?*
3. *In her article Menzies says ". . . much of the antipathy for bilingualism in Western Canada translates as antagonism against Ottawa for shoving its will down westerners' throats while continuing to ignore their own deep-seated grievances." Would you agree with this statement? Support your point of view with specific examples. To what extent would this sentiment be true in other parts of Canada?*
4. *Compare the points of view expressed in these two articles. With which do you agree? Be prepared to defend your answer.*
5. *Can bilingualism be a positive force for Canadian unity? Why or why not?*

DON'T GIVE US TOO MUCH

The following excerpt appeared in a publication from the Edmonton Journal *entitled "What does the West Want?" Its author, Mel Hurtig, is a prominent Western Canadian publisher.*

I believe the West has done very well by Confederation, especially when I visit Quebec and the Maritimes. Given the resources we have, with hard work, determination and goodwill, we can overcome all or most of our problems. But in the process we must not weaken the federal government to the point where it is so emasculated as to be unable to guide national development.

The multi-national corporation likes nothing better than balkanization and region competing against region, province against province, in giveaway schemes. Ottawa (be it Liberals or Conservatives in power), must be careful not to give away too much.

Many of the most pressing problems of the provinces and the regions cannot be solved without strong federal leadership. These include unemployment, inflation, foreign ownership, poverty and regional disparity. Diefenbaker in 1958 and Trudeau in 1968 were thrust into office by the Canadian people in their search for strong men who had faith in Canada and who knew where we were going. Neither delivered, both misunderstood their mandate.

And the result? An ad hoc Canada smothering in foreign ownership, eternally bickering within, wandering from debate on abortion to debate on capital punishment to the auditor-general's report and back to abortion again, and capital punishment again, etc., and etc., while the ship of state begins to submerge.

The West has many real problems, but the biggest problem of all is the combination of federal and provincial politicians who fit Donald Creighton's description.

"We can save two cultures in a single nation; but not two separate nations and ten quarrelling provinces. Our politicians have refused to acknowledge this truth, because like politicians the world over, they fear that if they tackle an important national issue, they will antagonize powerful interest or an influential minority. Nationalism is one of those causes, deep in people's heart, that ordinary politicians never dare to touch."

What is meant by?

"balkanization"

What do you think?

1. *What is Mr. Hurtig's point of view? Would you call him a centralist or a regionalist? Why?*
2. *To what extent do you think Mr. Hurtig's point of view is shared by other Westerners? Justify your response.*

ENGLISH-CANADA MUST BE PREPARED TO GIVE— BUT NOT TO GIVE AWAY THE STORE

The following excerpts are taken from a column by David Lewis, former leader of the New Democratic Party, and a professor of Political Science at Carleton University in Ottawa. They appeared in Maclean's Magazine *on August 22, 1977.*

Existing antagonisms in Canada are not the product of thoughtless Westerners, mendicant Easterners, grasping farmers or selfish labor leaders. The conflicts derive from legitimate grievances against central governments which have for decades broken as many promises as they have made to deal effectively with those grievances. What has been particularly irksome is that the relative situation has changed little since the end of World War II, despite the fact that during this period Canada has experienced immense economic and technical advance. The inequalities between classes and the inequities between regions persist. It is therefore necessary to break down not only the linguistic but also the economic barriers to the development of a common Canadian purpose.

However, these longer term considerations do not answer the problem of the immediate present: the urgent need to persuade the Québécois to reject separatism. There are now Canadians—academics, editorialists, former political spokesmen—who are urging immediate negotiations.

. . .

. . . To suggest that negotiations start now raises the obvious question as to who would negotiate with whom. The present Quebec government has not the slightest interest in negotiating a new kind of confederation except as it may be able to exploit such negotiations to advance its separatist cause. It would not be open—but simple-minded to present such a platform to the propagandists of Quebec independence.

As for the suggestion that we should plan for conditions after possible Quebec separation, it is the kind of defeatism that is self-fulfilling. Nothing could be more helpful to the separatist cause in Quebec than evidence that a significant number of Canadians in the other provinces are resigned to it. In our search for accommodation we must be careful not to reduce the federal institutions to impotence. Whatever constitutional changes we collectively agree to make, we must leave ourselves with a central parliament that retains the capacity to strengthen Canada's economic and cultural independence and to help Canadians in every region to achieve economic security and social equality. Without this capacity, there is little value in federalism, whatever its structure.

What do you think?

1. *From this document, to what does Mr. Lewis attribute the separatist tendencies in Quebec? How does he explain regional forces in the rest of Canada?*
2. *How does he believe these tendencies should be dealt with?*

Historical Background

5

THE 1940s, 1950s and 1960s

After the Second World War Canada as a nation entered into a period of economic growth. The general prosperity that Canada enjoyed in the 1940s, 1950s and 1960s was largely responsible for the reduced intensity of regional protest. Nevertheless, certain changes took place: Newfoundland became the tenth province of Canada, Quebec began to re-examine its own image in the wake of rapid industrialization, and the West continued to voice its grievances. In this section we will focus on these issues that commanded national attention in the postwar years.

Newfoundland and Confederation

1948 NEWFOUNDLAND GOES TO THE POLLS

BALLOT	
Responsible Government	◯
Commission Government	◯
Confederation	◯

In 1948 the people of Newfoundland found themselves faced with a decision of historic importance—determining the future form of government for their island. Newfoundland did not choose to become a partner in Confederation in 1867, preferring to remain a British colony. As such, it had enjoyed responsible government since 1855, with its own Prime Minister and General Assembly. However, the effects of the Depression were very severe in Newfoundland and led to a financial crisis. As a result, responsible government was suspended in 1934 and replaced by commission government. For 15 years Newfoundland was ruled by a governor and commission appointed by the government of the United Kingdom.

The 1948 Referendum presented Newfoundlanders with three options: they could return to independent government, retain commission government or become the tenth province of Canada. The following section deals with the situation in Newfoundland just before its entry into Confederation in 1949. What were the issues confronting the people of Newfoundland? What factors affected their final decision?

THE CENTRAL FIGURES IN THE PLEBISCITE SHOWDOWN

The Atlantic Guardian, *May 1948, presented the following sketch of the three main figures in the Confederation debate. J. R. Smallwood stood for Confederation, P. J. Cashin for responsible government, and C. A. Crosbie for economic union with the United States.*

a)   "Joey" Smallwood is undoubtedly the most outstanding figure in public life in Newfoundland today. . . .

. . . He knows that almost no Newfoundlander wants to join Canada for any reason except the belief that such a move is the quickest and surest way of putting more meat and potatoes on the tables of the majority of Newfoundlanders. He is forced to put to a skeptical, wary people, determined not to be "foxed" by anybody this time, reasoned and reasonable proof that they will be better off under Confederation than they would be remaining as they are or returning to Responsible Government ...

. . . There are other figures on the stage and perhaps some behind the scenes in this Confederation drama, but to the man in the street Joey Smallwood IS Confederation and the issue stands or falls with him. A little man with a good brain and a great heart, he deserves the respect of all who admire a sincere and courageous fighter for what he believes to be right.

b)   Major Peter J. Cashin has held the spotlight for a number of years as an agitator for the restoration of self government for Britain's Oldest

Colony. Fighting single-handedly and without much support at first from a frustrated population, he succeeded in keeping alive a spark of political consciousness during the "benevolent dictatorship" of Commission Government.

. . . From the beginning he was a bitter opponent of Confederation, championed by Joe Smallwood . . .

. . . But with the masses, particularly in and around St. John's, Major Cashin is fairly popular, and because of this he is a man to be reckoned with in the forthcoming showdown.

c) Chesley A. Crosbie has moved into the political limelight as the leader of a party rather vaguely dedicated to "closer economic union" with the United States . . .

The last minute plunge of Mr. C. A. Crosbie into the unexplored and unknown issue of Economic Union with the United States is simply another angle to the Responsible Government fight. Mr. Crosbie wants the country to get back its own government so that it can then talk to Washington as one Government to another. There appears to be a lot of support for the Crosbie plan, although there is no firm assurance that, having Responsible Government, Newfoundland would get anywhere with the United States.

What is meant by?

"Commission Government"
"Responsible Government"

What do you think?

1. *What did each of the main figures in the plebiscite debate feel the major issues were?*
2. *What effect did each feel his solution would have on the problem and why?*

WHAT WOULD CONFEDERATION MEAN TO NEWFOUNDLAND?

The following article by Ewart Young appeared in the Atlantic Guardian *in 1948.*

. . . In a little while the seven-man delegation now in Ottawa will be reporting back to the National Convention and through that body to the people of the Island, presumably with full details of the terms of union . . .

No one knows exactly what the terms are likely to be. It is possible, however, to set down a number of general observations that can be regarded as reasonably accurate in that they are based on policies and practices now in effect throughout Canada.

FAMILY ALLOWANCES. Take the matter of Family Allowances. Under Confederation every family in Newfoundland would receive about $6 per month for each child under 16 years ... Using the 60,000 registered school children as a basis for the family allowance payments, Newfoundland would receive something like $4,500,000 annually under this classification ...

OLD AGE PENSION. ... Current rate of payment in Newfoundland is $120 a year for man and wife (or $10 per month per couple) and $72 per year for man or widow (or $6 per month per person). Under Confederation the old age pension would amount to a minimum of $300 per year per person (or $25 per month).

TAXES. Personal income tax in Newfoundland is somewhat lower than in Canada, but corporation taxes are higher, 33% in Canada and 35% in Newfoundland. Canadian income tax, however, has recently undergone considerable revision, and under the new scale set for 1948 a married taxpayer with two children of family allowance age will not pay any tax whatever on an income up to $1,700 per year. Under Confederation the average Newfoundland wage earner making $150 per month would pay little or no income tax.

IMMIGRATION. At present Newfoundlanders can enter Canada to reside or work under certain conditions and subject to immigration and Customs regulations. Under Confederation all barriers between Newfoundland and Canada would be removed.

What do you think?

1. What would the advantages of Confederation be for a Newfoundlander?
2. What would the disadvantages of Confederation be?

CONFEDERATE PROPAGANDA

The following article appeared in The Confederate, *May 31, 1948.*

Are you in this List?

TO ALL MOTHERS. Confederation would mean that NEVER AGAIN would there be a hungry child in Newfoundland. If you have children under the age of 16, you will receive EVERY MONTH a cash allowance for every child you have or may have.

TO ALL WAR VETERANS. Canada treats her veterans better than ANY OTHER COUNTRY in the World. She has just increased their War Pensions 25%.

TO ALL WAGE-WORKERS. All wage-workers will be protected by Unemployment Insurance. Newfoundland, under Confederation, will be opened up and developed.

TO ALL OVER 65. You would have something to look forward to at the age of 70. The Old Age Pension of $30 a month for yourself, and $30 a month for your wife.

TO ALL LIGHT-KEEPERS. You will all become employees of the Government of Canada. Your wages and working conditions will be greatly improved.

TO ALL CUSTOMS OFFICIALS. You will become employees of the Government of Canada at better salaries and much better working conditions.

TO ALL FISHERMEN. The cost of living will come down: The Government of Canada will stand back of our fisheries.

TO ALL NEWFOUNDLANDERS. The cost of living will come down. Newfoundland will be linked up with a strong, rich British nation. Newfoundland will go ahead with Canada.

GIVE YOURSELF A CHANCE. GIVE THE CHILDREN A CHANCE
GIVE NEWFOUNDLAND A CHANCE. VOTE FOR CONFEDERATION
AND A HEALTHIER, HAPPIER NEWFOUNDLAND

AN APPEAL FOR CONFEDERATION

On Thursday, June 3, the toiling masses in Newfoundland will have the biggest and best chance they ever had in our country's 450 years' history.

They will have the best chance they EVER HAD to make Newfoundland a better place for themselves and their families.

Will they use the chance to help themselves?

. . . I believe that the great majority of the fishermen, loggers, miners, railroaders, mill-workers, teachers, shop and office workers, civil servants, laborers, and others who have to work for their living are closing their eyes and ears to the selfish few . . .

I believe that our people can see clearly now who are their friends, and who are their enemies.

For nearly three years I have fought and worked to get this chance for our people. Water Street and Water Street's politicians have fought me and tried to put me down. They have failed.

You have your chance, now . . .

Use this chance . . .

Vote for Confederation

Your sincere friend
Joseph R. Smallwood.

What do you think?

1. After reading the above article would you have voted in favor of or against Confederation? Why?

ANTI CONFEDERATE PROPAGANDA

The following articles were printed in The Independent *of St. John's on March 22, April 12, May 3, 1948.*

NEWFOUNDLAND FOR NEWFOUNDLANDERS.   We, a body of Newfoundlanders, with no other motives than honest convictions and the welfare of all classes and sections of Newfoundland at heart, have come together in the "Responsible Government League" with the return of *Responsible Government* as our aim.

We sincerely believe that in the years ahead, the interest of Newfoundland will be best served by an independent Government responsible only to the people of Newfoundland, a Government that is able to deal and negotiate for trade and other concessions with the Governments of the United States, United Kingdom and Canada, on behalf of a free and independent people.

Responsible Government is what our forefathers fought for and won nearly one hundred years ago. We feel that the present generation of Newfoundlanders has *a duty and a trust* to restore this temporarily-lost heritage . . .

Self Government is the People's Government
—If you want a Newfoundland policy formed by
Newfoundlanders for Newfoundland—Vote for
Responsible Government

WE SHALL PAY AND PAY PLENTY.   The Confederates are trying to persuade us that Confederation will not mean additional taxation—that we shall get the family allowances, and other things, without paying for them. *This is a gross deception* . . .

We shall pay and pay plenty. . . .

Let us not be fooled, men and women, we shall not get something for nothing by joining up with Canada. On the contrary, we shall be doubly taxed, taxed to pay our proportion of the cost of running the Dominion and taxed to pay the cost of running the Province.

WHAT DO YOU KNOW ABOUT CONFEDERATION? What do you know about Confederation that would persuade you to cast your vote for it in the coming referendum?

We have heard a lot about family allowances and pensions and things of that sort; but what will it mean to our earning power? How will it affect our industries? What assurance have we that once we enter Confederation the Canadian Government will take even the slightest interest in our affairs? How much more shall we be taxed? How will it affect our way of life?

. . . You don't know what is going to happen to you. You are governed no longer from St. John's but from Ottawa . . .

And these strangers will not try to understand your way of doing things, they will immediately begin to make you conform to their ways . . .

Yes it will be a great change.

Only one thing we know, it will bring us nothing that we shall not have to pay for and pay through the nose.

Can the Baby Bonus Save Newfoundland?

Many people are being led to believe that they can spend the money which may come to them through the Family Allowance as they like.

That is absolutely untrue.

The money can only be spent on the children—for food, clothing, education, etc.

Neither the father nor the mother dare spend a cent on themselves. If they do they may be punished . . .

In other words, the money is spent under government control and is not for free spending by the parents. You cannot do as you like with it, can't even buy a loaf of bread for yourself out of it.

ANOTHER TWIST TO RESPONSIBLE GOVERNMENT

The St. John's Sunday Herald, *March 28, 1948 carried the following:*

[Mr. Crosbie stated] . . . "the advantages in Economic Union with the United States far outweigh anything we might ever hope to get under Confederation. Therefore we, the people should not consider Confederation until we have had the chance to exercise our undeniable democratic right to deal with the U.S. Government.

" . . . It is necessary to return to self-government before Economic Union can be arranged . . . Immediately self-government becomes a reality, I will have the privilege of leading a party pledge to bring about Economic Union with the United States."

"This plan is for Economic Union and only Economic Union," he emphasized. "Newfoundland will retain her position as the oldest and most loyal member of the British Family of Nations."

What do you think?

1. *After reading the above articles would you have opposed Confederation? Why?*

It is interesting to note that in the first referendum on June 3, 1948, the vote was:

Responsible Government	44.55%
Commission Government	14.32%
Confederation	41.13%

On July 22 the vote was:

Confederation	52.34%
Responsible Government	47.66%

What do you think?

1. *Was the pro-Confederation vote large enough to justify Newfoundland entering Confederation? Why?*
2. *If the question arose today, do you think Newfoundlanders would vote the same way? Why or why not? What concerns would they have?*
3. *If in 1978, 52% of the population of Quebec favoured separation, should separation be permitted to occur? Justify your response.*

Quebec

In the aftermath of the Second World War, Quebeckers began a lengthy process of self-examination. The rapid shift from an agricultural to an industrial society had an enormous impact on the lives of the people of Quebec. New trends towards modernization in society conflicted with the image Quebec (and the rest of Canada) had had of itself for centuries. As a consequence, young intellectuals began to press for a reassessment of Quebec's place in Canada.

This period of reevaluation culminated in 1960 with the election of John Lesage as Premier of Quebec and the dawn of what has been called the "Quiet Revolution." What was the "Quiet Revolution"? Why did it occur? How was it a form of regional protest, if at all? How might the demands it generated have affected later counterdemands from other regions and provinces in Canada?

CITE LIBRE

In 1950, Cité Libre, a small magazine founded by Gérard Pelletier and Pierre Elliott Trudeau, appeared on the Quebec scene. It soon established itself as a journal of considerable note in social and intellectual reform circles and was an important influence on the thinking of Quebec progressives in the fifties. The following passage, written by Trudeau for the June, 1950 issue of the magazine, illustrates the tone and spirit of the journal. (Reprinted by permission of Pierre Elliott Trudeau.)

"But we have preserved the language and the faith of our fathers. That is something positive."

That is a lie which illustrates very well how we have confused quantity and quality. Our language has now become so poor that we no longer realize how badly we speak it . . . our faith, so tenuous, has ceased to be apostolic . . .

There are not many ways out of our quandary. We must stop trembling at the thought of external dangers, stop fortifying our traditions by sullying what is opposed to them, and consider by what positive actions we can uphold our beliefs.

We want to bear witness to the Christian and French fact in America. So be it. But let us sweep away all the rest. Let us submit to methodical doubt all the political notions of the past generations; the strategy of *survivance* no longer serves the flourishing of the City. The time has come to borrow from the architect the style that is called functional, to scrap the thousand past prejudices that clutter up the present and to start building for the new man. Let us throw down the totem poles and violate the taboos, or better yet let us consider them as non-existent. Let us be coldly intelligent.

What is meant by?

"survivance"

What do you think?

1. *What is the meaning of the passage? Why did Mr. Trudeau make this proposal?*
2. *What words used in the passage might describe the philosophy of the* Cité Libre?

THE TIMES ARE CHANGING

André Laurendeau's death in 1968 deprived French Canada of one of its most famous spokesmen. Laurendeau was the editor of Le Devoir *and one of the original commissioners for the Royal Commission on Bilingualism and Biculturalism. The following editorial was written by Laurendeau for the June 27, 1953, issue. (Reprinted by permission of* Le Devoir.*)*

One of my friends has lived abroad for several years. When he returned here he was conscious of modifications in the atmosphere. He said: But what has happened to French Canadians? When I left, it was language, traditions, and survival that were spoken of. They were what interested people. Now they are hardly spoken of anymore and I have the impression that they interest no one.

It is true the climate has changed. We practice oratorical patriotism much less. Certain clichés already well worn out for ten years have almost disappeared and when one hears them one smiles spontaneously as at old-fashioned dress. Does this signify profound changes? Or is it modesty, fatigue, or indifference?

The most important source I believe is restlessness, at least among those who are reflective. We have been knocked silly by the Industrial Revolution. We are still completely upset by it.

We are living through a time of reflection. We are meditating over the new conditions of our life, not in the manner of hermits in the desert or of philosophers in their cells, but from day to day, as we are touched by events. And we are testing ourselves in new spheres.

So we are speaking less of language, of tradition, and above all of *la survivance.* We are preparing ourselves to live in conditions which the age creates, to tackle problems which the old responses will no longer solve.

The most immediate problem of all is the economic one. Abbé Groulx, at the Club Richelieu on Thursday, called to mind in a very full account, reproduced entirely in *Le Devoir*, that the history of our economic life remains to be written.

It would be, it seemed to him, a history painful enough to read. . . . It would say that since 1760 we have been behind. We have been lacking that which is essential to an economy: a tradition of large businesses and the formation of large funds of money for capital. The problem was worsened in proportion as enterprises have become larger and more important. We have ended up convincing ourselves that big business necessarily eludes us. We have too often limited our ambitions to establishing and then selling, at a mediocre profit, small and medium-sized businesses.

"Well," says Abbé Groulx, in a felicitous aside, "the populace, and not just the populace, will lean fatally towards the culture where they make their living."

The historian brought to mind the two judgements held for two centuries by two men as little alike as is possible. Premier Papineau described the scene in Quebec in 1828: "They [the English] in Quebec have the energy and the necessary wealth to prosper." Durham in his famous report noted that the majority of the wage-earners "are French and in the employ of English capitalists." Write instead "Anglo-American capitalists" and the phrase remains appropriate for 1953.

But the times are changing. Today a large section of the intellectual and the active among French Canadians are scarcely interested in creating French-Canadian capitalists. They discard, by hypotheses, the present forms of capitalism. They believe in cooperation and in trade unionism and in political action stemming from these two movements. When they come almost to the end of their thinking, they wish to entrust to the state of Quebec, reformed of course, the administration of major natural resources. Fernand Dansereau has noted in a study published a few weeks ago that a nationalism that is new and probably unconscious animates these minds.

What do you think?

1. *What changes does Laurendeau feel have taken place in Quebec? How does he account for these changes?*
2. *Do you think Laurendeau would feel the Quebec response to changing conditions was regional or cultural? Why?*
3. *To whom was Laurendeau addressing his argument? Would he be addressing the same group of people today?*
4. *Keeping in mind the section on contemporary issues in Quebec you have already read, would you argue that the issues raised by Laurendeau are still valid today? Defend your answer.*

AN IMPERILLED CONFEDERATION

In 1967, Daniel Johnson, former Premier of the Province of Quebec, addressed the Confederation of Tomorrow Conference in Toronto. His remarks concerned what Quebec wanted in 1967. (From: Government of Quebec, Preliminary Statement by Mr. Daniel Johnson, Former Prime Minister: Confederation of Tomorrow Conference, (Toronto, November 1967).)

We are now living in a divided country searching for identity and racked by inner tensions.

Why is this so? Why, when a few short years ago most people did not have the slightest premonition of such a crisis, why are some of us now suddenly obliged to accept as a working hypothesis the hitherto unthinkable possibility of Canada's dissolution? What has taken place which can account for the astonishment in some circles, the dismay in others at such a development?

What has happened is that Quebec, mainstay of French Canada, questioning the validity of the country's political structure, seeks a reallocation of powers between the two orders of government and concrete recognition for French Canada of rights equal to those always enjoyed by English-speaking Canada. Such aspirations, expressed more forcefully and consistently than ever before, first surprised English-speaking Canada and then produced opposition to what seemed a threat to the established order. In fact, we have reached the point where quite a few French-speaking Canadians believe that persistent misunderstanding makes any statement of their aspirations to English-speaking citizens a waste of time. A considerable number among the latter, we realize, are satisfied with the present political system and hold that no concession should be made to the vague demands of what they believe to be a vociferous and extremist minority. Thus the two groups which a century ago established Canadian Confederation are becoming more firmly entrenched in their "two solitudes". More seriously still, these two solitudes are increasingly out of touch with each other's reality; in the end, lack of co-operation between them can destroy Canada.

. . .

French Canadians assume that the 1867 confederative act was designed to let them develop in accordance with their own culture.

One hundred years ago, the Fathers of Confederation entrusted to the provinces both those spheres of activity which, at the time, seemed properly to depend on local initiative and those which seemed essential to protect language, religion and culture.

Today, after a century's experience, French Canadians have become aware of three things. First of all, whenever members of their community living in provinces other than Quebec have sought to obtain rights equal to those enjoyed by English-speaking Canadians, the 1867 constitution has proved impotent ...

The second thing French Canadians have noticed is that there has always been a clear tendency for the federal government to take over, partly or wholly, responsibilities assigned to the provinces in the 1867 constitution. . . .

And thirdly, French-speaking Canadians realize that the 1867 division of responsibilities between governments no longer permits the French-Canadian nation to develop as effectively as it desires. . . .

Quebecers have always known that if their enterprises are to attain success in Canada, they must exert themselves more than other Canadians, who have the dual advantage of numerical superiority and favouring Canadian economic and political institutions. But in addition, they now find their road to full self-achievement encumbered with fresh obstacles, including some which, under present conditions, seem more difficult to overcome than those they have met in the past. In general, during the last decade, not a minority but a majority of Quebecers have become aware that their situation is likely to grow worse if they do not act promptly to remedy it.

In sociological terms, Quebecers have witnessed the disintegration of the way of life which traditionally protected them. They had survived in good part because they lived in isolation, locked in upon themselves, clinging to the past in a typically rural environment where the state's presence was marginal. Almost overnight, they found themselves in an industrial society requiring massive intervention by the state, open to the whole of North America and exposed to the influence of foreign, especially American, culture backed by such powerful means of communication as speedy transport, highways, cinema, radio and television.

In demographic terms, they have become aware that, even though they form some thirty per cent of Canada's population, they constitute a tiny group in comparison with the North American English-speaking community.

On the economic level, they have come to understand that the industrial society in which they were henceforth to live had not been created by them, but by others not sharing their cultural values. And also that, in a world where economic might confers enough de facto advantages to make de jure claims unnecessary, they were—not always through their own fault— seriously lacking in means for effective action.

In political matters, as we have already said, they have realized that Canada's structure itself worked to their disadvantage and that the 1867 constitution was far from giving them the protection they had traditionally anticipated.

Taking all this into account, it is incontrovertibly evident that our nation no longer has a choice. If it passively accepts the present situation, it will inevitably take the road to slow but sure assimilation into the great North American mass.

. . .

As French-speaking Canadians, we have an unshakeable conviction that we form a viable community sharing one of the greatest cultures in the western world, speaking an international language and endowed with vast human potentialities. That is why, despite all difficulties, we are resolved to preserve our identity. But there is more than this. The very act of asserting ourselves as a nation will certainly help greatly in giving Canada the identity she needs to distinguish herself from her powerful neighbour to the south. Moreover, we are convinced that, in future, nations like ours will have a role to play out of all proportion to their demographic strength.

. . .

Essentially, what French Canadians want is to be themselves and develop normally like any other people; in Quebec and in other parts of Canada. More particularly, they want to create in Quebec an environment conducive to their own growth. They also want it to be possible for members of their community settled in other provinces to develop as English-speaking Canadians can do in Quebec.

In a country like ours, we must begin by ensuring public education at all levels in Canada's two official languages wherever the English or French-speaking group is sufficiently large. Obviously, this does not rule out the necessity of providing the French or English-speaking groups with means of acquiring good command of the majority language in their environment. As for other government services such as departments, courts, administrative bodies, we believe the best way to avoid problems and render justice to the greatest number of people concerned is to deal with the question on a regional basis, without regard to provincial boundaries.

What do you think?

1. *What realities do Quebeckers have to face, according to Mr. Johnson?*
2. *How have these realities affected Quebec's demands?*
3. *How would the present government of Quebec respond to these demands?*
4. *Does Mr. Johnson propose any solutions to the issues he has presented? If so, what are they? If not, why do you think he didn't?*

WHAT DOES QUEBEC WANT—1970

Prime Minister Robert Bourassa addressed the Constitutional Conference in 1970 on the topic of "What Does Quebec Want?" (Reprinted by permission of the Hon. Robert Bourassa.)

. . .

Constitutional revision is forcing us to discover and invent new ways and means of doing things, capable of meeting the dual requirement of our federal system: respect for the two founding communities and balance of powers when dealing with the great pursuits of tomorrow.

QUEBEC'S IDENTITY. We want an invigorating federalism, one that decentralizes, one that places confidence in the governments that it joins together. We believe that between secession's easy-sounding truths and the pure and simple abandonment of our responsibilities to another government, the federative formula is the best one. To be sure, this is conditional on a strict respect for the special characteristics of our culture and the aspirations of the Quebec community. This requires, therefore, a flexible federalism, which will express our true freedom as Quebecers within the structures of a dynamic participation in the great plans involving Canada as a whole. We consider that such an option is to be preferred to the constraints which might well be the consequence of a political sovereignty severed from the realities of our times.

Our choice is made. But at the same time, it forces us to prove our case that it is the best suited to ensure the most favorable conditions of existence for the citizens we have the honour to serve. Not only the economic but also the social and cultural conditions of their existence.

I have confidence that the new federalism which will arise from our discussions will stimulate the flowering of our individual as well as our collective freedoms. Freedom of association, of participation, of voluntary delegation of powers, indeed, but also freedom to withdraw, not to commit ourselves when we deem that any given jurisdiction can be exercised in a better way, with more efficiency and greater coherence, by this or that order of government.

. . .

I can already appraise all the efforts that we will have to make towards reassessing the situation during the coming months. For it is obvious that the present structures of the Canadian federation are ill-suited to our requirements.

We will therefore have to conscript our energies in record time in order to arrive quickly at concrete solutions. We are given another chance to change some of the particularly antiquated and inoperative aspects of the type of federalism we now have. But our Quebec fellow-citizens will not tolerate any longer either the excessive slowness of the revision procedure of our constitution, or the lingering chaos which stem from it.

. . .

It is from this general point of view that the present Quebec Government is approaching the task of constitutional revision. Against an illusory sovereignty, it proposes instead a full freedom of action within federal structures respectful of the distinctive character of Quebec, its particular cultural traits but also its great need of catching up in the economic area.

The new federal contract, therefore, must satisfy these pressing requirements.

Indeed, this is the best way to attain one of the fundamental goals of the Canada of tomorrow: the preservation and development of the bicultural character of the Canadian federation.

. . .

In addition, it is also undeniable that all Quebecers want to organize their participation in social life and the improvement of their environment first of all within the framework of institutions conceived by them and in which they participate fully. Quebecers are holding on firmly to the possibility of expressing themselves collectively through public structures, hence a government, they control fully; they will never agree to give this up.

The constitutional policy of our government will therefore hold the premise that Quebecers require and want, on the one hand, to manage their own government in order to be allowed to develop their own cultural entity, where the whole of Quebec is involved, and on the other hand, to participate, where the whole of Canada is involved, in a prosperous bicultural federation, capable of managing its own affairs and ensuring a minimum of equality between its citizens and regions while making a contribution to the progress of the international community.

. . .

The new government of Quebec intends to make a dynamic contribution to constitutional revision, and this in the respect for its present constitutional powers and through its will to share in the policies of Canada as a whole. At one and the same time, it will make a double contribution by the enrichment of the Quebec personality, which it seeks faithfully to mirror, and by the effectiveness of its initiatives at the Canadian level.

Finally, our government sees in constitutional revision an unparalleled opportunity and, taking into account the circumstances which prevail in Quebec, perhaps the last opportunity to build a country that will match the aspirations of Canadians.

A country where citizens and governments will, in complete good faith and without reservations, work together in the pursuit of the aim which I took the liberty to outline briefly in the present statement and which seem to me to correspond to the highest interest of Quebec and of Canada. (translated from French)

What do you think?

1. *What does Mr. Bourassa claim Quebec wants? How does he propose to resolve the issue?*
2. *To what extent do you think the aspirations of Quebecers are valid? Why?*
3. *Do you think their demands are the result of regional or cultural protest? Why? How have the demands of Quebec influenced regional demands in the rest of Canada?*

The Prairie Provinces

WESTERN DISCONTENT

Although it is true that the postwar years witnessed little active protest, regional grievances did not completely disappear. The following document testifies that regional sentiment in the West was still strong. It is an excerpt from W. L. Morton, "Clio in Canada and The Interpretation of Canadian History," University of Toronto Quarterly, XV (3), April, 1946. (Reprinted by permission of the author and University of Toronto Press.)

. . . Indeed the sectionalism of the West is, in different terms, as justified as the French nationalism of Quebec or the British nationalism of Ontario. . . . Not only is there driven between East and West the blunt wedge of the Shield. Not only is there the clash of economic interest caused by difference in resources, climate and stage of economic development. There are also environmental differences so great as to be seldom appreciated. The West is plains country, with few, though great resources, a harsh and hazardous climate, and an inflexible economy. So domineering is this environment that it must change people and institutions greatly from those of the humid forest regions of the East. The West, for example, has long faced the problem of paying fixed rates of interest with returns from a very "unfixed" rainfall.

There is finally the fact that the West was annexed to Confederation as a subordinate region and so remained for sixty years. Such was the historical schooling of the West. It had, therefore, to fight its way up to self-government and equality in Confederation, nor is the process ended. No more than French Canada can the West accept a common interpretation of Canadian history or cultural metropolitanism. The West must first work out its own historical experience . . . and free itself, and find itself. Until it ceases to be an exploited or a subsidized region it cannot do so. In an imperfect world an unequal incidence of national policies is no doubt inevitable, but even in an imperfect world people may be allowed to shape an interpretation of history and a way of life in accord with their own experience.

If this view appears extreme, it is partly because Westerners seldom enjoy that blessed moderation which descends upon those who have dwelt long among the flesh-pots, and partly because metropolitan Canada has seldom appreciated the impact of Laurentian imperialism on the West . . . It was the fate of the West to become the colony of a colony which brought to its new imperial role neither imagination, liberality, nor magnanimity. To ensure returns from the £300,000 spent in "buying" the West, the natural resources were retained, contrary to British precedent, the protective tariff, that chief of Canadian extractive industries, was established, and the monopoly clause of the Canadian Pacific Railway charter was imposed. In the events which preceded the rebellion of 1885, Ottawa added neglect to subordination, and after the rebellion was suppressed, neglect from time to time was not unknown.

And Eastern aggression has continued in other and sometimes subtler ways. For two generations the West has been let by the Ontario-born. What this has meant it would be idle to attempt to estimate, but it may be that native Westerners will not be so susceptible to the blandishments of metropolitan "nationalism". On the other hand, the Westerner, like the medieval Scot, is poor. Similar in effect is the fact that the West like a colony, is used as a proving ground in which bright young men in business and the professions prepare themselves for higher positions in the head offices of the East. . . .

Be that as it may, the subordination of the West, when added to its sharp sectionalism, gives it an incisive and cogent character of its own. . . . It has no acceptable alternative to working out its own identity in terms of its own historical experience. It must realize its latent nationalism, a nationalism neither racial like the French nor dominant—a "garrison" nationality—like that of Ontario, but environmental and, because of the diversity of its people, composite. It may, of course, fail (as the French might have been assimilated), and, by the joint process of exploitation and loss of its natural leaders to the East and the United States, be reduced to a subject people, without character or spirit.

Yet if it takes up the old Canadian struggle for survival and self-government, it may survive and, with French Canada, end the Laurentian domination. When all of the "decisive" and subordinate areas have achieved survival and self-government, and have raised themselves to equality in Confederation, when Confederation is held together no longer by the "Protestant garrison" and protectionist imperialism, but by the consent of equals, when it ceases to be an instrument of domination and exploitation and becomes a means to co-operation and distributive justice, then there can be a common interpretation of Canadian history and a common textbook in the schools, French as well as English, East as well as West. Moreover, it must be a catholic, imaginative, and magnanimous interpretation. This is not only ideally desirable, it is practically necessary. The Canadian state cannot be devoted to absolute nationalism, the focus of homogeneous popular will. The two nationalities and four sections forbid it. The state in Canada must promote liberty of persons and communities, and justice, which is the essence of liberty . . .

What do you think?

1. *What historical reason does Morton cite to explain the existence of regional sentiment in the West?*
2. *What particular grievances does Morton address?*
3. *What kind of regional character does the author see in the West?*
4. *According to this article, what changes in attitude are required to make Confederation work better for the West?*

THE 1920s AND 1930s

The 1920s and 1930s were years of great upheaval in Canada, where regional problems were of great concern. The most vocal protest movements were centered in Western Canada and in the Maritimes. This phenomenon was influenced by many factors and even by events and attitudes of the recent past.

The Wilfrid Laurier years, from 1896 to 1911, had witnessed the continuation of John A. Macdonald's National Policy; settlement increased in the West and Canada prospered. However, by 1911, when Robert Borden replaced Laurier as prime minister, there were visible signs that all was not well in the Dominion of Canada. Western farmers began to organize and press for changes in tariff policy. Provincial politicians from British Columbia and the Maritimes demanded more financial aid from the Federal Government. The coming of the First World War interrupted this agitation, as attention turned to a common war effort. But once the war ended, the same grievances re-emerged.

These grievances became even more acute during the depression years. It is not surprising that the most vocal protest movements were organized in the Maritimes and the Western provinces, since the Great Depression affected those regions more severely than other areas of Canada. As conditions worsened, in the absence of any federal initiatives, regional protest movements began to formulate policy proposals to solve the problems in their own areas.

The following section documents some manifestations of regional protest in Canada between the two World Wars. How might this protest have contributed to a redefinition of the limits of federal power? Why did some Canadians come to accept more government intervention in the running of the economy? How do Canadians feel about such controls today?

British Columbia

In the 1930s British Columbia was governed by the provincial Liberal Party under Premier T. Duff Pattullo. Elected on a broad platform of social and economic reform, Pattullo was influenced by Franklin Roosevelt's "New Deal" program in the United States and proposed his own "Little New Deal" for British Columbia. His government argued that B.C. was not a province like the others and resented having its prosperity sapped to support the other regions of the nation. This section examines separatist sentiment in British Columbia in the thirties, as well as regional demands for increased recognition within Confederation.

A DOMINION OF BRITISH COLUMBIA

The Vancouver Sun, *May 14, 1934 issued a secessionist threat in the front page editorial "A Dominion of British Columbia".*

What is the political and economic future of people in this province? That is a question which is being asked in every store and club in Vancouver and throughout the country. The question is hardly a party one, it is not a new one, but events of the last few days have forcibly brought it before our people.

Premier Bennett's refusal to extend to the Government of British Columbia the same credit help that was given to the C.P.R. was one incident. The other, Ottawa's disclosure that an outside owned tobacco monopoly had, in 5 years, paid out some 32 million dollars in dividends while at the same time reducing to Canadian growers a tobacco price per pound from 30¢ down to 15¢.

These are only samples of a series of events which show British Columbians how they and their rich province are being exploited. That young student tobacco grower, what chance had he to get ahead while he was being bled white by the tobacco monopoly? What chance have the people of this province to get ahead with development thwarted, with trade stifled by high duties, and with tax and transport levies that seem designed to kill rather than encourage industry?

Unless some understanding and quotas and agreements are arrived at with the money centres and political powers of Canada, something more serious than talk must be given the idea of forming a DOMINION OF BRITISH COLUMBIA, which will include the Yukon, Vancouver Island, and, if they want to join us, the Province of Alberta.

In transportation, in finance, in industry, and in political recognition, too, Canada, from the Great Lakes west, as a "receiving" entity, simply does not exist.

Our ability to produce and pay is openly admitted. President Beatty, at the recent annual meeting of the C.P.R., stated that 50% of the freight revenue came from the West: and what applies to railway freight applies to most other businesses. But when it comes to sharing emoluments and control and executive position, we are not on the map. Hardly an executive salary or ranking directorship in any Canadian institution is now held by men west of the Lakes.

The centralizing policy of the East may have been all right in the growing, building, prosperous days of Canada, but to allow this exploiting and unequal sharing to settle down into a permanent policy, and economy for CANADA is, to independent-minded, social-minded, British-minded, British Columbians, unthinkable.

Canadians in this end of Canada are a slow-thinking, slow-acting, patient people. Like the tobacco-grower student, we "take our medicine like a man" until the dose becomes unsupportable.

The cruel exploitation of tobacco growers in Eastern Canada is only a mild sample of what has been done to Western holders of Turner Valley oil properties by Canada's oil monopoly; to Peace River and Pacific development, and generally in preventing British Columbians from sharing their rightful heritage.

It is certainly time for a re-survey and declaration of future plans and policy.

The national debt of Canada totals about $3 billions.

On the basis of this province's 700,000 population, our share of this debt would total about $180 millions. Interest on this debt would cost taxpayers in interest about eight million dollars a year. Instead of eight millions per year, what British Columbia now pays the Federal Treasury in excise and duties and various taxes, is well over 30 million dollars annually.

What do we get for that money?

Confederation was formed on a basis of very low tariffs. This province could, on a basis of the B.N.A. Act, buy and sell and trade unhampered with the world. A scheming, exploiting East has changed all this.

Now we must try and sell our lumber and minerals and wheat and fruits in world markets, but are compelled to buy all our goods from and do all our business with Eastern Canada.

Although there are markets for tens of millions worth of our Western products in England and Japan and China, we British Columbians cannot exchange a seagrass rug with Japan without paying several hundred per cent duty; we cannot bring in a bamboo chair from China; we cannot exchange cotton or woollen goods or machinery with England without being taxed unpayably high duty.

The financial and industrial manipulators in St. James Street do not seem to realize THAT THEY ARE BUILDING UP IN ENGLAND AN ANTAGONISM AGAINST CANADIAN PRODUCTS that is reducing to peonage the people who live in this Western half of Canada.

To meekly state that British Columbians have been unjustly dealt with, is not enough. The day of sending from Vancouver protesting Board of Trade and public delegations to St. James Street and to Ottawa, must come to an end.

What is now required is a re-survey of CANADA, a planned economy that will allow this province to develop trade in England and abroad, and a re-allotment to this end of Canada of its rightful share in the directing and executive positions and spending of Canada.

This fine rich Pacific Coast province is not going to be prevented from buying and selling to Britain, our natural market; we are no longer going to be hindered in developing trade with Japan and China and India.

The Okanagan and Fraser Valley fruit farmer is not the docile habitant of Quebec; our loggers and miners in this province are real men; while the great middle classes in our British Columbia cities average up a people unequalled on earth.

IF WE ARE FORCED TO IT BY EASTERN CANADA, WE CAN SEPARATE AND PAY OUR OWN WAY AND GO IT ALONE; AND WE CAN BE SURE WE WILL HAVE 100 PER CENT BRITISH SUPPORT.

Victoria and Vancouver are world seaports. This province is a great hunting and sporting country. And regardless of the tongues and races in the rest of Canada, we are and propose to remain, a British people.

There must be a more equitable sharing among Canadians of things Canadian, or else this province must look about in self-defence to find ways and means to federate these parts into a DOMINION OF BRITISH COLUMBIA.

What do you think?

1. *What are the B.C. grievances alluded to in this editorial? How do they reflect regional concerns, if at all?*
2. *What kind of attitude does the author of this editorial have to Canadians in other parts of Canada? Are his views justifiable?*
3. *Why was British Columbia threatening to secede?*
4. *What kind of federal action did the author feel was necessary in order for there to be "a more equitable sharing among Canadians of things Canadian"?*

B.C. WANTS SPECIAL CONSIDERATION

In two letters to the Canadian Prime Minister, R. B. Bennett, in 1933 and 1934, Pattullo stated his province's opinion on the situation. (Pattullo Papers, Pattullo to R. B. Bennett, December 18, 1933 and June 1, 1934.) (Reprinted by permission of the Minister of Supply and Services.)

. . . We are an empire in ourselves, . . . and our hills and valleys are stored with potential wealth which makes us one of the greatest assets of the Dominion.

I have an idea . . . that the West understands the East better than the East understands the West, for the simple reason that most of the Westerners were born in the East and have kept in touch with conditions there. . . .

. . . I am aware that the great bulk of the people of Ontario and Quebec know nothing of British Columbia, that they view us somewhat patronizingly as a part of Canada which must be tolerated while responsible journals suggest that we go to Ottawa begging and coming away with a bag full of eastern money. They do not stop to consider the hundreds of millions that have been poured into the pockets of eastern manufacturers by the western provinces.

What do you think?

1. *Your perception of the way others see you may influence how you see yourself and how you deal with your problems. What kind of image does Pattullo think Canada has of British Columbia?*
2. *In what ways might this perception have influenced B.C.'s response to its own problems?*
3. *Can you think of any other examples in Canada where external perceptions might have affected regional behaviour? Explain.*

DOMINION-PROVINCIAL RELATIONS IN 1938

"British Columbia in the Canadian Federation" was a submission of the Pattullo government to the Royal Commission on Dominion Provincial Relations in 1938. Part II of the submission is a historical survey of B.C.'s demands for better terms: Part VII contained the province's recommendations.

The position we take is not that the Dominion Government has violated the Terms of Union, or that we are entitled to compensation for lack of fulfillment in any substantial respect, as the performance of a legal contract could be construed; but we do contend that in the development of the constitution, in its actual operation, from the date of Confederation in 1871, that a state of affairs has grown up in British Columbia and in the Dominion, as the result of the union between the two, that has established a moral right and a sound constitutional claim on our part for increased recognition—and a state of affairs that was not anticipated by either party to the Federal compact.

Eastern Canadians were for a long time wholly ignorant of British Columbia, and very indifferent about its welfare. In fact, generally speaking, the mental attitude of the people towards the Province for about thirty-five years was not only of a negative character, but to a very considerable extent unfavourable; not intentionally so, but, because they did not understand the real situation and had been prejudiced on account of a long political fight in which British Columbia and the Canadian Pacific Railway were the principal issues. Hence, even if various Governments had been more favourably disposed, the mental attitude of the people as a whole would have prevented a betterment policy being carried out. British Columbia was not only commercially isolated, but she was politically isolated as well.

For a proper knowledge of the case it is necessary to consider the conditions which existed at the time British Columbia entered Confederation, and the mental attitude in which the Terms of Union between the Province and Dominion were framed. Public sentiment, as represented in Parliament, was prejudicial to more favourable terms being granted. A large section of Canada was utterly opposed to union with British Columbia on the terms under which the construction of a trans-continental railway was rendered obligatory. It was only upon grounds of large public policy of a national character—the rounding out of Confederation—that their adoption was justified. It was almost universally conceded that the Province, physically handicapped as it was, would not pay its way in Confederation, and it was strongly contended that the construction of the Canadian Pacific Railway—an essential demand of British Columbia—was too great a sacrifice on the part of the Dominion, and that the railway when built would prove unremunerative. Consequently, the financial terms conceded to British Columbia were the least favourable possible, and without any adequate knowledge of its financial requirements. . . .

The subsequent course of events has shown that British Columbia has not only paid its way in Confederation, but has contributed in forty years about $35,000,000 in excess of what it has cost the Dominion; that the Canadian Pacific Railway has been instrumental more than any other factor in raising up Canada to the proud position which it occupies today, with benefits vastly greater to the rest of Canada than to British Columbia; and that the Settlement Act gave a realizable asset to the Dominion thirty times greater than the expenditure which it involved.

The Government of British Columbia submits as incontrovertible that the original and amended Terms of Union having been based upon assumptions which have proved groundless, and that as the very opposite of what had been anticipated has transpired, . . .

[The submission put forward twenty-six recommendations, some of which were:]

1. Power should rest in the Parliament of Canada to amend the British North America Act upon a basis to be agreed between the Provinces and the Dominion.

2. The special position of British Columbia in the Confederation of Canada should receive immediate consideration and the terms upon which British Columbia entered into Confederation adjusted in order that British Columbia may be in a position of equality with the other Provinces of Canada when considering new adjustments and relationships in Dominion and Provincial authority. . . .

. . .

6. The Provinces should be granted authority to raise their own revenues by whatever means deemed necessary in the light of circumstances and requirements. This, if carried out, would place beyond question all taxes as now levied and would authorize the imposition of other taxes, such, for example, as the business turnover tax or the retail sales tax. . . .

What do you think?

1. What claims was B.C. making from Confederation in the 1930s? How do these claims differ from current demands in B.C. and in the other provinces? How are they the same?
2. Which claims do you feel are most justified? Why?

Prairie Protest and Western Political Parties

The Western Canadian prairie region has traditionally claimed that it was an unequal partner in Confederation and that it has been discriminated against by the policies of Central Canada and the Federal Government. In this reaction it closely resembles the Atlantic region. Partly due to late settlement and the inconsistent application of federal policies, the prairies did not have the same tradition of institutional structures evident in other parts of Canada. In fact, it should be noted that Central and Eastern Canada already had established political, economic and social structures before Confederation, while Alberta and Saskatchewan did not even exist as provinces until 1905. Thus, the development of such structures in the prairie provinces is essentially a 20th century phenomenon, in particular, a product of the interval between the two World Wars. This section examines some aspects of this important development by focusing on the discussion of local issues and the establishment of political parties reflecting the regional interests of the Prairie provinces.

THE FARMERS PLATFORM OF 1921

"The Farmers Platform of 1921" was also known as "The New National Policy." It provided the basis of farm organization demands when these groups supported the Progressive Party in the 1921 election. The party won 64 seats, 38 of them in the prairie provinces. High on the list of priorities of this party was their tariff policy, as stated in the 1921 platform.

THE TARIFF

3. Whereas Canada is now confronted with a huge national war debt and other greatly increased financial obligations, which can be most readily and effectively reduced by the development of our natural resources, chief of which is agricultural lands; . . . And whereas the war has revealed the

amazing financial strength of Great Britain, which has enabled her to finance, not only her own part in the struggle, but also to assist in financing her Allies . . . , this enviable position being due to the free trade policy which has enabled her to draw her supplies freely from every quarter of the globe and consequently to undersell her competitors on the world's market, . . . we believe that the best interests of the Empire and of Canada would be served by reciprocal action on the part of Canada through gradual reductions of the tariff on British imports, having for its objects closer union and a better understanding between Canada and the Motherland and at the same time bring about a great reduction in the cost of living to our Canadian people; . . .

. . .

DEFINITE TARIFF DEMANDS

Therefore be it resolved that . . . as a means of remedying these evils and bringing about much-needed social and economic reforms, our tariff laws should be amended as follows:

a) By an immediate and substantial all-round reduction of the customs tariff.

b) By reducing the customs duty on goods imported from Great Britain to one-half the rates charged under the general tariff, and that further gradual, uniform reductions be made in the remaining tariff on British imports that will ensure complete Free Trade between Great Britain and Canada in five years.

c) By endeavouring to secure unrestricted reciprocal trade in natural products with the United States along the lines of the Reciprocity Agreement of 1911.

d) By placing all foodstuffs on the free list.

e) That agricultural implements, farm and household machinery, vehicles, fertilizers, coal, lumber, cement, gasoline, illuminating fuel and lubricating oils be placed on the free list, and that all raw materials and machinery used in their manufacture also be placed on the free list.

f) That all tariff concessions granted to other countries be immediately extended to Great Britain.

g) That all corporations engaged in the manufacture of products protected by the customs tariff be obliged to publish annually comprehensive and accurate statements of their earnings.

h) That every claim for tariff protection by any industry should be heard publicly before a special committee of parliament.

What do you think?

1. *How would the policies outlined above benefit the West?*
2. *Were the Progressives successful in getting their program implemented? Why or why not?*

THE NATURAL RESOURCES QUESTION

Chester Martin, a professor of history at the University of Manitoba, published The Natural Resources Question *in 1920 and drew attention to this grievance of the Prairie Provinces. By 1929, the Federal Government had transferred control of natural resources to Alberta, Saskatchewan and Manitoba.*

Indeed there is a sense in which the provincial control of the public domain served an even more fundamental purpose.

It is more than the cornerstone of Confederation. It was part of the foundation, the very bed-rock upon which the whole edifice was built, for without responsible government and its first corollary, the 'grant of full rights over the land,' the provinces which entered into Confederation in 1867 would never have been in a position to aspire to a British and transcontinental Dominion.

Now while it is seldom that a great principle has been so discerningly built into the foundations of a nation, it is doubtful if a parallel can be found to the half-century of devious expedience during which this fundamental principle has remained in abeyance in the case of Manitoba. Beyond a doubt this Province has been the Cinderella of Confederation; it has been her misfortune for fifty years to sit among the ashes and aspire only to the commonplace rights and privileges of the more fortunate provinces of the Dominion. She inherited from the Riel Insurrection an unenviable prejudice from the rest of Canada that was as meaningless as it was unjust. Within her boundaries for fifty years have been fought out the bitter controversies of Quebec and Ontario. . . . Railway communications east and west were a by-product of the terms of union with British Columbia, and the public domain was withheld because the Canadian Pacific Railway 'must be built by means of the land through which it had to pass.'

With regard to 'land revenues' it was twelve years before any fiscal concessions were made to alleviate the poverty in that respect which had been imposed upon the province 'for the purpose of the Dominion.'

. . .

It is submitted that the time has come to right this half-century of vested wrong by an Imperial amendment . . . which shall leave this province like the other provinces of the Dominion 'supreme' over its own lands 'directly under the Crown as its head.' . . . 'The Natural Resources Question' may thus be said, without false modesty, to constitute one of the most important problems of the Dominion. Its settlement would set the seal of full provincial status under the *British North America Act* of 1867 upon three Canadian "colonies", and would enable the Dominion, with its house in order to move forward discerningly among the British nations of the Empire and the other nations of the world.

What do you think?

1. *Historically, why did the "natural resource issue" exist on the Prairie provinces?*
2. *Why was the control of natural resources such an important issue in the prairie provinces?*
3. *In light of later developments, do you think this transfer was in the best interests of Canada? Why or why not?*

PROGRESSIVE PARTY IN CANADA

In 1950, W. L. Morton published a history of organized farm protest entitled The Progressive Party in Canada. *(Reprinted by permission of the author and the University of Toronto Press.) He offered the following interpretation of the effects of the Progressive Party:*

. . . Did the restoration of the old parties in 1930, then, and the rise of the C.C.F. and Social Credit parties, essentially composite parties like the old, mark a complete defeat of the Progressive revolt against the party system? To a great extent it did. Yet the old order of Macdonald and Laurier, when party affiliation was hereditary and party chieftains were almost deified, was not restored. The two-party system did not return in its former strength. The rules and conventions of parliament made provision for more than two parties. The electorate became more independent, indeed, to the point of political indifference. The authority of the whip became lighter, the bonds of caucus weaker, than in the old days. These were effects of the Progressive movement, and constituted its mark on Canadian political life. . . .

Yet the Progressive insurgence was not merely a sectional protest against a metropolitan economy, it was also an agrarian protest against the growing urban domination of the Canadian economy and of national politics. As such, it was closely allied to the sectional protest. As an agrarian protest, the Progressive movement was a response to the industrialization of the economy, and the commercialization and mechanization of agriculture. . . .

In a larger view, also, the Progressive movement marked a profound transformation. Behind the sectional protest lay not only resentment of the National Policy and of its agents, the political parties. Behind it lay also resentment of the inequality of the provinces of the continental West in Confederation. They had been created with limitations, imposed "for the purpose of the Dominion." They entered Confederation, not as full partners, as sister provinces, but as subordinate communities, subject to the land, fiscal, and railway policies of the metropolitan provinces and the special interests of the French Canadian in the French dispersion in the West. They were, in short, colonies under the form of provinces "in a federation denoting equality." The Progressive party was a full-blown expression of the West's resentment of its colonial status. As such, it was one phase of the development of the Canadian nation. . . .

The transfer of the natural resources in 1930, the purpose of the Dominion having been fulfilled, marked the end of the colonial subordination and the achievement of equality of status by the West in Confederation. This, too, was a response to western pressure embodied in the federal Progressive party and the provincial governments the movement threw up. The Progressive movement, in short, marked the achievement of political maturity by the West, and the symbols of equality could no longer be withheld. . . .

What do you think?

1. *Why did the Progressive movement arise in the West? What effect has it had on regional protest?*
2. *What does Morton think was the significance of the Progressive Party?*
3. *What effects of Progressivism can you detect in Canada today?*

UNITED FARMERS OF SASKATCHEWAN—PLATFORM

The Great Depression severely affected the three Prairie provinces. Debt payments, falling prices, and the loss of foreign markets were compounded by drought and grasshoppers. By 1931, new solutions were being proposed to deal with the situation. The Toronto-based Saturday Night *informed its readership of some of the proposals and assessed them. On January 24 and March 24, the activities of the U.F.C. (United Farmers of Canada)-Sask. Section were analyzed.*

Solution of the prairie economic and political problems has been undertaken with much gusto by the radical orators of the Saskatchewan United Farmers. . . . These expert promoters of theories unfolded carefully prepared remedies to suppress depression in Canada. . . . Unable to trust any of the numerous present parties in the inauguration of the precious plans, the leaders contended that the only safe course is a brand new political group— carefully nourished and controlled within the unadulterated ranks of their own brethren. Truck or trade with Conservatives, Liberals, Progressives, or lesser lights, naturally would not provide the same attractive avenues for new aspiring office-seekers. They want to be installed safely in the drivers' remunerative seat themselves. . . .

The epoch-making historical platform is planned for both provincial and federal consummation. The various fantastic planks may be open to all manner of individual interpretations by politicians and taxpayers, but that does not worry the new aspirants for power—and the limelight. The planks are all numbered, contradictory, and reduced to the vaguest simplicity, as follows:

FEDERAL

1. Pegged grain prices.
2. Federal stabilization board.
3. Downward revision of freight and express rates.
4. Socialization of currency and credit.
5. Completion and operation of the Hudson Bay route, and terminal elevators and harbor facilities, by September 1, 1931.
6. Free transport to Churchill.
7. Federal assistance in adjustments between creditor and debtor.
8. Supplementary federal 100 per cent pool legislation, if necessary.
9. Government regulation of the Grain Exchange, and abolition of speculation.
10. Nationalization of the Canadian Pacific Railway, and revaluation of Canadian National Railways assets.

PROVINCIAL

1. Legislation preventing foreclosures, evictions or seizures, until the next session of the legislature.
2. Aids to adjustment between creditors and debtors by powers granted to the debt adjusting commissioner.
3. Inclusion of all citizens in those entitled to assistance under the Debt Adjustment Act.
4. Absolute security of tenure on home quarter section.
5. Enlargement of debt adjustment commission, to include two commissioners and a chairman.
6. Introduction of province-wide crop insurance.
7. Introduction of a Primary Products Act.
8. Nationalization of all land and resources as rapidly as possible.

     Ultimate objective (both provincial and Dominion)—*Social ownership and co-operative production for use—not for profit. ...*

     The platform also sets a new precedent in prairie agrarian politics. Free trade, long the predominating issue, has now given way to protectionist theoretics in a most extreme form. Farmer organizations will have some difficulty harmonizing their stock doctrines of free trade with urgent demands for combinistic and compulsionistic legislation—aimed at eliminating competition and personal liberty in commercial trading.

The ill-digested idea of a provincial compulsory hundred per cent grain pool, . . . has already created organized reaction among western farmers, and been declared *ultra vires* by the courts and constitutional authorities. There is no suggestion of any proposed compensation for the millions of capital invested by grain marketing companies and subsidiaries, which have been conducting a necessary and indispensable grain marketing service for nearly three-quarters of a century. This evidently, is one way of realizing the idle dream of a socialized state, non-profit-making to the producer,—and their dictators manipulating the money bag. . . .

And so we find the newest political bogeyman trying to spread his self-important shadow across the country. They are to be the great rallying influence for all extremists. . . .

What is meant by?

"*ultra vires*"

What do you think?

1. *Does the author of this article have a regional bias? If so, what is it?*
2. *How would you react to these reports of political activity in the Prairie provinces if you were a reader of* Saturday Night *in 1931 in Central Canada? if you were a reader of* Saturday Night *in 1931 in south-west Saskatchewan or south-east Alberta? Why?*
3. *How might you account for these "radical proposals"?*
4. *To what extent do you think those who put forward these proposals were influenced by the Depression? by regional issues?*

THE SOCIAL CREDIT PARTY

The Social Credit Party in Alberta, under the leadership of William Aberhart, swept the provincial election of 1935 and elected the majority of federal Members of Parliament from Alberta later that year. The Social Credit monetary theory was accepted by a debt-ridden population in spite of the apparent conflict of the theory with the federal power over money and banking. Most of the subsequent Alberta legislation was later disallowed or declared unconstitutional.

The following is an account of an early Aberhart speech as reported in the Calgary Herald *in January, 1934.*

Income for everybody, sufficient for food, shelter and clothing, regardless of occupation or lack of it; the competitive system retained but with its worst features removed; private enterprise permitted but not allowed to expand beyond the public good, such were some of the results seen in application of the principles of the so-called Douglas system to the conditions of Alberta.

Three principles are essential to the plan, but would be applied differently according to the circumstances of the country which adopted them, Mr. Aberhart said.

The basic idea is that all citizens of a country own its natural resources and are entitled to a share in their distribution, instead of permitting a few financiers to exploit them. From this it follows that a government must function for the benefit of all the citizens instead of favoring privileged classes, whether manufacturers, producers, or bankers. Every citizen is a consumer and so the consumer must be the first consideration of a government.

On the security of the natural resources the government would credit every man and woman each year with enough to feed, shelter and clothe them during the year. In payment for the necessities of life everyone would be given non-negotiable notes on his account in this government credit house, which would then be transferred to the credit of whoever presented them. Such credits would have to be spent each year for any unspent remainder would be eliminated yearly. . . .

An automatic price control would be maintained by the government which would make hoarding of products impossible. For as the amount of goods increased the price would have to decline, thus keeping a balance between production and consumption. The producer would be guaranteed the cost of his product but there would be no profit allowed, only a commission. Those who wished to engage in production of a certain kind, against the advice of an advisory board, would be at liberty to do so, but would not be furnished with loans from the government credit house as would those who followed advice.

The result of these measures would be to keep up a constant purchasing power; to prevent alternate inflation and deflation at the will of the banks; to keep a constant flow of credit available for the productive industries and for distribution of their products. . . .

What do you think?

1. *In what ways was the rise of Social Credit in Alberta an indication of Western discontent?*
2. *What grievances do you think Social Credit sought to overcome? Do you think Mr. Aberhart's proposals were reasonable? Why or why not?*

NEW HOPE FOR THE WEST

"New Hope for the West" was the title of an article by John M. Imrie published in the Queen's Quarterly *in 1937. It was written in response to*

the appointment on April 14, 1937 of a Royal Commission to investigate Dominion-Provincial Relations.

To the prairie provinces more than to any other part of Canada, the national commission on the division of financial powers and responsibilities as between the federal and provincial governments [Rowell-Sirois] presents a new hope and a new opportunity for economic betterment.

Both are needed sorely in the prairie west. The depression was more severe in that area than in any other part of Canada. Moreover, there it brought into bold relief certain disabilities of long standing, some due to mistakes in early settlement, others to the unequal incidence of various national policies, others again to the survival of an old tradition that "the West can pay more."

It was shortsightedness on the part of several groups, some governmental and some private, that allowed these disabilities to continue unchecked until there had developed from them a sense of grievance and finally an attitude of protest. This, more than anything else, explains the rise and spread of social credit in the west and accompanying tendencies towards default and repudiation.

It is high time that these disabilities were given serious consideration on their own merits and by a judicial body free from sectional or political bias. . . .

It is not my purpose to deal in this article with the more obvious points in the case of the prairie provinces individually and collectively. . . . I choose instead to outline a few of the broad background pictures that should be presented by the prairie west.

To begin with, there should be given with the revealing brush of an artist the picture of an early land settlement on the western plains; the mistakes in early settlement policies; the fact that these were evolved and applied at a time when Ottawa controlled the natural resources of the prairies; and their effect on present economic conditions in the prairies and on the financial responsibilities of prairie governments. . . .

Then there should be traced the origin, continuance and effect of an old tradition that "the West can pay more". This had such power thirty years ago that many advertisements in national publications would conclude with price quotations somewhat like this: "Price 25 cents (west of the Great Lakes 35 cents)." In those days there was justification for the higher rates in the west. It cost more to do business there, population was scattered; freight rates were higher; overhead had to be distributed over fewer units. The actual extra cost was less on the whole than the extra levied charge. But in those days there was little objection from prairie people—soil was virgin, crops were good, part-time employment was plentiful, money flowed freely.

Whatever justification there was thirty years ago for charging higher prices, higher interest rates and higher freight rates in the west has been lessened greatly through changes in the picture meanwhile. On the one hand, the density of settlement has been greatly increased and the cost of doing business has been lessened. On the other hand, the west is no longer a country of virgin soil where two or three crops will put a new settler "on easy street", and no longer may the average farmer earn extra money on construction work on new railways or mushroom towns. Moreover agricultural prices during recent years have been far lower relatively on a "real money" basis than those of twenty-five or thirty years ago. It should be possible to persuade the commission that the tradition "the West can pay more" has outlived its original measure of justification and that its abandonment in part at least, is one of the processes necessary to ensure the financial independence of the three prairie provinces.

. . .

Another point to which the attention of the Commission should be directed is that two at least of the three prairie provinces have had for many years an unfavourable trade balance. . . . Such a condition, in more or less degree, is natural during the development period of a new area. It is natural also that after settlement reaches a certain point activities develop beyond primary production, efforts should be made to achieve a more balanced economy. Campaigns for the establishment of local industries that are waged from time to time in the prairie provinces are reflections of this desire. But there are definite limitations on what may be manufactured in the west due to distance from raw materials and to competition from factories more favorably located in relation to population and markets.

It is a realization of this limitation that has led to agitation in the prairie west from time to time for a system of regional or provincial tariffs. The argument presented is similar in principle to that used to justify a national tariff. There is, of course, a fundamental difference between national and regional tariffs and I do not believe the latter could be set up on any large scale without destroying the very basis of Confederation. But, if the prairie west is to be denied in the interest of Confederation the right to tariff protection related to the needs and aspirations of its own area, as I believe it must be denied, and at the same time is to be required to pay the excess cost of a tariff policy that benefits two provinces in particular, that is a factor to be considered in any sound analysis of the financial powers and taxation bases of the federal and provincial governments.

. . .

. . . Canada's great national task to-day is to devise a formula that will permit and promote the full and concurrent development of each of the several parts of Canada without involving undue or disproportionate sacrifice by any part or parts.

What do you think?

1. *Why does Imrie consider the appointment of the Rowell-Sirois Commission to constitute "New Hope for the West"?*
2. *What issues does Imrie see as being the root of Western problems?*
3. *What has been the result of these problems?*
4. *How does Imrie propose to correct the West's grievances?*

The Maritime Rights Movement

The Maritime region had enjoyed a period of great prosperity during the First World War as a result of the Canadian war effort. However, a postwar recession greatly altered the situation. The Conservative Party of Nova Scotia, having been defeated in the provincial election of 1920, attempted to rejuvenate itself politically by reviving the issue of Maritime Rights. The Conservatives were returned to power in 1925, and in 1926 the Federal Government appointed a Royal Commission to investigate Maritime claims. What seemed at first the victory of the movement was as much psychological as it was political. As later developments showed, the victory did little to actually solve Maritime problems.

INDEPENDENCE WOULD IMPROVE NOVA SCOTIA'S ECONOMY

The issue of Maritime Rights revived the arguments of regional patriots. These are outlined in an important speech by F. W. Corning, Conservative House Leader, delivered in the Nova Scotia Legislature on April 23, 1923.

Restore our province as an independent, self-governing British dominion, make us once more free and independent in the matter of trade and commerce, competent to protect ourselves sanely and wisely from the products of Ontario and Quebec as well as other lands, then there would undoubtedly be a great revival in business and local manufacturing in this province. Instead of decreasing, as at present, our population would increase. In a comparatively short time, in my opinion, we would have a million people in Nova Scotia. Farming would become remunerative. Manufacturing, commerce and foreign trade would quickly and actively develop. Enterprise would flourish. Distributing houses, banks and other institutions would quickly spring up.

What do you think?

1. *According to Corning, what positive effects would the re-establishment of self-government have on the Maritimes?*
2. *Given what you have already read about developments in Canada in general and the Maritimes in particular, how reasonable do you think Corning's predictions were?*

THE MARITIME RIGHTS PRINCIPLE

The movement generated pamphlets written in support of the general principle of Maritime Rights. The following are excerpts from F. B. McCurdy, Nova Scotia's Right to Live *(1924), and A. P. Paterson,* The True Story of Confederation, *(1926).*

WE CLAIM OUR PLACE

In order that it may succeed, Confederation must function in the spirit in which the Dominion of Canada was conceived—for the benefit of all Canadians and not for the principal advantage of Ontario and Quebec. Otherwise Nova Scotia's position at any rate becomes intolerable. Surely it is primarily the function and duty of our Provincial Government and our Provincial Representatives to ascertain and advocate the removal of the disabilities of the Province, instead of leaving our position and case to be investigated by the Dominion Government and the Railway managements as has been weakly suggested by one or more of our Provincial Ministers. . . .

. . . Please let me for a moment speak for the Maritime Provinces, and perhaps in a special sense for our own province of Nova Scotia. At first, let me say that we claim our place, and are proud to claim our place, as a member of the Dominion of Canada. And as a member of the Canadian Confederation, we are anxious always to promote the common welfare, asking only our fair share of the common weal. But the unfair and unsympathetic treatment of our case by the *Journal* and other newspapers chills and discourages. . . .

How, I ask, can Canada expect ever to be a nation unless she uses her own resources and facilities at hand to create a self-contained economic whole, instead of, for instance, utilizing and enriching American ports situated in a foreign land, and by burning huge quantities of American coal? . . .

. . .

Unless the central provinces of Canada are ready to join in the creation of an economic whole which will allow the residents of all parts to earn a livelihood in times of peace then those who are robbed of their opportunities by the self-interest of the bigger brothers will be driven to seek their own remedy. . . .

But in what measures has this system of Protection to industries alone helped us? It compels Canadians, east and west, to buy the manufactured goods of Ontario and Quebec, but it still permits them to use American ports of entry and export for their goods, if so be they can wring a further profit thereby—and we who live . . . by the sea must watch with what philosophy we can command the edifying sight of Canadian imports and exports being carried through a foreign country, which refuses to trade with us, in a one-sided manner whereby all profit accrues to them, while our own unequalled harbors are left empty and idle, our longshoremen go unemployed, and our transportation interests languish.

. . .

When Nova Scotia protested in 1868 against being coerced into a union that she claimed was oppressive and unnatural, she was asked to try out Confederation. For fifty-seven years it has been under trial. With what result?

The fathers of Confederation and those who have directed public policies since the birth of the Dominion have failed to devise a policy that would sustain even a reasonable growth in Nova Scotia.

. . .

What we need, if we would thrive, is the opportunity to live our own lives, to develop our own resources and to increase our own culture under fiscal arrangements that are suited to our needs, that will ensure us a square deal, so lacking in the cumulatively unfair Canadian fiscal history in the past fifty years.

PAYING TRIBUTE

. . . Since Confederation, the Maritimes have faithfully contributed their full quota toward every National undertaking,—railways, canals and even the Western immigration activities which have lured such tragic numbers of their own people from their own farms.

. . .

. . . there is a strong tendency toward secession in the Maritimes. As a matter of fact, an inflammable condition is rapidly developing in all three Maritime Provinces, which, lacking leadership, is not serious at present. Nevertheless, should anything happen to produce strong leaders for secession, it would be exceedingly difficult and perhaps impossible to prevent it. . . .

The people of the Maritimes feel that they are being deprived of their rights under Confederation. They know that, separated from Canada, and as a Maritime Dominion under its own Government, their position in the British Empire would be very important. They also know that, for her own protection, Canada would be obliged to maintain her rail connection to Maritime ports; and that from a commercial standpoint, if present conditions continue, commercial separation would be greatly to the advantage of the Maritimes. . . .

It may be that for their present economic decrepitude the Maritimes themselves have been somewhat to blame, for it is only of recent months that they united to tell their fellow-countrymen throughout Canada something of their impossible handicaps. Formerly, a conspicuous lack of such Maritime unity—induced by party politics and local squabbles over purely local differences—resulted in an absence of co-operation in their infinitely more vital National concerns; a circumstance, by the way, which played nicely into the hands of Central Canada. Now, however, there has been a complete and most welcome change: The Maritimes are united and are working in harmony for fair play and national unity. They are also conscious, for the first time, of a complete change in the attitude of their fellow-countrymen toward them. It is now a very sympathetic attitude which seems to promise better, brighter and more equitable things for the three Provinces by the sea.

The Maritimes believe that Confederation must be held together by sentiment; by the strong presence of a truly National Spirit, assured and supported by an equitable Federal agreement. They contend that if Canada is to become a nation imbued with a truly National Spirit and inspired by a truly National Soul, selfish sectionalism, so often displayed in the past, must absolutely cease.

It is true that the conditions under which Nova Scotia and New Brunswick were brought into Confederation were not calculated to develop the National Spirit. Yet it is quite certain that these Provinces have exhibited a true National Spirit and adhered closely to true National Ideals. Can this be said of Central Canada? . . .

What do you think?

1. *What complaints do the writers of these pamphlets have?*
2. *What results do these writers predict if Maritime claims are not acted upon? Why?*
3. *How justifiable are these claims in your opinion?*

THE CLAIMS OF NEW BRUNSWICK

The following is taken from the New Brunswick submission to the Commission: A Statement of its claims with Respect to Maritime Disabilities within Confederation *(1926).*

. . . The claims of the Province of New Brunswick to special consideration are based not so much upon a comparison of what the Province receives from the Dominion Government with the subsidies in various forms received by other Provinces, nor upon the additions of territory which have been given to other Provinces, as they are upon the basic principle that Confederation was undertaken in the belief that it would result in increased prosperity to all its members. It is evident that no province would have entered the Union under any contrary expectation.

. . . Because of the fiscal policy of the United States of America certain of our products are practically barred from that great and near market.

. . . But we believe that all might join in an attempt to secure for wood and wood products reciprocal entry free of duty into both countries. We believe that consumers in the United States would look with favor upon this proposal.

. . . The necessity of special rates westward to give Maritime Province manufacturers a fair opportunity in Western markets requires simply the application of a system which the Inter-state Commission appears to have found to work satisfactorily in the United States.

. . . The importance to the Province of the taking over of this railway National Trans-continental by the Dominion will be realized when it is understood that the drain caused by the annual deficit absolutely cripples the slender finances of the Province. . . .

. . . The people of the Maritime Provinces ask that their harbours be utilized as the outlets of Canada to the extent that was contemplated at the inception of Confederation. Today the harbour of Portland, Maine, is being used to a large extent as a terminus of the Canadian National Railway. We have yet to learn that the State of Maine has become a part of the Canadian Federation, or is entitled to share in the benefits caused by our union.

. . . There has been during the same time, and there is today, a large exodus from the Maritime Provinces, partly caused by the natural movement towards larger centres of opportunity, but largely because of the unfortunate conditions which have prevailed in the Maritime Provinces for some years. It is submitted that the Canadian Immigration Department should specially organize a service for the Maritimes, to be carried on wholly at the expense of the Dominion. Agricultural settlers of a good class should be sought and should be limited to British and Scandinavian people, and the repatriation of the Acadian French who have emigrated from New Brunswick.

. . . In addition to the other suggested forms of relief, the subsidy to the Province should be increased, so as to enable the Province to carry on its administration without increasing deficits or resorting to direct taxation. An examination of the expenditures of the Province will show that many of the items, such as education, are not receiving as much assistance as is necessary, while none are conducted in a manner even approaching generosity. It might be well to fix a limit of population, below which, and until it is reached, there should be a large increase in the per capita subsidy. Such rate of subsidy might decrease when the population attained a certain figure. If then the Province enters upon a period of greater development and returning prosperity which, it is confidently anticipated, would be the result of adoption by the Federal Government of the suggestions contained in this memorandum, there would in time be a partial discontinuance of the increased assistance.

What do you think?

1. *How effective do you think the measures proposed in the New Brunswick submission would be in overcoming the claims of unfair treatment prevalent in these documents? Why?*

THE DUNCAN REPORT

The Liberal Prime Minister, William Lyon Mackenzie King, appointed the Royal Commission on Maritime Claims (The Duncan Commission) to "... focus the discussion into a practicable program, to take stock of what has been done, what has been left undone, and of what still may be done." The Commission's Report was presented to the prime minister in the fall of 1926. In 1927, the Federal Government revised and increased the amount of financial aid to the region, and reduced freight rates.

. . . The outstanding fact, it seems to us, is that the Maritime Provinces have not prospered and developed, either in population, or in commercial, industrial and rural enterprise, as fully as other portions of Canada. We are unable to take the view that Confederation, is, of itself, responsible for this fact. The trend and nature of economic development generally throughout the last sixty years has made within the Maritimes changes in the structure of business and employment which are unrelated to Confederation, and which would have taken place whether or not the Maritime Provinces had been independent units outside of Confederation. Even within Confederation there has been such a measure of responsibility resting on each province for its own development that much at least of what has happened within the Maritime Provinces must be related to their responsibility and not to the responsibility of the Dominion.

We are far from saying that the Dominion, within its sphere of control, has done all for the Maritime Provinces which it should have done. But it must not be overlooked that the task which has been placed upon the Federal authorities in bringing such a vast territory as Canada to its present point of growth and prospect has been colossal. . . . It is not possible in such an undertaking as the making of Canada, with its geographical and physical conditions, and its variety of settlement and development, to maintain always an accurate balance, apportioning to every section of this extensive country the exact quality of benefit and quantity of advantage which would be theoretically and justly desired. But reasonable balance is within accomplishment if there be periodic stocktaking. We venture to regard the present occasion as such a period of stocktaking, so that in the future progress of the common great enterprise the prospects of the Maritime Provinces may be brought into line with the prospects of other parts of Canada and the prospects of the Dominion as a whole.

What do you think?

1. How does the point of view of this report differ from the attitudes of other Maritime spokesmen?

THE CLAIMS OF PRINCE EDWARD ISLAND

The Duncan Commission and the 1927 revision did not completely undermine Maritime agitation. "The Claims of Prince Edward Island 1927" helped to ensure that the debate continued.

Almost the total revenue of Prince Edward Island up to the time of Confederation was obtained from Customs Duties. This source of revenue was surrendered to the Federal Government, and the underlying and fundamental basis for this giving up of our revenue-producing capacity was that we should receive an equivalent. That was undoubtedly the principle of Confederation.

The question arises—Did we get it? Up to 1873 our population was increasing (having doubled in the 30 years previous), manufacturing industries were growing up, the Colony was in a most prosperous position. We had established our own trade routes and markets, chiefly with Great Britain and the United States. Suitable public buildings, roads, wharves, breakwaters, lighthouses and other public works had been constructed. A stock and experimental farm had been fully equipped, and generally the Colony was as prosperous and progressive as any community in British North America.

We had done all these things, had carried on our business and PAID OUR WAY out of the revenues collected. Apart from the Railways, the trifling debt carried by the Colony represented a part of the expenditure incurred by the transactions relative to buying out the lands from the proprietors, and will be dealt with later. Otherwise, we were not a cent in debt and still prospering. . . .

Since 1873 the subsidies received by us from Canada have been increased by 94%,—in the same time our local expenditure has been increased by 266%. . . .

Before Confederation our revenues were quite sufficient to meet expenditure without resorting to local taxation, and yet we were forced soon after Confederation to resort to local taxation, which, in a purely farming community means Provincial suicide if too heavily imposed.

Many citations can be submitted to show the existence of an understanding that in Confederation we would not need to resort to heavy local taxation. . . .

The process of centralization of wealth and industry which has been taking place ever since Confederation, robs P. E. Island. An ever-increasing proportion of the savings of our people is being invested in the capital stock of industrial and other concerns and carried out of our circulation to the Central Provinces, to incidentally increase their Provincial revenues. We receive very little from our succession duties, and still less from Company taxes, per capita, than any other Province.

Not only have we contributed largely of our money to the building up of the Western Provinces, but many of our most valuable assets—the young men of our Provinces—have gone in the same direction. As a result, in P.E.I. we have, in every 1,000 of our population, about 60 persons over 70 years of age, while Alberta has but eleven per thousand. . . .

Many of our public services are suffering for want of sufficient revenue. An instance is the matter of Public Health. Our Hospitals are insistently demanding increased aid,—we have not the money, and practically nothing can be done for any branch of Public Health.

Moreover, we are greatly handicapped by our roads. We have no gravel or permanent roads in P. E. Island, because we must bring all the gravel for such operations from the Mainland at an alarming cost. The demand for better roads is insistent, and, although reasonably good work has been accomplished with the material at hand, the results have not been satisfactory. One of our chief branches of farming is the raising of seed potatoes, a commodity that is shipped largely in the fall and spring when our roads are at their worst. The result is that, owing to such heavy traffic during these seasons, many of the roads leading to shipping centres become almost impassible, and our shippers are severely handicapped. . . .

What do you think?

1. What do you consider to be the main complaints of PEI? Are they justified? Why?

THE ECONOMIC PLIGHT OF NOVA SCOTIA

Norman McL. Rogers was a professor at Queen's University, Kingston, when in 1934 he prepared the following "Submission on Behalf of the Nova Scotia Government to the Royal Commission of Economic Inquiry."

It has been assumed generally that the lack of economic progress in Nova Scotia has been the result of the failure of enterprise in this province.

This is a superficial view of the true situation. It would at least be closer to the truth to say that the lack of enterprise is the accumulated result of a long period of gradual but persistent economic debilitation.

A condition of economic decline is almost certain to be reflected in the statistics of population. The comparative population figures for the provinces of Canada as revealed by the decennial census since 1871, indicate the failure of Nova Scotia to maintain a satisfactory growth and the more significant fact of an absolute loss of population in the decade 1921-1931. . . . Either through the greater allurements of urban life in the United States and in the central provinces, or through lack of diversified and remunerative employment in Nova Scotia, the most active element of its population has been drawn away from the province to contribute to the upbuilding of foreign countries and other sections of the Dominion. A movement of this character has a cumulative effect on the morale of a community. . . .

It is important to observe that tariff protection in Canada confers special benefits upon the central provinces of Ontario and Quebec. . . . It has to be acknowledged that in their geographical incidence subsidies given to industry in the form of tariff protection are distributed unequally among the various provinces of the Dominion. . . . The Canadian tariff system, despite its baptismal title of "The National Policy" has been developed without any clear relation to its effects upon the economy of the provinces as such. . . .

. . .

In addition to the injury suffered by Nova Scotia under the incidence of the protective tariff, there are handicaps arising from the interrelation of tariff policy and freight rates, which have aggravated the difficulties of the Maritime Provinces and of Nova Scotia in particular. It has been pointed out that the protective tariff, as applied to a country of great length and of narrow breadth, has encouraged an immoderate concentration of manufacturing in the central provinces of Ontario and Quebec. As a result the consumer in Nova Scotia is not only prevented from availing himself of the geographical advantage of the province in relation to purchase in foreign markets accessible by water, but is also placed under a relative disadvantage as against consumers in Ontario and Quebec because of the added freight rates on the purchases he is compelled to make in the home market by reason of the long rail haul from the factories of central Canada to the Atlantic seaboard. Consumers in Ontario and Quebec are either relieved of these charges, or they are of slight importance as an element in the cost of the goods purchased. . . .

It is urged that Nova Scotia is entitled to relief and compensation not merely in pursuance of the assurances given on the occasion of its entrance into the Canadian Federation, but also on the broad equitable ground that a federation defeats its primary purpose if through its constitutional arrangements or through policies instituted by the national government it accomplishes the gradual debilitation of one or more of the provincial communities of which it is composed. . . .

What do you think?

1. *Rogers seems to blame the "characteristics of an economic age" for many of the Maritime problems. How does that help to explain why the Maritime region today is one of the main beneficiaries of federal subsidies?*
2. *Would the Maritimes be better off without federal grants? Explain.*
3. *Do you see any parallels between the situation in the Maritimes and the situation in the Prairies? Explain.*

MARITIMES REQUEST COMMISSION TO EXAMINE FINANCIAL ARRANGEMENTS

A further Royal Commission (known as the White Commission) was appointed in September 1934 to investigate the financial arrangements between the Federal Government and the Maritime Provinces, after the prime minister received this letter from the three Maritime provincial premiers:

. . . The undersigned Premiers of the three Maritime Provinces respectfully request that a commission be now set up to take under consideration and deal with the recommendation of the Duncan Commission that there be a revision of the financial arrangements between the Dominion Government and the Maritime Provinces.

You will recall that this matter was discussed with you after the last Inter-Provincial Conference in January, 1933, by the then Premier of New Brunswick, Hon. Mr. Richards, the late Hon. F. C. Black, Acting Premier of Nova Scotia and Hon. Dr. MacMillan, of the Prince Edward Island Government, at which time it was understood that a commission would be set up. We are unanimously of the opinion that this commission should be set up forthwith.

Yours very truly,

L.P.D. Tilley, Premier of New Brunswick

Angus MacDonald, Premier of Nova Scotia

W.J.F. MacMillan, Premier of Prince Edward Island . . .

[The Commission defined the scope of its inquiry:]

The subject with which we are to deal is, we think, one calling for broad equitable consideration having regard to the exceptional geographical and, in a sense, isolated position of the Maritime Provinces in relation to the rest of the Dominion and the economic disabilities imposed upon them in consequence whereby they claim to have failed to share proportionately with the other Provinces the benefits and advantages of Confederation, and having regard also to the alleged more favourable treatment accorded by the Dominion to other members of the Union in respect of financial subsidies and territorial enlargement. . . . It is manifestly in the national interest that the feeling of discontent in this regard which has so long prevailed in greater or less degree and has become at times acutely intensified should be permanently allayed by such measures of amelioration as may be just and equitable to the end that so vital, essential and integral a part of Canada may be enabled to share equally with the other Provinces the benefits and advantages of Confederation. . . .

[The Commission's *Report* submitted in 1935 considered the general claims of the Maritimes, and recommended some changes:]

We are concerned only with the matter of revision of financial arrangements. The broad economic problems of the Maritimes like those of the other Provinces are for the Government and Parliament to consider and deal with. Increase of money grants to individual Provinces will not alone bring about prosperous conditions within their areas although it may indirectly assist by promoting, through educational and public welfare services, economic efficiency or by reducing taxation within the Province and thus lessening the burden upon trade and industry. . . .

As an assessment in detail of each of the claims presented before us is, for the reasons given, manifestly impracticable, we adopt the only course available to us, viz., to consider equitably the claims in the aggregate assigning to each its due weight according to our best judgment and making our recommendation in the form of special additional annual subsidies to the Maritime Provinces respectively as a final equitable settlement of the claims brought before us for adjudication. These additional annual subsidies so recommended are to be in substitution for the interim annual subsidies recommended by the Duncan Commission. They should commence in the fiscal year 1935-6 and the interim annual subsidies recommended by the Duncan Commission should cease at the end of the fiscal year 1934-5.

The additional annual subsidies which we recommended are as follows:—

To Nova Scotia $1,300,000
To New Brunswick . . . . $ 900,000
To Prince Edward Island . . . . $ 275,000

What do you think?

1. *Why was the White commission reluctant to reach wide-ranging conclusions about Maritime claims?*
2. *If you were the Canadian prime minister in the 1920s and 1930s how would you have responded to the arguments put forward by the Maritimers? Why?*

The Case for Centralization

As economic conditions worsened during the depression years, provincial governments found it difficult to cope with the problem alone. The Federal Government was urged to step in and assume certain responsibilities previously delegated to the provinces. As a result, the power to make decisions of national importance became increasingly centred in Ottawa.

Protest from many quarters convinced many Canadians of the need to have a centralized Federal Government to enact laws and make reforms. Why would people have reacted this way in the 1930s? How would a more centralized government have benefited Canada? How did the provinces react to having their powers decreased? What seeds of future protest may have been sown in this move towards centralization?

THE LEAGUE FOR
SOCIAL RECONSTRUCTION MANIFESTO

Perhaps not so surprisingly, in the 1930s in Canada the socialists were some of the strongest supporters of centralization. The following excerpt is from the league for Social Reconstruction's Manifesto, and is taken from a book entitled The Dirty Thirties *(ed. Michael Horn, ©1972, Copp Clark).*

The League for Social Reconstruction is an association of men and women who are working for the establishment in Canada of a social order in which the basic principles regulating production, distribution and service will be the common good rather than private profit.

. . .

Such measures as the following are among the essential first steps for the achievement of the new social order:

(1) The creation of a National Economic Planning Commission as the Principal organization for directing and co-ordinating the operation of the whole economy in the public interest.

(2) Socialization of the machinery of banking and investment to make possible effective control of credit and prices and the direction of new capital into socially desirable channels.

(3) Public ownership (Dominion, provincial or municipal) of transport, communications, electric power and such other industries as are approaching a condition of monopoly, and their operation, under the general direction of planning commission, by competent managements divorced from immediate political control.

(4) The development of co-operative institutions in every sphere of economic life where they are appropriate, notably in agricultural production and marketing and in the distribution of necessities to consumers.

(5) The establishment of import and export boards for the regulation of foreign trade.

(6) Social legislation to secure to the worker adequate income, leisure, freedom of association, insurance against illness, accident, old age and unemployment, and an effective voice in the management of his industry.

(7) Publicly organized health, hospital and medical services.

(8) An aggressive taxation designed not only to raise public revenues but also to lessen the glaring inequalities of income and to provide funds for the socialization of industry.

(9) The amendment of the Canadian constitution, without infringing upon legitimate provincial claims to autonomy, so as to give the Dominion Government adequate power to deal effectively with urgent economic problems which are essentially national.

(10) A foreign policy designed to obtain international economic co-operation and to promote disarmament and world peace.

What do you think?

1. Which articles of this manifesto are specifically related to centralization?
2. In which areas of responsibility did the L.S.R. feel the national government should be involved?
3. Why do you think the L.S.R. would have been likely to take such a centralist stand? Do some independent research to support your conclusions.

PROPOSALS ON UNEMPLOYMENT POLICY

H. M. Cassidy, a leading economist, made a number of concrete proposals to lessen the problems caused by unemployment. In the following extract he presents some of his suggestions for improving the unemployment situation and argues in favour of a strong central government to put these proposals into operation. (Source: H. M. Cassidy, "An Unemployment Policy—Some Proposals," in Canadian Problems as seen by Twenty Outstanding Men of Canada *(Toronto: Oxford University Press, 1933).)*

SOME CONCRETE PROPOSALS

It seems to me that in Canada we must work out a generous and humane system of relief, a scheme of unemployment insurance, and a programme of employment stabilization, all of them on national lines under the leadership and the direction of the Dominion Government.

The Dominion must take the lead because unemployment is beyond dispute a national problem which can be only dealt with effectively by national action. In the earlier part of the depression (and to some extent still) there was much talk from Ottawa about unemployment being a provincial or municipal responsibility, and the B.N.A. Act was cited in support of this position; while members of provincial governments have claimed (incorrectly) that the relief of the unemployed was legally the responsibility of the municipality. Such claims are absurd, in the face of the problems that beset us. Should members of a family quarrel about whose responsibility it is to put out the fire that is destroying their home? Whatever the B.N.A. Act says or does not say about unemployment (and, incidentally, it touches directly on the subject not at all, although it does cover it by indirection), the Federal Government must get on with the task of dealing effectively with the problem, or else Conservatives may see, before very long, a type of Dominion Government they will not like. If the B.N.A. Act requires revision, to make possible more effective action by the Dominion, let it be revised. A document drawn up in 1867 to fit the circumstances of the day need not be expected to be entirely adequate for 1933. It might be changed in a number of ways, I think, to increase Federal powers and to make possible the more effective government of the country, without impairing unduly the Federal nature of our constitution and without touching at all the minority guarantees that make up one of its leading characteristics.

RELIEF

To deal first with the relief system. The granting of public relief must be continued, and the system must be improved and co-ordinated under national and provincial direction. . . .

The municipalities, I think, should continue to administer relief—except that in rural districts county or district welfare units should be established to take over the work from numbers of small municipalities. The local authorities should be required to assume responsibility for the relief of distress in their communities, subject to general rules laid down by the Dominion and the provinces. . . . Their duties towards those in distress must be clearly defined by the Dominion and the provinces if reasonable uniformity is to be achieved.

But the municipalities cannot be expected to bear the whole burden of relief charges. They must continue to receive financial assistance from the two senior branches of government. It would be reasonable, I think, for the municipalities to assume a certain portion of the expense, say not to exceed half a mill or so on the local tax rate, while the provinces bear the greater part of the remaining burden and the Dominion also contributes. I should make it clear that I suggest this as a policy when unemployment is less severe than at present. For the present it is probably necessary that the Dominion should assume at least a third, or even more, of the total charges.

. . .

UNEMPLOYMENT INSURANCE

But we should not look to relief as the major method of providing maintenance for those who are involuntarily unemployed. Unemployment insurance should be adopted, as soon as possible, to perform this function.

The method of insurance is to make financial provision in advance for such predictable contingencies as death, accident, fire or bad weather. Unemployment insurance represents an attempt to apply this principle to the hazard of unemployment. It exacts contributions to a central fund from all the employed workers of a given group, or in their behalf, and it provides that those who lose their jobs shall receive benefits from this fund. Thus it spreads the essentially social burden of unemployment over the whole group of workers (and over industry and the state, in so far as these contribute to the scheme) rather than concentrating it upon those individuals who for one reason or another lose their jobs.

. . .

Unemployment insurance must certainly be national in scope. For any province that sets up a system which involves charges on industry (as any adequate system must) would handicap its industrialists to the advantage of those in other provinces. The Dominion, therefore, must pass legislation to make the system effective over the whole country. Under the B.N.A. Act as it stands this is impossible, except with the consent of the provinces. The best plan, I think, would be to confer the appropriate authority upon the Dominion by amendment of the constitution and for the Dominion to assume the burden of all state charges to the scheme as well as full responsibility for administration. If this were done, it would seem reasonable to have the provinces and the municipalities bear the main burden of relief expenses, as has been suggested above. But if amendment of the B.N.A. Act cannot be arranged easily, the Dominion can probably set up a national system by passing legislation to provide substantial subsidies to those provinces that will adopt model insurance acts. While I think that this method is preferable to no action at all, it is open to various administrative objections, and I much prefer the frank and honest method of amending the constitution to confer on the Dominion full authority to deal with what is beyond question a national issue.

. . .

THE STABILIZATION OF EMPLOYMENT

The third aspect of the programme that I propose is more fundamental than the other two, in that it definitely aims at prevention rather than the mere alleviation of distress. . . .

It is essential, . . . that there should be a co-ordinating, directing agency for the attack on unemployment. And this agency must be permanent. Unemployment is not a problem to be considered only when it occurs on a vast scale. . . . This is a task of the first magnitude, so important in the modern state that it demands the full attention of a group of the most able men to whom the work can be delegated. Such responsibility can only be assumed in Canada by the Dominion Government.

I would suggest, therefore, that the Government establish a Dominion Board of Employment Stabilization, to be assisted by an Advisory Council and an expert staff. . . . The Board would be a centre of information, and therefore the brain of a stabilization programme. It would collect statistical and other relevant information, it would study the problem of stabilization in all of its aspects, and it would advise government and private industry upon appropriate measures that should be carried out. While the Board would have no powers of compulsion, I think it is reasonable to suppose that it would come to have substantial influence over government and industry, particularly if it were permitted to issue reports to the public and thus to gain the support of public opinion. Compulsion would certainly be necessary to put into effect various of the measures that the Board might recommend, but this would be provided by the Dominion through legislation dealing with the measures in question.

. . .

But I do not wish to extend the list of suggestions further, nor to discuss in detail the possible usefulness of each one. It is the method rather than the specific measures to be undertaken that I want to emphasize. It seems to me that the plan I propose involves the harnessing of intelligence to the problem of employment stabilization. I am confident that a great deal of success in this direction could be achieved by the right kind of governmental control, and a great deal by co-operative measures on the part of private industry. But I don't think that much success will be achieved without a thinking, planning agency, such as I have described, at the centre of things.

What do you think?

1. *What concrete proposals does Cassidy make for dealing with the unemployment problem?*
2. *Why does he argue that a strong central government is necessary to deal with the situation?*
3. *What kind of centralized government does he describe? Be specific.*

FEDERALISM AND THE B.N.A. ACT

There was much concern in the 1930s over the limitations imposed on the Federal Government by the British North America Act. In the following passage, N.A.M. MacKenzie argues for a reassessment of the B.N.A. Act and the role of the central government in order to encourage more rapid solutions to national problems. (Source: N.A.M. MacKenzie, "The Federal Problem and the British North America Act," in Canadian Problems as seen by Twenty Outstanding Men of Canada *(Toronto: Oxford University Press, 1933))*

It is stated from time to time either that The British North America Act is perfectly satisfactory and should not be amended in any way or that it is obsolete and archaic, and that it does not permit either the Dominion or the provinces to deal satisfactorily with a great number of subjects, among them, insurance, the control of the sale of stocks and shares, social legislation, including unemployment insurance, the settlement of industrial disputes, and in the field of external affairs, the making of treaties. That there is a real limitation upon the powers of the Federal Parliament and Government in these and other fields is unquestionable but whether changes should be made or not is decidedly a matter of opinion. Here, however, it is desirable to look at the Act itself and see just what it does provide. As pointed out above, the intention of the Fathers of Confederation was that all matters of national importance should be in the control of the Central Government. In actual practice, however, due partly to the views of the Privy Council, in a whole line of decisions and partly to the growing strength of the provinces, many matters of national importance have been held to be within the exclusive competence of the provinces. . . .

. . .

. . . in all fairness to the Act itself and to those who framed it, most of those matters essential to the national welfare are included within the twenty-nine enumerated heads. Among them are "the regulation of trade and commerce" (though here again the Privy Council have intervened in defence of provincial rights and have relegated "trade and commerce" to the limbo of forgotten things), "the raising of money by any mode or system of taxation," "navigation and shipping," "the regulation of seacoast and inland fisheries" (but not the proprietary interest in the fish themselves), "currency and coinage," "banking," and all matters associated with finance; "copyrights," "naturalization and aliens," "marriage and divorce," (but not the forms of marriage,) "the criminal law," etc. It is only in regard to new developments brought about by a changing economic and social order that the defects in the B.N.A. Act become apparent, e.g., the whole field of social legislation, the control of radio and aviation, the development of hydroelectric power and again in the field of external affairs. . . .

Hydro-electric development might be declared to be a work or works for the general advantage of Canada and so brought under federal control but this would undoubtedly meet with strong opposition from the provinces. At the same time the whole question of the development and particularly the export of power is of the utmost importance to the whole of Canada, as it affects our relations with the United States and should be subject to federal regulation.

Much more could be said with regard to the whole question of subsidies, of natural resources, of provincial issues which become federal issues, e.g., the question of "Maritime rights" and "the western wheat pools," but I have already said enough to provide you with some basic facts at least, and some controversial suggestions, and I prefer to leave the rest for our discussion at the end of my remarks. . . .

The British North America Act has on the whole been an admirable solution of the problems of a federation of British colonies in North America, and if you are satisfied with things as they are, and feel that under the existing constitution you can work out a satisfactory solution of our common problems, then there is nothing more to be said on the subject. . . .

I must confess that I am not satisfied with the existing machinery for I consider it inadequate for our present purpose. Without surrendering any of the fundamental privileges that are so precious to the provinces, I believe it is possible and necessary to work out a method for more rapid common action in many fields of legislation and government. Provincial conferences are slow and unsatisfactory and should be superseded by other devices. The simplest of these, of course, is to give to the Dominion the temporary or permanent power to legislate in regard to any matter of national concern, save for a few excepted subjects, like education and language. If the Dominion Parliament proves too cumbersome a body for emergency action, it is quite possible for that body to delegate certain of its powers to the executive, as it has done in the past, and is doing to an increasing degree today.

This would require the amendment of the B.N.A. Act, but if that is desired by the people of Canada, it is a very simple matter to arrange for.

In addition, the Act should be amended so as to give the Dominion full powers in regard to the making of treaties and conventions and the enacting of the legislation necessary to carry out such treaties.

What do you think?

1. *According to MacKenzie, what circumstances made it necessary to consider amending the B.N.A. Act?*
2. *What specific issues would benefit from a more centralized form of government?*
3. *Why might some of MacKenzie's suggestions have been considered controversial in the 1930s?*

CENTRALIST POLICIES ENACTED

The Federal Government, pressed on all sides to act, began to introduce reform measures of national scope. As Edwin R. Black describes in the next section, this move toward legislating broad-scale changes signalled the consolidation of power in federal hands—centralization. (Source: Edwin P. Black, Divided Loyalties *(Montreal: McGill/Queen's University Press, 1975))*

The advent of the economic depression in the nineteen-thirties brought calls for government action. Primary responsibility for relief and welfare measures was constitutionally that of the provinces, but they were unable to cope with the problem financially. Demands arose that the federal government intervene regardless of the legal distribution of powers. Spokesmen for important segments of the population began to hearken back to the centralist designs of the state's founders. A Liberal-Conservative summer school was told in 1933 that the Fathers of Confederation had aimed at, and thought they had achieved, through the B.N.A. Act, "a form of government which, while preserving some of the visible emblems of autonomy in the provinces, would actually be a strong centralized government," with virtually unlimited powers to deal with crises. The same speaker Professor Norman A. Mackenzie, said:

> I believe it is possible and necessary to work out a method for more rapid common action in many fields of legislation and government. . . . The simplest device is to give the Dominion the temporary or permanent power to legislate in regard to any matter of national concern, save for a few excepted subjects, like education and language.
>
> . . .
>
> In addition, the Act should be amended so as to give the Dominion full powers in regard to the making of treaties and conventions and the enacting of the legislation necessary to carry out such treaties.

Mackenzie King, the opposition leader, spoke of the unarguable necessity of Ottawa's assuring the enjoyment of a national minimum standard of living. Toward this objective, his party proposed creation of a national commission to direct all relief work. It also promised, if elected, that the government would undertake rigorous supervision of provincial spending of federal relief funds. "As to permanent measures," said King, "the Liberal party is pledged to introduce policies which will serve to provide employment by reviving industry and trade, and to introduce a national system of unemployment insurance," and to set up a closely controlled central bank under federal ownership. . . .

The Conservative prime minister, R. B. Bennett, fought strongly against the centralists' stand. He asserted that centralization was constitutionally impossible and continued to channel relief measures through the provinces. Then, as the 1935 election neared, Mr. Bennett announced what was for many observers an astonishing *volte-face* on his part: that the time had come for "a radical change in the policy of the Administration." A measure of government control of the economy was needed, he said, and outlined a legislative program on which his opponent, Mackenzie King, congratulated him—not, however, without disputing its constitutionality. Mr. Bennett's legislation was enacted promptly. It included a Trade and Industry Act, the Employment and Social Insurance Act, the Minimum Wage Act, the 48 Hour Week Act, the One Day's Rest in Seven Act, and the Natural Products Marketing Act. The prime minister felt that this legislation had sound legal footing. . . .

These measures sought to consolidate in federal hands certain powers which traditionally had been judicially assigned to provincial areas of authority.

. . .

Presentations made to the Royal Commission on Dominion-Provincial Relations evidenced the widespread support for a centralist view of confederation. In the prairie provinces, both official government briefs and private representations expressed the view that the duties and taxing powers of the federal authority should be greatly expanded. Westerners said that only Parliament could effectively deal with the legislative problems of relief, social insurance, and regulation of wages and hours. The gist of the submission from the centralist-minded provinces was that confederation was designed to give the federal government, along with the most important revenue sources, all the important and expensive duties, and that those tasks which had been insignificant in 1867 but were now large national problems should be transferred to the central legislature.

Except for those from Quebec, the private citizens who testified before the commission were centralist almost unanimously, and particularly was this view held by the businessmen who thought centralized government could cut costs and reduce taxes. The Vancouver Board of Trade urged that a plebiscite be held in each province on the question of abolishing the legislature in favour of an Ottawa-appointed and controlled commission. The Canadian Legion demanded that the federal government be given jurisdiction in all matters of national importance "even though to do so it is necessary to encroach upon property and civil rights, or other powers delegated to the provinces." The Native Sons of Canada suggested that the purpose of Confederation was to "establish a national unit" and to "obliterate the provincial boundaries and fuse the colonial units" then existing.

What do you think?

1. *Why did most Canadians support the move to centralized government?*
2. *What arguments can you propose against such a move?*
3. *Why would increased federal authority pose a constitutional problem?*

4. What similarities or differences are there between the views held by many Canadians today regarding the constitution and those held in the 1930s?

ROWELL-SIROIS COMMISSION

The Royal Commission on Dominion-Provincial Relations, commonly known as the Rowell-Sirois Commission, was appointed in 1937 to examine "the economic and financial basis of Confederation and the distribution of legislative powers in the light of economic and social developments". The commission published its report in 1940, and made the following recommendations about transferring more taxing power to the Federal Government. (Source: Report of the Royal Commission on Dominion-Provincial Relations, Book II: Recommendations. *(Ottawa: King's Printer, 1940))*

. . . we shall have to recommend that certain functions now under the jurisdiction of the provinces should be allocated to the Dominion on grounds of the need for uniformity throughout Canada, or of the economy incidental to unified administration, or of the unequal financial ability of provinces to perform them. But in so doing we carefully respect the federal system. We aim throughout to safeguard the autonomy of the provinces, and to ensure to each province the ability to decide issues of peculiar importance to itself. We emphasized throughout this whole section the importance of limiting the transfer of jurisdiction to the Dominion to what is strictly necessary. . . .

1. PERSONAL INCOME TAXES

The personal income tax is the most highly developed modern instrument of taxation. It can be more delicately adjusted to individual circumstances, and thus made fairer in its incidence, than any other tax. It adjusts itself automatically to economic fluctuations. It can raise a given revenue with less burden on the national economy than any other tax because it is drawn from surplus income rather than made a burden on costs. . . . And it has become an integral part of modern economic, political and social policy. It is the most effective method yet devised, within the framework of the capitalist economy, for achieving the social and humanitarian objectives of our civilization; for applying wealth which is made possible only by organized society for the benefit of society as a whole; for preserving the freedom of individual initiative and at the same time making possible the financing of those services which can be most economically provided by the community as a whole. . . .

The unsuitability of provincial (and municipal) jurisdiction in the income tax field is only partly due to the obstacles which it creates to the development of a business-like and efficient tax structure for the country as a whole. The income tax, because of the nature of the Canadian economy, is productive only in some units. Those provinces in which a provincial income tax is, or would be, relatively unproductive feel aggrieved because they think that income earned within their jurisdiction is, through the operation of national policies, concentrated in more fortunate provinces where it may be taxed for provincial purposes. . . .

The Commission thinks it desirable that the income tax should be used in accordance with modern practice, as the equalizer and chief instrument of adjustment in the whole tax system. . . . The rate and the appropriate curve of progressivity necessary to reform and control the tax structure can only be achieved if this equalizing instrument of taxation is under one authority. That authority can only be the Dominion. . . .

The Commission accordingly recommends the provinces and *ipso facto* their municipalities should withdraw entirely from the personal income tax field. . . .

2. CORPORATION TAXES

The primary criticism of the present system [of corporate taxation] is that business has been made an object of taxation in itself. It is one thing to use the corporate organization as an agent to collect taxes cheaply and simply from final recipients of wages, interest and dividends, but in Canada business itself is taxed. Some $20 million of total Dominion and provincial corporation taxes comes from specific taxes which bear no relation to net profits, and have naturally become fixed charges, embodied in the overhead. As such they increase the costs of production of all Canadian business, impair its competitive power, and crush out marginal enterprises. . . .

The second major criticism of the present system is the inevitable inequity, lack of uniformity, and lack of efficiency arising from the divided jurisdiction. Corporate business has naturally adapted itself to the national policies and local concentrations of power and income which we have noted as so characteristic of the Canadian economy. Several provinces have consequently been led to devise elaborate formulae, differing in almost every province and in relation to every business, which can be applied to whatever assets fall within their jurisdictions, or which, in more extreme cases, will extract as much as the corporation can pay before it is clearly advantageous for it to sacrifice its investment and withdraw completely from the province. But in many cases once the initial investment has been made the corporation cannot withdraw. . . .

The Commission accordingly recommends the complete withdrawal of provinces from the corporation tax field as defined below. . . .

It has been the aim of the Commission to frame proposals which will, if implemented, place jurisdiction over the social services in the hands of the governments most likely to design and administer them, not merely with the greatest economy and the greatest technical efficiency, but with the regard for the social, cultural and religious outlook of the various regions of Canada, which is essential to genuine human welfare. The financial proposals have been designed to enable every province of Canada to rely on having sufficient revenue at its command in war-time as in peace-time, in years of adversity as in years of prosperity, to carry out the important functions entrusted to it.

. . . The Commission does not consider that its proposals are either centralizing or decentralizing in their combined effect but believes that they will conduce to the sane balance between these two tendencies which is the essence of a genuine federal system and, therefore, the basis on which Canadian national unity can most securely rest.

What do you think?

1. Why did the Commission recommend that the provinces withdraw from the fields of personal income tax and corporate tax?
2. How might the provinces have reacted to such a proposal decreasing their sources of income?
3. In what ways did these recommendations indicate a definite trend towards centralization in government?

TOWARDS A BETTER INTEGRATED STATE

Alexander Brady, writing in the Canadian Historical Review, *offered a well-reasoned analysis of the probable effects of the Rowell-Sirois Commission's Report on increasing centralization in Ottawa. (Source: Alexander Brady, "Report of the Royal Commission on Dominion-Provincial Relations," Canadian Historical Review, XXI (September, 1940))*

Opinions presented before the Commission differed widely as to the exact point at which to strike the new balance. In its principal recommendations in Plan I the Commission unmistakably suggests an extensive shifting of power to the federal authority. Such notably is the case in the recommendation that income taxes, corporation taxes, and succession duties should exclusively be levied by the Dominion; that the Dominion should assume the entire debt of all the provinces, provided that an annual payment be made by the provinces to the Dominion of revenue from self-supporting debt. It is worth recalling here the truism that the power to tax is the basis of most other political power. The financial centralization implied in these recommendations would directly and indirectly enhance federal authority, focus the eyes of the electorate upon Ottawa and divert their gaze from the provincial capitals, preparing the way for a future and further transfer of specific legislative powers. On the other hand, the recommendations in regard to social services reveal a jealous concern for provincial autonomy. The Commissioners are clearly anxious to be considered champions of the provinces. The relief of employables should be transferred to the Dominion, and in the case of some other services, such as minimum wages and maximum hours, federal administration may be desirable. But these measures are all to be reviewed as exceptions. "It is fundamental to our recommendations that the residual responsibility for social welfare functions should remain with the provinces, and that Dominion functions should be deemed exceptions to the general rule of provincial responsibility." Here obviously is a desire to strike the balance at a point suggested by administrative efficiency and by the necessity of making the provincial administrations responsible for the welfare of their own citizens, while at the same time the wealthy provinces are expected to share their wealth (through federal taxation) with the less fortunate.

One may wonder whether a balance which candidly rests on the premise of provincial egality will not prove to be too delicate and difficult to maintain, owing to the clash of centrifugal and centripetal forces. Indeed, even the establishment at present of the type of balance recommended will be difficult enough, apart from its maintenance in the future. In 1930, for example, Ontario and Quebec with 60 per cent of the total population in the Dominion collected 87 per cent of the total succession duties. Naturally these provinces will be reluctant to see such duties become exclusively a federal form of taxation. Their spirit of generous sharing is likely to be weak. Of course with other provinces they receive compensations, but their surrender of jurisdiction will be made only under the future pressure of more than ordinary circumstances, for the chief provincial administrations are still jealous centres of power. If centrifugal influences thus hamper the achievement of the new federal balance, centripetal forces when once it is attained may soon upset it. The division of jurisdiction in social services suggested by the Commission seems in logic impressive enough, but in operation the public is likely to look to the federal authority for increased social services because of its decisive control over finance. There seems little point in talking about "social welfare functions remaining with the provinces" if in the final analysis the chief taxes to pay for an expansion in these functions are collected by the Dominion. Ottawa becomes the real distributor of benefactions, and the public will not be ignorant of the fact.

However precarious may prove to be the balance suggested by the Commission and however difficult to operate, it is to be welcomed on the whole as a step towards a better integrated state. It would make possible for Canada the formulation of a far more co-ordinated national economic policy. In the future its inevitable influence would tend toward greater integration. In the nature of things it cannot be a permanent goal, for in twenty-five years some of its arrangements are likely to be obsolete. The true end of Canadian development must be national unity with such centralization in legislative power and decentralization in administrative discretion as the necessities of statehood at the time dictate.

What do you think?

1. According to Brady, what would be the general effect of the Rowell-Sirois Commission's recommendations, if acted upon?
2. What new areas of jurisdiction would the Federal Government assume? What areas would remain under provincial control?
3. Why did Brady consider the balance suggested by the Commission to be "delicate" and "difficult to operate"?
4. Brady stated, "In the nature of things it [the balance suggested by the Commission] cannot be a permanent goal, for in twenty-five years some of its arrangements are likely to be obsolete." Almost forty years have passed since Brady made this statement. In the light of recent events, do you think Brady's suspicion has been realized? Do some independent research to support your thesis.

What do you think?

1. Do you think the move towards centralizing more power in the Federal Government was beneficial to Canada? Why or why not?
2. Was the trend towards centralization a response to regional needs or was it a response to a national crisis that displaced regional concerns? Explain your answer.
3. Do you think a strong central government can still be sensitive to a region's needs and problems? Why or why not?
4. What measures, if any, can a strong central government adopt to ensure that all regions of a country are fairly represented in policy-making?

THE 1880s

In 1879 the Conservative government of John A. Macdonald introduced the National Policy. Among its proposals the program included a system of protective tariffs for Canadian products, the construction of a transcontinental railway and a western land and settlement plan.

These policies became a major cause of regional protest in the 1880s when the prosperity they had forecast did not materialize. Although a world-wide depression largely contributed to the National Policy's failure to ensure national standards of wealth, several regional movements placed the blame on the shoulders of the Federal Government. What resulted from this controversy was a redefinition of the provinces' role in Confederation—a redefinition that greatly affected the formation of particular regional identities and the expression of local grievances.

This next section addresses itself to the major issues that faced Canada in the 1880s. Why was there so much regional discontent in that decade? What forms did it assume? What is the connection between economic depression and regional protest, if any?

PROVINCIAL RIGHTS MOVEMENT

As early as 1868 Macdonald predicted the conflict between federal and regional forces, as well as the fate awaiting any provincial rights movement that might challenge the federal power. The following is excerpted from a letter Macdonald wrote to a friend on October 26, 1868.

. . . I fully concur with you as to the apprehension that a conflict may, ere long, arise between the Dominion and the "State Rights" people. We must meet it however as best we may. By a firm yet patient course, I think the Dominion must win in the long run. The powers of the General Government are so much greater than those of the [Federal Government of the] United States, in its relations with the local governments, that the central power must win. . . .

My own opinion is that the General Government or Parliament should pay no more regard to the status or position of the Local governments than they would to the prospects of the ruling party in the corporation of Quebec or Montreal. . . .

What do you think?

1. *How did Macdonald propose to deal with the "states' rights" people?*
2. *What effect do you think his opinion as expressed here might have had on states' rights people?*
3. *Would Macdonald's prediction be accurate today? Explain your answer.*

THE NATIONAL POLICY OF 1879 AND FEDERAL POWER

As leader of the opposition in 1878, John A. Macdonald presented his proposed National Policy to the House of Commons. It became the major plank in the Conservative Party platform during the general election that same year. The Conservatives won the election on the promise that they would put this policy into action.

. . . but that this House is of the opinion that the welfare of Canada requires the adoption of a National Policy, which, by a judicious readjustment of the Tariff, will benefit and foster the agricultural, the mining, the manufacturing and other interests of the Dominion; that such a policy will retain in Canada thousands of our fellow countrymen now obliged to expatriate themselves in search of employment denied them at home, will restore prosperity to our struggling industries, now so sadly depressed, will prevent Canada from being made a sacrifice market, will encourge and develop an active interprovincial trade, and moving (as it ought to do) in the direction of a reciprocity of Tariffs with our neighbours, so far as the varied interests of Canada may demand, will greatly tend to procure for this country, eventually, a reciprocity of trade. . . .

. . . The resolution speaks not only of a reasonable readjustment of the tariff but of the encouragement and development of inter-provincial trade. That is one of the great objects we should seek to attain. Formerly, we were a number of Provinces which had very little trade with each other, and very little connection, except a common allegiance to a common Sovereign, and it is of the greatest importance that we should be allied together. I believe that, by a fair readjustment of the tariff, we can increase the various industries which we can interchange one with another, and make this union a union in interest, a union in trade, and a union in feeling. We shall then grow up rapidly a good steady and mature trade between the Provinces, rendering us independent of foreign trade, and not, as New Brunswick and Nova Scotia formerly did, look to the United States or to England for trade, but look to Ontario and Quebec,—sending their products west, and receiving the products of Quebec and Ontario in exchange. Thus the great policy, the National Policy, which we on this side are advocating, would be attained.

What do you think?

1. *According to Macdonald, what was the purpose of the National Policy?*
2. *a) What proposals were contained in the National Policy?*

b) *How might these proposals have affected Canada? regional discontent?*
3. *To what degree was Macdonald's policy equating national interest with the interests of Central Canada? Explain.*

Manitoba

MANITOBA BILL OF RIGHTS

Macdonald's National Policy conflicted with the local aspirations of Manitoba's government and business community, in particular on the issues of land claims and railways. As a response to this disagreement, the following resolution—a "Bill of Rights"—was passed unanimously by the Manitoba Legislature on April 2, 1884.

Resolved, that this House, having had under consideration the despatch of the Secretary of State for the Dominion of Canada to His Honour the Lieutenant-Governor of the Province of Manitoba, of the date of 2nd April, instant, regrets that the Federal Government have not seen their way clear to acknowledge the right of this Province to the control of her lands, and to place her in the same status as the originally confederated provinces. In addition to her first claims, it is absolutely necessary for the requirements of this Province, that a re-adjustment of her capital account and financial status should at once be made. And that a delegation of this House, composed of the Hon. Mr. Speaker and such members of this House, as are members of the Executive Council, that this House may appoint, to at once proceed to Ottawa to meet the committee, as suggested in the said despatch of the second of April, to procure from the Government of Canada a settlement of the rights of this Province, as claimed by its Legislature.

(The instructions, popularly referred to as a "Bill of Rights", were:)
1. To urge the right of the Province to the control, management and sale of the public lands within its limits, for the public uses thereof, and of the mines, minerals, wood and timber thereon, or an equivalent therefor, and to receive from the Dominion Government payment for the lands already disposed of by them within the Province, less the cost of survey and measurement.
2. The management of the lands set apart for education in this Province, with a view to capitalize the sum realized from sales, and apply the interest accruing therefrom to supplement the annual grant of the Legislature in aid of education.
3. The adjustment of the capital account of the Province, decennially according to population—the same to be computed now at 150,000 souls,

and to be allowed until it corresponds to the amount allowed the Province of Ontario on that Account.

4. The right of the Province to charter lines of railway from any one point to another within the Province, except so far as the same has been limited by its Legislature in the Extension Act of 1881.

5. That the grant of 80 cents a head be not limited to a population of 400,000 souls, but that the same be allowed the Province until the maximum on which the said grant is allowed to the Province of Ontario be reached.

6. The granting to the Province extended railway facilities—notably the energetic prosecution of the Manitoba Southwestern, the Souris and Rocky Mountain, and the Manitoba and North-Western railways.

7. To call attention of the Government to the prejudicial effect of the tariff on the Province of Manitoba.

8. Extension of boundaries.

What do you think?

1. Why did Manitoba want control of land and the right to a railway policy?

2. In what ways were these demands related to regional sentiment?

3. Compare these demands with the current demands of the Prairie Provinces.

THE RIEL REBELLION OF 1885—DEMANDS

The unsettled problem of Métis land claims, the Canadian Pacific Railway monopoly, the treatment of Indians on reserves and the grievances of whites toward settlement policy all contributed to the rebellion in the spring of 1885, the second such insurrection led by Louis Riel. The actual rebellion was short-lived, and Riel was tried and hanged for treason on November 16, 1885.

The following petition was drafted by Métis and white settlers under Riel's direction and forwarded to the Dominion government in Ottawa in late 1884.

To His Excellency the Governor General of Canada, in Council.

We, the undersigned, your humble petitioners, would respectfully submit to Your Excellency-in-Council, the following as our grievances:

1. that the Indians are so reduced that the settlers in many localities are compelled to furnish them with food, partly to prevent them from dying at their doors, partly to preserve the peace of the territory;

2. that the Half-breeds of the territory have not received 240 acres of land each as did the Manitoba Half-breeds;
3. that the Half-breeds who are in possession of tracts of land have not received patents therefor;
4. that the old settlers of the N.W.T. [North-West Territories] have not received the same treatment as the old settlers of Manitoba;
5. that the claims of settlers on odd numbers, prior to survey and on reserves, prior to the proclamation of such reserves, are not recognized;
8. that settlers are charged dues on lumber, rails and firewood required for home use;
9. that customs duties are levied on the necessaries of life;
14. that no effective measures have yet been taken to put the people of the North-West in direct communication with the European markets, via Hudson's Bay;
15. that settlers are exposed to coercion at elections, owing to the fact that votes are not taken by ballot;
17. . . . (h) that the N.W.T., although having a population of 60,000, are not yet granted responsible government, as was Manitoba when she had less than 12,000 of a population; (i) that the N.W.T. and its Premier Province [Manitoba] are not yet represented in the Cabinet, as are the Eastern Provinces; (j) that the North-West is not allowed the administration of its resources as are the eastern provinces and British Columbia. . . .

In conclusion, your petitioners would respectfully state that they are treated neither according to their privileges as British subjects nor according to the rights of people and the consequently as long as they are retained in those circumstances, they can be neither prosperous nor happy.

Your humble petitioners are of opinion that the shortest and most effectual methods of remedying these grievances would be to grant the N.W.T. responsible government with control of its own resources and just representation in the Federal Parliament and Cabinet.

Wherefor your petitioners humbly pray that Your Excellency in Council would be pleased to cause the introduction, at the coming session of Parliament, of a measure providing for the complete organization of the District of Saskatchewan as a province, and that they be allowed as in '70, to send delegates to Ottawa with their Bill of Rights; whereby an understanding may be arrived at as to their entry into Confederation, with the constitution of a free province. . . .

What do you think?

1. *What similarities exist between this petition and present attitudes in the Northwest Territories?*

2. Are the Northwest Territories today better prepared for provincial status than the North West of 1885 was? Why or why not?
3. To what extent was the Rebellion of 1885 the result of regional grievances?

Ontario and Provincial Rights

Other regions of Canada have often suspected that their own claims and concerns are secondary to the interest of Ontario. In fact, regional protests have frequently been directed against this central province as much as against the Federal Government in Ottawa. It is sometimes forgotten that Ontario has also questioned its own role within Confederation and disagreed with the Federal Government over the degree of power it has a right to exercise. In the 1880s Ontario actually led the provinces in defining the distribution of federal and provincial powers under sections 91 and 92 of the British North America Act. The decisions of the Judicial Committee of the British Privy Council, at that time the final judge in the interpretation of the B.N.A. Act, confirmed the provinces' claims. As a result, the power of the federal authority was somewhat restricted.

Some of the issues concerning Ontarians in the 1880s are presented in the next section. How did Ontario perceive itself in the 1880s? What effect did this perception have on regional agitation? How accurate was it to equate the interests of Ontario with national interests at that time? How accurate is such an assessment today?

CONFEDERATION SUITS ONTARIO

The following speech was made by Alexander Mackenzie, the first Canadian Liberal Prime Minister, in the Ontario legislature. It was reported in the Toronto Globe on February 8, 1872.

. . . He was bound to say that he advocated Confederation not merely as a great political measure essential to the continuation and perpetuation of British political power on this continent, which was his principal object, but as the system of government most suitable to our condition, and under which we would be able to obtain certain great advantages in the administration of our own affairs. It was the constant complaint prior to 1867 that we were subjected as a people to unfair influences. We were placed in the position of contributing from two-thirds to three-fourths of the revenue of the country, while we were always unable to obtain for local purposes, such as we tax ourselves for under the present system, one-half of the actual revenue of the united provinces. In this respect he believed the change effected by the confederation of the provinces was extremely beneficial to us as a province; and he hoped to the Province of Quebec also, by stimulating its people to greater exertions in regard to local affairs, instead of depending upon the general resources.

What do you think?

1. *According to Mackenzie, why did Ontario enter Confederation? Do you think this type of speech, if read or heard by someone outside Central Canada, would support the standard interpretation about the intentions of Ontario? Why or why not?*

MOWAT AND THE MANITOBA BOUNDARY DISPUTE

The Liberal administration in Ontario under the leadership of Oliver Mowat was frequently at odds with the Federal Government in the 1880s. The following excerpt is from the Toronto Globe reports of Mowat's speeches in the legislature regarding the annexation of what is now Northwestern Ontario (the Manitoba Boundary Dispute).

Why is it that our rights in that territory are so persistently withheld from us? I would like to know some reason, some real reason . . . What is the meaning of the Dominion Government? Is it to make Ontario the smallest of the great Provinces? . . . Does not the Dominion owe the greater part of its prestige to Ontario? (applause) Is not Ontario the great taxpayer—the Province that puts more money into the Treasury than she takes out of it? (applause) Why the difficulty, the obstacle that stands in the way? . . . I cannot account for it except that there is a little hostility somewhere against this Province as a Province . . . There is hostility somewhere, and those who ought to stand up for Ontario are not doing so . . . Well, it is for the people of Ontario to say whether they will yield or not . . . If they have been asleep, I venture to say that they are aroused now—(applause)—and that they will be asleep no more, and that they will not rest until every mile of awarded territory is surrendered to us—(renewed cheering)—and our constitutional freedom and our Provincial rights are both respected and secured for ever. (loud and long-continued cheering.) (January 28, 1882)

What do you think?

1. *Why was Mowat so opposed to the Federal Government?*
2. *What effect would Mowat's point of view have on regional sentiment in the 1880s? How has it affected present-day views of Ontario?*

THE *GLOBE* COMMENTS

The Toronto Globe *was an avid supporter of the Liberal Party and of Mowat's campaign against federal power. The following are sections from its editorial comments.*

On 20th June next the electors of Ontario will be called upon to decide these questions:—

Shall Ontario remain the Keystone Province of Confederation?

Shall Ontario, at the dictation of a handful of French Blues, be degraded to the position of a fifth-rate Province?

Shall Ontario be reduced in size till she is less than one-half of the area of Quebec, less than two-thirds of the area of Manitoba, less than one-fourth of the size of British Columbia, and less than one-half of the size of fifteen or sixteen new Provinces hereafter to be created?

Shall Ontario be deprived of the railway terminus on Lake Superior, with the city which is certain there to spring up?

Shall Ontario be robbed of 60,000,000 acres of fertile land?

Shall Ontario lose the revenue of $125,000,000, the sum which the pine alone, to say nothing of other valuable timber, on the disputed territory is computed to be worth?

Shall Ontario be defrauded of a mineral region the wealth of which may exceed anything else in the known world?

Shall Ontario be driven to adopt direct taxation for Provincial purposes?

In a word, will Ontario suffer herself to be dismembered and despoiled in order that the Bourbons at Ottawa may be sustained in power by French votes?

The future of this Province lies trembling in the balance. And the Confederation will scarce withstand the shock of a corruptly-gained verdict endorsing the vile robbery proposed to be committed. (May 20th, 1882)

The greatest political gathering ever held in Canada is now in itself a thing of the past, but owing to the peculiar circumstances under which it was held bids fair to have the most far-reaching and enduring effects. For some time past there has been a general and growing feeling of alarm at the attitude of the Dominion Government towards Provincial rights under the British North America Act. If those rights cannot be maintained intact, then Confederation must be pronounced a failure, and with this alternative before them the members of the Convention speaking for the vast majority of the people of Ontario, while proclaiming their earnest desire to maintain the federal union of the Provinces, announced their stern determination to see that the sphere of local self-government is not in any way curtailed. The event proves that Mr. Mowat did not miscalculate the real feeling of the people in this matter, and he has now been assured that what they want is a continuation of the policy of resistance to Federal encroachment. (January 5, 1883)

Men of Ontario! Up and be doing! This nation cannot stand if the central authority at Ottawa is to dominate our local affairs. An end must be put to organized aggression of the Dominion Government upon Provincial rights. Only upon condition that Provincial rights are respected is there any hope of building up a Canadian nationality. Let those rights be further encroached upon, let some other Province than long-suffering Ontario be pinched, and the work of the statesmen of the last generation will be scattered to the winds. . . . (February 5, 1883)

Tomorrow the people of Ontario will decide whether for the next Parliamentary term their affairs will be managed by those who have administered them so well for the last twelve years, or will be committed to new, inexperienced, and untrustworthy hands. They will decide whether a determined stand is to be made for the maintenance of Provincial rights, or these rights are to be disgracefully abandoned at the dictation of the majority in another Province. They will decide whether territory awarded to Ontario by a competent board of arbitrators, after a full investigation, is to be taken away from her for no other reason than that Quebec does want her to have it. They will decide whether our present excellent license law is to be maintained, or the dictation of the Dominion Government is to be submitted to in a matter which has ever since Confederation been dealt with by the Provincial legislature. (February 26, 1883)

What do you think?

1. *What grievances are expressed in these editorials?*
2. *What perceptions of Ontario do these editorials reveal? what perceptions of the Dominion government?*
3. *Do you see any similarities between the attitudes presented here and present-day attitudes in Ontario? Justify your answer.*

The Maritime Provinces

BUSINESSMEN REACT TO NATIONAL POLICY

The Federal Government investigated the state of the Canadian economy in 1885 and issued a report on its findings a year later. Entitled Reports Relative to Manufacturing Interests in Existence in Canada, *it included the following comments about the operation of the National Policy by various businessmen in the Maritimes.*

NEW BRUNSWICK BUSINESSMAN REACTS ... S. R. Foster & Son of the nail and tack works [St. John]; ... "The National Policy has, in my opinion, proved the salvation of the infant industries. During the American war the demand for various manufactured products stimulated existing factories and encouraged the starting of new ones, and for ten years prosperity reigned in these lines in the Lower Provinces. I say ten years advisedly, for although the war continued only four years, war prices prevailed during the balance of the decade. Then came a period of languishing; and the advent of the National Policy lifted the drooping spirits of the industrial classes and gave new courage to the men who controlled them. Had it not been for the National Policy our own business, which was suffering, would have been 'snuffed out' along with many industries. Ever since the advent of the National Policy we have gradually been gaining." ...

NOVA SCOTIA BUSINESSMEN REACT ... R. Taylor, of the Halifax Boot and Shoe Factory; ... "Business is dull. Confederation is one cause of this dullness, and the National Policy is another. The duties on certain articles used in manufacturing boots and shoes, such as serge, elastic, and findings in general, is objectionable. These articles are not made in the Dominion, nor even in the United States, except, perhaps, in the case of a few articles. There is not sufficient encouragement to warrant any one engaging in their manufacture. We get our supplies from England. Serge was duty free before the National Policy came into force." ...

A. Robb & Sons' Amherst stove and machine works; ... One of the members of the firm, the manager of the works, says:—"Our field lies in the Maritime Provinces, and also to some extent in Quebec and Newfoundland. Since 1878 we have nearly doubled the extent of our business. The National Policy has helped us directly, by keeping American stoves out of our local markets, and indirectly, by keeping American stoves out of Upper Canada. The effect of this latter upon the Upper Province manufacturers is to keep them more to their home markets. The opening of the North-West has also been a help in this way, as it has attracted the energies of the Upper Canadians more to that territory and kept them so fully employed as to leave little chance for the accumulation of surplus stock for use in competition with Lower Province work. In the meantime, we are developing our energies down here and growing stronger. . . .

PRINCE EDWARD ISLAND BUSINESSMEN REACT Hickey & Stewart's tobacco factory; ... "The National Policy helps our business to the extent that it keeps out American manufacturers. Of course that is an advantage. Confederation has, however, given us the Western Provinces as competitors, and, as a result, the rivalry is keen, though we manage to maintain our hold on the Island and other Maritime Provinces."

Dorsey, Goff & Co., boot and shoe manufacturers; . . . "The Island is not affected so much by the troubles of the outside world as some other Provinces or districts; yet, to some extent, the hard times do bear upon the prices of certain products. We find a market altogether in the Island for the work of our factory, and we manage to compete successfully with the Upper and neighboring Provinces.

"The National Policy keeps out American manufacturers, and prevents our American cousins from making the Island a slaughter market for their surplus stock." . . .

What do you think?

1. *According to these businessmen, was the National Policy a benefit or a hindrance to the economic development of the Maritime region? Why?*
2. *Do you think these businessmen would feel that the National Policy was a unifying or divisive factor in Canada? Why?*

THE NOVA SCOTIA REPEAL MOVEMENT

Premier W. S. Fielding of Nova Scotia was critical of the operation of the National Policy and the Confederation settlement. The financial problems of his government led to the introduction of a Repeal Resolution on May 8, 1886. After some debate the Resolution was passed.

. . . That, previous to the union of the provinces, the province of Nova Scotia was in a most healthy condition; . . .

That after nineteen years under the union, successive governments have found that the objections which were urged against the terms of the union at first apply with still greater force now than in the past years of the union and the feelings of discontent with regard to the financial arrangement is now believed by this house to be more general and more deeply fixed than ever before.

That Nova Scotia previous to the union had the lowest tariff and was, notwithstanding, in the best financial condition of any of the provinces entering the union;

That the commercial as well as the financial condition of Nova Scotia is in an unsatisfactory and depressed condition;

That it seems evident that the terms of the "British North America Act" combined with the high tariff and fiscal laws of the Dominion are largely the cause of this unsatisfactory state of the finances and trade of Nova Scotia;

That there is at present no prospect that, while the province remains, upon the existing terms of union, a member of the Canadian federation, any satisfactory improvement in the foregoing respects is at all probable;

That previous to 1867 negotiations were in progress for an union of the maritime provinces, but were interrupted by the negotiations for the larger union;

That it now appears, as it did then, that the interest of the people of the several maritime provinces now incorporated with Canada are in most respects identical;

That the members of the branches of the legislature of Nova Scotia are of the opinion, and do hereby declare their belief, that the financial and commercial interests of the people of Nova Scotia, New Brunswick and Prince Edward Island would be advanced by these provinces withdrawing from the Canadian federation and uniting under one government;

That if it be found impossible after negotiations for that purpose, to secure the co-operation of the respective governments of the sister provinces in withdrawing from the confederation and entering instead into a maritime union, then this legislature deems it absolutely necessary that Nova Scotia, in order that its railways and other public works and services may be extended and maintained as the requirements of the people need them, its industry properly fostered, its commerce invigorated and expanded and its financial interests placed upon a sound basis such as was the case previous to confederation, should ask permission from the imperial parliament to withdraw from the union with Canada and return to the state of a province of Great Britain, with full control over all fiscal laws and tariff regulations within the province, such as prevailed previous to confederation;

That this house thus declares its opinion and belief in order that candidates for the suffrages of the people at the approaching elections may be enabled to place this vital and important question of separation from Canada before them for decision at the polls. . . .

What do you think?

1. *What were the grievances that led to the introduction of the resolution?*
2. *How do these grievances bear out the claims made at the time of Confederation?*
3. *Has the situation (with respect to these grievances) in the Maritimes changed today? Explain your response.*
4. *The Maritimes Repeal Resolution passed in the legislature. In 1976 Quebec elected a government that includes separation from Canada in its party platform. Compare these secessionist movements in the two provinces.*
5. *Why is separation considered a possible solution to regional grievances?*

NOVA SCOTIA NEWSPAPERS COMMENT ON REPEAL MOTION

There were various responses to Repeal in the local and regional press. The following are samples of the newspaper comments at that time.

Morning Chronicle, Halifax, Monday, May 10, 1886.

The repeal resolutions passed in the house of assembly on Saturday night with such an overwhelming majority [that it] will inspire the hearts of our people with a long smothered hope. From the 1st of July, 1867, down to the present hour there has been nothing to modify the feelings of resentment which the people down by the sea have felt at their forced union with Canada. We were strangers then, and we are strangers still, so far as common interests and those feelings which inspire brotherhood are concerned. . . . The people of Nova Scotia know the Ontario and Quebec man, but we know him principally in the shape of the commercial traveller. He comes here to sell, but he buys nothing save his hotel fare, and in this respect he makes a rather ostentatious display. He is usually a genial enough sort of person, has a diamond ring, smokes fat cigars, "sets them up with the boys" in an offhand way, and generally conveys the impression that in his own estimation he is a very superior being, whose condescending patronage it is a great privilege to enjoy. He spreads himself periodically throughout this province, in number he equals the locust, and his visit has about the same effect. He saps our resources, sucks our money, and leaves a lot of shoddy behind him. He has been able—at least the people whose agent he is—to have laws passed that compel us to buy his wares or submit to a tremendous fine. . . . Now, we submit that this sort of acquaintance with our upper provinces friends is not such as to inspire bonds of fealty and affection. Such bonds never have and never will exist. Our interests—the very genius of our people, all our instincts, everything that is calculated to foster and encourage national spirit, are so utterly foreign and dissimilar that fusion is absolutely impossible. The attempt to build up a Canadian nationality has been the most complete miscarriage that can be pointed to in the history of civilized communities. . . . It has been a waste of substance and resources, and Nova Scotia has suffered the most of all. This fact has burned itself into the minds of our people, and they have concluded that [in] so far [as] they are concerned the union must be dissolved. . . . How long are the proud spirited people of Nova Scotia going to submit to a condition of vassalage, galling to the quick, a vassalage forced upon them by treachery and brought about by corruption? Not long.

The Daily Examiner, Charlottetown, Tuesday, May 11, 1886.

Succession [sic] resolutions have passed the Nova Scotia Legislature. We regret that the present majority—led by Mr. Fielding, have in such a way compromised themselves, and trust that the people of Nova Scotia, at the polls, will speedily make them wish they hadn't. That the financial relations of the Dominion with the several Provinces, are not now on a satisfactory footing may be admitted; but the dignified course to pursue, in the premises is to demand the appointment of an independent commission to settle them on a just basis—not to go whining about secession. That the Government has in the past five years been making unfairly large expenditures in the Northwest, may also be admitted; but the bargain with British Columbia is now fulfilled—the C.P.R. is almost complete—and the government will now be able to devote more attention to the requirements of other parts of Canada—including those of Nova Scotia and P. E. Island. To complain that trade is not "booming" in Nova Scotia is certainly foolish in view of the profound depression existing in the Mother Country and the industrial distress of the States. How could Nova Scotia out of the Union improve her commercial position? The repealers of Nova Scotia have not answered this question. From every point of view their actions appear to be over-hasty and ridiculous.

What do you think?

1. *What arguments were used by the newspapers to support or attack Repeal?*
2. *How, if at all, have the grievances changed between 1886 and the present?*

NOVA SCOTIA ELECTION OF 1886

With Repeal as the central issue, Fielding called a provincial election. His Liberal Party took 29 of the 38 seats. Nova Scotia observer, J. F. Stairs, commented to John A. Macdonald on the result in a letter June 17, 1886. (J. F. Stairs to Sir John A. Macdonald, Confidential, Halifax, June 17, 1886.)

My Dear Sir John
You must have been as much astonished at the result of our election as we ourselves were. The fact is we have not got over it yet.
. . . but after we discussed all reasons we must acknowledge that the great reason was Repeal, and this fact makes the position a very serious one.
Possibly in some counties our opponents were not serious in this issue, success will I am afraid make their party a united one. They have aroused all the old feelings of 1867. Many of them arc talking as strongly now against the Dominion as the most rabid Irishman could against Ireland's union with

England, and the grit party in Nova Scotia will now surpass anything that party has ever attempted in Canada in the way of disloyalty and efforts to break up the Union. I am sure now the leaders will push the agitation to the bitter end. They will endeavour to draw New Brunswick and P.E.I. into it with Nova Scotia, in which I think they will not succeed, and will then go it alone. I am very much worried about the situation, would like to know what the Dominion Government will say to a request for repeal from Nova Scotia, and what course you advise your friends here to pursue.

. . . Nova Scotia must not get one cent of financial help as better terms upon the thrust of Repeal.

What do you think?

1. *Why was Stairs surprised at the outcome of the election? What effect did he think the victory of the Repeal supporters would have on Canada?*
2. *How would you describe Stairs's reaction to the Repeal situation? What effect would his kind of reaction have on the contemporary situation in Quebec?*

FIELDING ENDS REPEAL AGITATION

Fielding refused to act on Repeal until the results of the federal election of February 22, 1887 became known. As it happened, the Nova Scotia Conservatives opposed to Repeal returned 14 members, while the Repeal Liberals elected seven. Based on his party's poor showing in the election, Fielding decided to call an end to Repeal agitation.

. . . I have felt, since the February election, that the hands of the government were tied. . . . I am persuaded that our true policy is to tell the people of Nova Scotia that they had the matter in their own hands, that they had a glorious opportunity of asserting their desires on this question, and of placing themselves in a fair position to secure the accomplishment of those desires, that they lost that opportunity, and that, until they are prepared to take up the question again with greater firmness, and repair the damages of the February election, this repeal movement can have no reasonable hope of success.

What do you think?

1. *Was repeal a viable political issue in 1886 and 1887? Today? Why?*

The Interprovincial Conference of 1887

The Interprovincial Conference was held at Quebec City in October 1887 and was attended by the Liberal premiers of Manitoba, Ontario, Quebec, New Brunswick and Nova Scotia. Twenty-two resolutions on issues of provincial rights and autonomy were approved. The Macdonald government in Ottawa simply ignored these resolutions. But by the very action of convening such a conference, the provinces demonstrated the "Compact Theory" of Confederation. (This theory maintains that the Canadian union is a league of sovereign states which by solemn compact have delegated certain powers to the central government. Since the central government is viewed as a creation of the provinces, each province must give its assent before any constitutional changes can be made).

INTERPROVINCIAL CONFERENCE—STATEMENT

Whereas, in framing the British North America Act 1867, and defining therein the limits of the Legislative and Executive powers and functions of the Federal and Provincial Legislatures and Governments, the authors of the Constitution performed a work, new, complex and difficult, and it was to be anticipated that experience in the working of the new system would suggest many needed changes: that twenty years' practical working of the Act has developed much friction between the Federal and Provincial Governments and Legislatures, has disclosed grave omissions in the provisions of the Act, and has shown (when the language of the Act came to be judicially interpreted) that in many respects what was the common understanding and intention had not been expressed, and that important provisions in the Act are obscure as to their true intent and meaning; and whereas the preservation of Provincial autonomy is essential to the future well-being of Canada; and if such autonomy is to be maintained, it has become apparent that the Constitutional Act must be revised and amended; therefore the representatives and delegates of the Provinces of Ontario, Quebec, Nova Scotia, New Brunswick and Manitoba duly accredited by their respective Governments, and in Conference assembled, believing that they express the views and wishes of the people of Canada, agree upon the following Resolutions as the basis upon which the Act should be amended; subject to the approval of the several Provincial Legislatures:

1. That by the British North America Act exclusive authority is expressly given to the Provincial Legislatures in relation to subjects enumerated in the 92nd section of the Act; that a previous section of the Act reserves

to the Federal Government the legal power of disallowing at will all Acts passed by a Provincial Legislature; that this power of disallowance may be exercised so as to give to the Federal Government arbitrary control over legislation of the Provinces within their own sphere; and that the Act should be amended by taking away this power of disallowing Provincial Statutes, leaving to the people of each Province, through their representatives in the Provincial Legislature, the free exercise of their exclusive right of legislation on the subjects assigned to them subject only to disallowance by Her Majesty in Council as before Confederation; the power of disallowance to be exercised in regard to the Provinces upon the same principles as the same is exercised in the case of Federal Acts; . . .

(Toronto *Globe* March 9, 1888)

The Confederation has its origin in a bargain between certain Provinces, in which bargain the Provinces agreed to unite for certain purposes and to separate or continue separated for others. The Provinces party to the bargain were at the time of the compact independent nations in the sense that they enjoyed self-government subject to the Imperial veto upon their legislation, to the Imperial appointment of the Governor-General, and to the Queen's command of the forces. The Dominion was the creation of these Provinces; or, in other words, was created by the British Parliament at the request of the Provinces. The Dominion being non-existent at the time the bargain was made, was plainly not a party to the bargain. It cannot then, be a party to the revision of the bargain. The power to revise the created body must lie in the hands of those who created that body. The over-whelming majority of those who created the Dominion being in favour of the revision of the Confederation compact, the British Parliament is not entitled to look any further or to consult the wishes of the Dominion Government in the matter.

What do you think?

1. *How does the so-called Compact Theory of Confederation differ from the view held by John A. Macdonald?*
2. *Would the system of government as proposed by the Interprovincial Conference have subdued regional tensions or aggravated them? Why?*

THE 1860s AND 1870s:
THE CONFEDERATION YEARS

The Dominion of Canada came into being with the enactment of the B.N.A. Act on the first of July, 1867, and included the provinces of Ontario, Quebec, New Brunswick and Nova Scotia. The Confederation of British North America had been partly intended to eliminate the sectional rivalries and political deadlock that had existed in the united Canadas [Ontario and Quebec] during the 1860s. But between 1867 and 1873, the new Dominion acquired more territories, and thus made it necessary to expand the original definition of Confederation.

This section examines some regional responses to the Confederation proposal and reactions to the expansionist politics of the new Dominion. Did Confederation itself lay the foundation for future regional protest in Canada? Was Confederation a factor in the emergence of regional identities? Did Confederation fail to provide a national identity for Canadians?

The Case for Confederation

MACDONALD ARGUES FOR COLONIAL UNION

John A. Macdonald was one of the architects of Confederation. In September 1864 at Charlottetown, Prince Edward Island, he explained what he saw as the purpose of uniting the provinces of British North America.

The question of "Colonial Union" . . . absorbs every idea as far as I am concerned. For twenty long years I have been dragging myself through the dreary waste of Colonial politics. I thought there was no end, nothing worthy of ambition; but now I see something which is well worthy of all I have suffered in the cause of my little country. . . . There may be obstructions, local difficulties may arise, disputes may occur, local jealousies may intervene, but it matters not, the wheel is now revolving and we are only the fly on the wheel, . . . we cannot delay it—the union of the colonies of British America, under one sovereign, is a fixed fact. . . .

The dangers that have risen from this system we will avoid if we can agree upon forming a strong central government—a great central legislature —a constitution for a union which will have all the rights of sovereignty except those that are given to the local governments. Then we shall have taken a great step in advance of the American Republic. If we can only obtain that object—a vigorous general government—we shall not be New Brunswickers, nor Nova Scotians, nor Canadians, but British Americans, under the sway of the British Sovereign. . . . In the conference we have had [the Charlottetown Conference] we have been united as one man—there was no difference of feeling, no sectional prejudices or selfishness exhibited by any one;—we all approached the subject feeling its importance; feeling that in our hands were the destinies of a nation. . . .

In the case of a union, this railway must be a national work, and Canada will cheerfully contribute to the utmost extent in order to make that important link, without which no political connection can be complete. What will be the consequence to this city [Halifax], prosperous as it is, from that communication? Montreal is at this moment competing with New York for the trade of the great West. Build the road and Halifax will soon become one of the great emporiums of the world. All the great resources of the West will come over the immense railways of Canada to the bosom of your harbour. But there are even greater advantages for us all in view. We will become a great nation; and God forbid that it should be one separate from the United Kingdom of Great Britain and Ireland. . . .

Union must take place some time. I say now is the time . . . I will feel that I shall not have served in public life without a reward if before I enter into private life, I am a subject of a great British American nation, under the government of Her Majesty, and in connection with the Empire of Great Britain and Ireland.

What do you think?

1. *Why did Macdonald propose "colonial union"?*
2. *How did he propose to avoid the mistakes of the United States that had plunged that country into a civil war over sectional rights?*
3. *What devices did Macdonald propose to use to bring together so vast a territory?*

STRONG CENTRAL GOVERNMENT ESSENTIAL

During the years immediately preceding Confederation, Macdonald argued vigorously for a strong central government. The first document is an extract from his Quebec conference statements, the second from the Confederation Debates.

In framing the constitution care should be taken to avoid the mistakes and weaknesses of the United States' system, the primary error of which was the reservation to the different states of all powers not delegated to the General Government. We must reverse this process by establishing a strong central Government, to which shall belong all powers not specially conferred on the provinces. Canada, in my opinion, is better off as she stands than she would be as a member of the confederacy composed of five sovereign States, which would be the result if the powers of the local Governments were not defined.

We have strengthened the General Government. We have given the General Legislature all the great subjects of legislation. We have conferred on them, not only specifically and in detail, all the powers which are incident to sovereignty, but we have expressly declared that all subjects of general interest not distinctly and exclusively conferred upon the local governments and local legislatures, shall be conferred upon the General Government and Legislature. . . .

What do you think?

1. Why did Macdonald argue for strong central government?

DELEGATION OF POWERS IN B.N.A. ACT

Sections 91, 92 and 93 of the British North America Act dealt with the problems of provincial and federal powers.

THE DISTRIBUTION OF CONSTITUTIONAL POWERS

DOMINION POWERS

91. It shall be lawful for the Queen, by and with the Advice and Consent of the Senate and House of Commons, to make Laws for the Peace, Order, and good Government of Canada, in relation to all Matters not coming within the Classes of Subject by this Act assigned exclusively to the Legislatures of the Provinces; . . .

ILLUSTRATIONS:

1. The Public Debt and Property
2. The Regulation of Trade and Commerce
3. The raising of Money by any Mode or System of Taxation
5. The Postal Service
7. Militia, Military and Naval Service, and Defence
10. Navigation and Shipping
12. Sea Coast and Inland Fisheries
14. Currency and Coinage
15. Banking . . . and the Issue of Paper Money
24. Indians and Lands reserved for Indians
25. Naturalization and Aliens
26. Marriage and Divorce
27. The Criminal Law

PROVINCIAL POWERS

92. In each Province the Legislature may exclusively make Laws in relation to Matters coming within the Classes of Subjects next hereinafter enumerated; that is to say:

1. The Amendment from Time to Time . . . of the Constitution of the Province except as regards the Office of Lieutenant-Governor

2. Direct Taxation within the Province in order to the Raising of a Revenue for Provincial Purposes
5. The Management and Sale of the Public Lands belonging to the Province and of the Timber and Wood thereon
8. Municipal Institution in the Province
9. Shop, Saloon, Tavern, Auctioneer, and other licences
10. Local Works and Undertakings other than such as are of the following Classes:
    a) Transportation facilities linking two provinces
    b) Transportation facilities linking Canada and other countries
    c) Facilities which the Parliament of Canada declares to be for the welfare of Canada or more than the single province
12. The Solemnization of Marriage in the Province
13. Property and Civil rights in the Province
14. The Administration of Justice . . .
16. Generally all Matters of a merely local or private Nature in the Province

93. In and for each Province the legislature may exclusively make laws in relation to Education. . . .

What do you think?

1. *According to the B.N.A. Act does the federal or provincial government have more power? Justify your response.*
2. *What possible conflicts do you see in this distribution of power? Explain.*

Anti-Confederation Movement in the Atlantic Provinces

Despite Macdonald's persuasive arguments and the support of several prominent Maritime and Newfoundland leaders for Confederation, strong anti-Confederation sentiment existed in New Brunswick, Nova Scotia, Prince Edward Island and Newfoundland in the 1860s. This reaction against union influenced both the regional identity of the Atlantic provinces and their attitudes toward Confederation.

MARITIME NEWSPAPERS COMMENT ON CONFEDERATION PROPOSAL

Maritime protests against Confederation were often expressed in the local press. The following are excerpts from contemporary newspapers writing on the topic of planned union.

HALIFAX *MORNING CHRONICLE*, JANUARY 11, 1865 Before deciding to hand over to the Canadians the patronage and revenues of Nova Scotia, let us enquire whether there is anything in our present condition to compel us to make this transfer.

Prior to the introduction of Responsible Government into this Province, Downing Street claimed the authority which it is now proposed to erect at Ottawa. How did we like that? Why, so little that our best men gave the flower of their lives to the struggle by which the system was changed. Huntington and Howe, Young and Uniacke, Doyle and DesBarres, and all their sturdy compatriots, in two or three Parliaments, fought out the great battle by which the appointment of our own officers—the control of our own revenues—the management of our own affairs—was secured to Nova Scotians. We possess and exercise these high powers now, in as full and ample a measure as the freest people on the face of the earth. And shall it be said that the labours of these men were in vain—that their policy was unsound, and that their lives have been wasted?

Why should anything be done? Nova Scotia, secure of self-government, can even bear with serenity an Administration that certainly tries her patience at times, for a year or two longer. She has been blessed with a good crop, an abundant fishery, a healthy season, her mining interests are extending; her shipyards have been busy all the year; her railroads are beginning to pay, and her treasury is overflowing, affording ample means to push forward public improvements just as fast as it is wise to push them, with the little surplus labour we have.

. . .

It is said that the Canadians have outgrown their Constitution. Well, if they have, what of that? If they are in trouble let them get out of it; but don't let them involve us in distractions with which we have nothing to do. Are not the Canadians always in trouble? Did not Papineau keep Lower Canada in trouble for twenty years, and McKenzie [sic] disturb the Upper Province for about the same period? Then did not both Provinces break out into open rebellion, which it cost the British Government three of four millions sterling to suppress? What would have been the situation of the Maritime Provinces then, had they been controlled by the Canadians? Would they not have been compromised by these outbreaks, and might they not all have been made the theatres of civil war? But they were not under Canadian influence. They maintained their loyalty unsullied. . . .

Now, is this the country for Novascotians to unite with, and to whose entire control we should hand over the management of our affairs? Here we have peace and order, everybody worships God as he pleases, and everybody obeys the law. There are no armed midnight processions—no villains chalking our doors at night—no arms secreted—no Fenians drilling—and everybody sleeps in his bed securely, with no man to make him afraid. In the name of common sense, then, are we to peril all these blessings, and mix ourselves up with distractions, the end of which no living man can foresee?

JOSEPH HOWE ON CONFEDERATION

Joseph Howe was the leading opponent of Confederation in Nova Scotia. The following excerpt is from a statement made in 1866, from J. A. Chisholm, The Speeches and Public Letters of Joseph Howe (Halifax, 1909/Vol. II).

Let us see what these Canadians desire to do. They are not, as we have shown, a very harmonious or homogeneous community. Two-fifths of the population are French and three-fifths English. They are therefore perplexed with an internal antagonism which was fatal in the unity of Belgium and Holland, and which, unless the fusion of races becomes rapid and complete, must ever be a source of weakness. They are shut in by frost from the outer world for five months of the year. They are at the mercy of a powerful neighbour whose population already outnumbers them by more than eight to one, and who a quarter of a century hence will probably present sixty-eight millions to six millions on the opposite side of a naturally defenceless frontier. Surely such conditions as these ought to repress inordinate ambition or lust of territory on the part of the public men of Canada. The wisdom of Solomon and the energy and strategy of Frederick the Great would seem to be required to preserve and strengthen such a people, if formed, as it appears they desire to form themselves, into "a new national-ity." While they discharge their duties as unobtrusive good neighbours to the surrounding populations, and of loyal subjects of the empire, Great Britain will protect them by her energy in other fields should the Province become untenable; but it is evident that a more unpromising nucleus of a new nation can hardly be found on the face of the earth, and that any organized communities, having a reasonable chance to do anything better, would be politically insane to give up their distinct formations and subject themselves to the domination of Canada.

. . .

But it may be asked, do not the Maritimes Provinces desire this union? and, if the question includes the Quebec scheme of confederation it is soon answered. . . . When franchises were conferred upon the people of the Maritime Provinces, and legislatures given to them, these could only be yielded up by voluntary consent, or be forfeited by misconduct. When self-government was conceded, it could never afterwards be withdrawn, unless upon ample proof, elicited by legal forms or deliberate parliamentary inquiry, that it has been grossly abused. Even the colonial legislators themselves, entrusted for a definite time with limited powers and sacred trusts, could not strip the people of their rights without their own consent, or transfer to others the power of legislation, any more than the aldermen of London could annihilate the constitution which limits their sphere of action, or than the common councillors of Bath could transfer the government of that city to Bristol.

. . . Until the people of Nova Scotia, Prince Edward Island and Newfoundland forfeit, by corruption or abuse, the privileges conferred, or voluntarily relinquish them, they cannot be reclaimed by the Crown or swept away by Parliament without a breach of faith; nor can they be transferred by the local legislatures, any more than an estate can be transferred by trustees whose powers are limited in the deed by which the trust has been created.

Unfortunately these plain principles of legal construction and constitutional law have, in dealing with the Maritime Provinces, been strangely overlooked. When all the parties to the Quebec scheme of confederation found that they had made an egregious blunder, they should have abandoned the project and left the Province in peace; and above all, the Government of England should have withdrawn from a controversy into which, for no imperial objects, as has been clearly proved, they had been artfully drawn. . . .

What do you think?

1. *Why was Howe opposed to Confederation?*
2. *Although both Howe and Needham opposed union with Canada, they each used different tactics in presenting their views. To whom or to what did Needham appeal? To whom or to what did Howe appeal? Which argument do you find more convincing? Why?*

CHARLES TUPPER ATTACKS HOWE

Charles Tupper was the leading pro-Confederate in Nova Scotia. The following is from a published letter of his in 1866.

Mr. Howe has ventured to affirm throughout his *brochure,* [*Confederation Considered*] that this policy of a Union between Canada and the Maritime Provinces is an ambitious and unscrupulous attempt at "spoliation" and "appropriation" on the part of Canada. What must be thought of his temerity in making such a statement, when viewed in the light of the fact, that when Mr. Howe was Leader of the Government of Nova Scotia, in 1861, he moved the resolution . . . , declaring "that many advantages may arise" from such a Union, and wrote an official letter to the Government of Canada based upon that resolution, which had been unanimously carried in the Assembly of Nova Scotia, asking Canada to entertain his overtures for Union, and proceeded to Quebec, in 1862, a Delegate to press his suit?

Now, when the policy of Union, for which for many years he professed such devotion, is likely, in other hands, to be more successful, he denounces it as an attempted "spoliation." If this Union of the Provinces be a "spoliation" on the part of Canada, no man has more to answer for in connection with it than Mr. Howe. For twenty years he has been advocating the construction of an Intercolonial Railway and the Union of the Provinces, as the best means of advancing their interests, promoting their prosperity, and the only means of securing, in any part of British America, the permanence of British institutions. . . .

. . .

Mr. Howe not only treats the proposed Confederation as an attempt at "spoliation" on the part of Canada, but says the ambition of her public men overleaps that of "Bismarck or Louis Napoleon." Does he not perceive that if it be true, as he asserts, that Canada is shut out from the sea during the winter months, and can never become a really great country, and that the equally balanced state of the Legislature between Upper and Lower Canada made a change in her Constitution indispensable, it was not strange that she should seek, in a Confederation, the means of obtaining access by railway to the ocean, and of removing that embarrassing provision of her present Constitution by which the two great sections of the country were equally represented in the Legislature irrespective of their growth or population? The reflection that Mr. Howe had himself endeavoured to induce Canada to unite with the Maritime Provinces, for the obvious reason that it would make the latter the "ocean frontage" for a great country lying behind them, teeming with wealth and industry, ought for ever to prevent him from charging Canada with attempted "spoliation." That neither Canada nor the Maritime Provinces can ever attain any real greatness, except in such a combination as is now proposed, cannot but be seen by anybody in the least acquainted with the position they occupy relatively to each other. . . .

Mr. Howe endeavours to excite hostility against Canada among British manufacturers by saying:—

Then certain persons in the manufacturing towns had been disgusted with the high duties which Canada had imposed on British productions. They were angry and did not stay to reflect that, if Canada were in error, the Maritime Provinces ought not to be punished for her faults, seeing that they had never followed her example.

It would only have been ingenuous had Mr. Howe repeated what he said on this subject a year ago at Detroit, when defending the Canadian Tariff:—

Now in the Provinces our people are naturally anxious to improve their internal communications, and bring them up to a level with other portions of the continent. Yielding to this pressure, the Government of Canada has expended large sums in the construction of railroads and canals. But the money being expended, of course the interest has to be paid, and that this might be done, changes have been made in the tariff from time to time. The necessities of Canada from these large expenditures compelled her to raise her import duty.

He might have added that, when Nova Scotia and New Brunswick have completed the public works contemplated under existing enactments, their indebtedness per head will be as large as that of Canada. But assuming that it be true that the policy of the Maritime Provinces is much more in favour of Free-trade than that of Canada has been, is it not the interest of every British manufacturer to throw that Free-trade leaven into the Canadian Legislation? It would have been but just had Mr. Howe admitted the well-known fact, that from the date of the Quebec Conference down to the present hour, the greatest strides have been taken in Canada in the direction of Free-trade, ...

The impossible nature of the task to which Mr. Howe addressed himself is well illustrated by the extravagant hyperboles and incongruous statements with which his pamphlet abounds. Its readers cannot fail to be impressed with the fact, that every argument advanced is not only in distinct contradiction with every sentiment in which, in a truly British American Spirit, Mr. Howe has advocated a Union of the Colonies throughout his public career, but, what is still more striking, that the reasons he now advances to sustain the various points of his present position effectually refute each other. . . .

When Mr. Howe wishes to prove that Canada, Nova Scotia, and New Brunswick, dependent upon each other for the advancement of all, and drawn together by a common interest and a common danger, had better remain isolated, he presents the United States as riven by internal discord and breaking up into a half-dozen different and antagonistic Governments; yet on the next page, when he endeavours to prove that Great Britain and a United British America will be unable to protect and preserve the latter, he reunites the scattered fragments of the Great Republic and declares with equal confidence that it will not only "stagger on for some years," but that a quarter of a century hence the American Union will exhibit a consolidated power, numbering sixty-eight millions of people.

It is obvious that both of these statements cannot be prophetic. . . .

. . . where, I would ask, can he expect to find another Nova Scotian who would be content with a position of isolation so utterly fatal to that progress and importance to which, with her great natural resources and position, as the Atlantic frontage of British America, she may now look confidently forward?

What do you think?

1. *What arguments does Tupper use to refute Howe? How successful are they?*
2. *Why does Tupper think that Nova Scotia would be better off within the new federation?*

REPEAL AGITATION IN THE MARITIMES

Even after Confederation in 1867, anti-Confederate sentiment did not die down in the Maritimes. As these editorials indicate, protest movements were being orga.~ized to repeal Confederation in Nova Scotia and New Brunswick.

NEW GLASGOW *CHRONICLE* SEPTEMBER 25, 1867   The general election of last week, in which were involved such momentous issues, has resulted in the most overwhelming defeat of the Canadian Party in Nova Scotia. The men who had forced Confederation upon this Province, who had set at defiance the well-understood wishes of the people, who had sternly declared the people should not decide the question at the polls, who had outraged public opinion in a manner never before known in the history of Nova Scotia, where are they? With two exceptions they are truly "among the missing." . . . After weary months of waiting the people's turn came. They were required to render a verdict upon the actions of their rulers. Have they not brought in a verdict of "GUILTY, without extenuating circumstances?" The people have spoken upon the question of Confederation, and what have they said? They have said with a unanimity never before known in the history of a free people that they are opposed to the measure of Confederation and to the manner in which it has been brought about. They have declared that they desire no political connection with Canada, that they wish to manage their own affairs, that they desire to remain loyal subjects of their gracious Queen. And they have declared that the legislature of the Province had no right nor power to take away the constitution of the country, without the sanction of the popular voice. . . . In a word we desire to have Responsible Government with all the blessings and privileges restored to us. Those privileges, while we did enjoy them, we never abused, and we cannot consent that they should be ruthlessly taken from us without just cause. We want to be restored to our former status as an independent Province of the British Empire.—In order to accomplish this, the Act of Union, so far as Nova Scotia is concerned, must be repealed. This is all we ask, and we will be satisfied with nothing less.

NEW BRUNSWICK *REPORTER* MAY 29, 1868   With very little of the ostentation which marked the occasion of its opening, the first session of the first Parliament of the Dominion came to a close last Friday. Most of the members had left for their homes, when the principal matters had been determined, some before, thus rendering the closing scene tame enough. In looking back at this session as the test of Confederation, we wish it were in our power to say that it has been satisfactory, and that the future looks bright and encouraging. But we cannot. Whether too much was promised, or too much expected, certain it is the facts fall far short of the expectations, and the very best friends of Confederation shake their heads ominously. For this state of affairs the men, and not the measure, are responsible; the omissions and commissions of Parliament are not the sins of Confederation. The cause for which we struggled in this Province necess-tated [sic] no tax upon the necessari[e]s of life, no bill stamps, no newspaper postage, and although these may not be of vital importance in themselves, the very fact that our representatives stood up against their adoption and were powerless to prevent it, is in itself, sufficient to damp the ardor of Unionists in New Brunswick. We were told at the outset that Canada's necessity was our opportunity; but the worst of it is, Canada has too many necessities, while New Brunswick has the delightful opportunity of paying her proportions. This would be cheerfully done were the measures of the day in harmony with the interests of New Brunswick, and were our representation regarded instead of being ignored. We expected that Confederation would induce a line of national instead of sectional policy; that it would give a general impetus to trade, emigration and commerce; that men like Cartier would see something more noble in the Union of the British Provinces, than a mere opportunity to advance the interests of their respective localities. But we have been disappointed; not in the cause which, being right, is sure to succeed eventually, but rather in the petty, selfish policy of some of the men who have given caste to the first operation of Confederation.

What do you think?

1. What was the future of Confederation as seen in these editorials?

JOSEPH HOWE AND THE END OF THE REPEAL MOVEMENT

After Confederation, Joseph Howe attempted to harness the existing anti-confederate sentiment in order to obtain repeal from the British authorities. When it became evident that the British would not grant repeal, Howe launched a campaign to secure "better terms" for Nova Scotia within Confederation. The repeal movement itself withered soon after Howe joined the Macdonald administration in January 1869. The following is a portion of a speech given by Howe on February 12, 1869.

Men of Hants,—In the speeches addressed to you previous to the general election, I almost invariably defined three lines of action:
1. To defeat the delegates who had framed the British America Act.
2. To endeavour to get the Act repealed; and
3. Should we fail in the effort to repeal the Act, that we should endeavour to modify and improve it.

To accomplish the first I strained every nerve. . . .

. . . In 1868, as a member of another delegation, I laboured with equal zeal and energy to repeal it. . . .

Both these missions failed. . . .

In the despatch which the Duke of Buckingham addressed to Lord Monck in June last, while distinctly refusing to repeal the Act of Union, he threw upon the Canadian ministers the obligation to inquire into the working of that Act, with a view to such modifications and changes as would make it more acceptable to the people of Nova Scotia. . . . When some of those ministers came down here in August, and solemnly pledged themselves before a committee of the convention to make the attempt, I claimed for them a fair hearing and due consideration for any propositions they might make. In taking this line I acted in the spirit of my third proposition, that "if we failed to accomplish the repeal of the Act, we should endeavour to modify and improve it."

. . . The results are now before you. In addition to the $60,000 added to the Quebec scheme by the labours of the delegates sent to England in 1866, we have now obtained for ten years a sum amounting, in round numbers, to $160,000 per annum, making, since I put my hand to this work $220,000 or £55,000 a year recovered for Nova Scotia.

Before the ten years expire, should it appear that, if from any cause, injustice is being done in money matters, the Canadians have now shown that they can be relied upon to reconsider the whole case, and to do substantial justice. . . .

. . . in August last the Premier offered me a seat in the cabinet. That offer was renewed, and pressed upon me again in October. But I felt that it would be time enough to think of honours and emoluments for myself when I had tested the sincerity of his professions to do justice to my country, within the scope and boundary of his acknowledged powers of action. He did do justice. . . . Sir John A. Macdonald, with some show of reason, pressed me again to take office. He said, "We have now done justice so far as we could in monetary matters, and are prepared to deal fairly with Nova Scotia in all other branches of the public service, as rapidly as we get the power; but I want your advice and assistance in order that this may be effectually done; and, what is more, I want some guarantee to give to Parliament that, when they have voted this money, the arrangement will not be repudiated by Nova Scotia.

I felt the fairness of this argument. . . .

What do you think?

1. *Why did Howe join the Macdonald government after having opposed it for so long?*

FIVE YEARS AFTER

The Saint John Daily News *May 3, 1872 assessed the prevailing mood of New Brunswick and Nova Scotia after five-years within Confederation.*

All is quiet in Nova Scotia. Its quarrels with the Dominion are composed. Its grievances have been substantially redressed. Its anti-politicians are conciliated. Its irreconcilables have disappeared from the public view. Repeal seems but the unquiet memory of a far-gone age. Annexationism is as dead as Tubal Cain. Nova Scotia currency has been assimilated to that prevailing in other Dominion provinces, and nobody has been ruined in consequence, and its people are in the enjoyment of a goodly degree of prosperity.

In New Brunswick, it would be difficult to find fuel in any appreciable quantity to kindle a Dominion Opposition flame. Our industries are generally prosperous. Our School Law has not been vetoed. Our Ballot box has not been withdrawn. Our demand for better terms has been treated respectfully, and will be acceded to in good time. The Dominion Government is showing a disposition to do us ample justice at all points. The Baie de Verte Canal is a 'fixed fact' of the near future. The requirements of Trade and Commerce in our Harbor are meeting with due attention from the Dominion Government, and minor, though important and much needed, public improvements elsewhere in the Province are about to be undertaken by the Dominion Public Works Department. The Dominion Government has certainly made some mistakes during its career, but so far as New Brunswick is concerned, they have been condoned or rectified to a large degree. And it is palpable to every observer that at this moment the Dominion Government upon the whole stands better with the people of New Brunswick than at any previous time since the Dominion was inaugurated.

What do you think?

1. What, according to the newspaper, was the mood of the Maritime Provinces in 1872? What were the reasons for this mood?

Quebec

As in the case of the Maritimes, public opinion was divided over the issue of Confederation in Lower Canada. Supporters of Union argued that Confederation would allow Lower Canada to manage its own affairs free from the interference of Upper Canada. On the other hand, anti-Confederates feared that the French culture and language would eventually be submerged in a Confederation dominated by an English-speaking majority.

SUPPORTERS OF CONFEDERATION

The following are two extracts outlining pro-Confederation arguments in Lower Canada. The first is taken from the Confederation Debates *of 1865; the second is from the newspaper* Le Journal de Quebec.

J. DUFRESNE, MARCH 10, 1865 ... I accept them [the Seventy-two Resolutions] for many reasons, but chiefly as a means of obtaining the repeal of the present legislative union of Canada, and securing peaceable settlement of our sectional difficulties. I accept them, in the second place, as a means of obtaining for Lower Canada the absolute and exclusive control of her own affairs. I accept them, thirdly, as a means of perpetuating French-Canadian nationality in this country. I accept them, fourthly, as a more effectual means of cementing our connection with the Mother Country, and avoiding annexation to the United States. I accept them, fifthly and lastly, as a means of administering the affairs of the colony with greater economy. Such are my reasons for accepting the Confederation scheme submitted to us by the Government. . . .

LE JOURNAL DE QUEBEC, DECEMBER 17, 1864 We want to be a nation one day, and as that is our necessary destiny and the goal to which we aspire, we prefer the political conditions of which we will be a vital element and in which we will still be in existence, rather than to be thrown into the midst of an immense people, like a drop of water lost in the ocean, where in a few years we would lose our language, our laws, and even the memory of our glorious origins.

What do you think?

1. What did the pro-Confederationists think Confederation would mean for a) Quebec? and b) the French in Canada?
2. What similarities and differences exist between these demands and those made by present-day spokespeople for French Canada.
3. What differences and similarities do you see between the concerns and reactions of Lower Canada to Confederation and the Atlantic and the West?

OPPONENTS OF CONFEDERATION

The following selections are taken from the Confederation Debates *of 1865 and the French language newspaper* Le Pays. *They outline some of the reasons for anti-Confederation sentiment in Lower Canada.*

ANTOINE A. DORION, MARCH 6, 1865 ... I am opposed to this Confederation in which the militia, the appointment of the judges, the administration of justice and our most important civil rights will be under the control of a General Government, the majority of which will be hostile to Lower Canada, of a General Government invested with the most ample powers, whilst the powers of the local government will be restricted, first, by the limitation of the powers delegated to it, by the Veto reserved to the central authority and further, by the concurrent jurisdiction of the general authority or government. . . .

HON. LOUIS AUGUSTE OLIVER FEBRUARY 13, 1865 ... My opinion is, that as much power as possible should have been entrusted to the local governments, and as little as is consistent with the functions it will have to discharge to the Central Government, and my reason for entertaining this opinion is, that the Supreme Government, with its power of purse and its control of the armies, will always be more disposed to stretch its prerogatives and to trench upon the domain of the local governments than to narrow down and retain its authority. The scheme then, in my opinion, is defective in that it invests this order and gives to the General Government too much power and to the local government too little. As it is now, if the scheme goes into operation, the local governments will be in danger of being crushed (écrasés) by the General Government. The tendency of the whole scheme seems to be one of political retrogression instead of advancement ...

JOSEPH XAVIER PERRAULT MARCH 3, 1865 ... I say, Mr. Speaker, that the scheme of Confederation is not expedient. But even if the scheme of Confederation was expedient, I maintain that the object of it is hostile. I gave an historical sketch of the encroaching spirit of the English race on the two continents. I pointed out the incessant antagonism existing between it and the French race. Our past recalled to us the constant struggle which we had to keep up in order to resist the aggression and the exclusiveness of the English element in Canada. It was only through heroic resistance and a happy combination of circumstances that we succeeded in obtaining the political rights which are secured to us by the present Constitution. The scheme of Confederation has no other object than to deprive us of the most precious of those rights, by substituting for them a political organization which is eminently hostile to us ...

LE PAYS, DECEMBER 29, 1864 ... 1. Because the new system would be expensive and complicated; 2. Because it would imperil the institutions and the religious faith, as well as the autonomy, of the French-Canadian nationality, guaranteed by solemn treaties and Imperial statutes; 3. Because it would impose on this province pecuniary obligations which were incumbent exclusively and by law on the other provinces of British North America, and very onerous material sacrifices, such as direct taxation, without procuring in return in this region any real tangible benefit; 4. Because it would very probably instigate, sooner or later, throughout the said provinces, and particularly in this region, civil troubles and perhaps very serious ones.

What do you think?

1. *Why did these people oppose Confederation? How valid do you think their arguments were?*
2. *Of the points of view recorded in these two sets of documents, which has history borne out? Which would you have found more convincing? Why?*

Manitoba

The Canadian government successfully negotiated the purchase of the Northwest from the British government and the Hudson's Bay Company in 1869. Many residents of the Red River settlement opposed this transfer of ownership even before the actual purchase was finalized and by October of 1869 began to actively resist the Canadian authorities. This joint effort by white settlers, Métis and Indians resulted in the admission of the province of Manitoba to Confederation in 1870.

PROVISIONAL GOVERNMENT DECLARED, 1869

The "Declaration of the Inhabitants of Ruperts Land and the North-West" of December 8, 1869 proclaimed a provisional government at Fort Garry under the leadership of John Bruce and Louis Riel.

Whereas, it is admitted by all men, as a fundamental principle, that the public authority commands the obedience and respect of its subjects. It is also admitted, that a people, when it has no Government, is free to adopt one form of Government, in preference to another, to give or to refuse allegiance to that which is proposed. . . .

. . . this people, ever actuated by the above-mentioned principles, had generously supported the aforesaid Government [the Hudson's Bay Company] and gave to it a faithful allegiance, when, contrary to the law of nations, in March, 1869, that said Government surrendered and transferred to Canada all the rights which it had, or pretended to have, in this Territory, by transactions with which the people were considered unworthy to be made acquainted.

And, whereas, it is also generally admitted that a people is at liberty to establish any form of government it may consider suited to its wants, as soon as the power to which it was subject abandons it, or attempts to subjugate it, without its consent to a foreign power; and maintain, that no right can be transferred to such foreign power. Now, therefore, first, we, the representatives of the people, in Council assembled in Upper Fort Garry, on the 24 day of November, 1869, after having invoked the God of Nations, relying on these fundamental moral principles, solemnly declare, in the name of our constituents, and in our own names, before God and man, that, from the day on which the Government we had always respected abandoned us, by transferring to a strange power the sacred authority confided to it, the people of Rupert's Land and the North-West became free and exempt from all allegiance to the said Government. Second. That we refuse to recognize the authority of Canada, which pretends to have a right to coerce us, and impose upon us a despotic form of government still more contrary to our rights and interests as British subjects, than was that Government to which we had subjected ourselves, through necessity, up to a recent date. Thirdly. That, by sending an expedition on the 1st of November, ult., charged to drive back Mr. William McDougall and his companions, coming in the name of Canada, to rule us with the rod of despotism, without previous notification to that effect, we have acted conformably to that sacred right which commands every citizen to offer energetic opposition to prevent this country from being enslaved. Fourth. That we continue, and shall continue, to oppose, with all our strength, the establishing of the Canadian authority in our country, under the announced form; . . . and, furthermore, we do declare and proclaim, in the name of the people of Rupert's Land and the North-West, that we have, on the said 24th day of November, 1869, above mentioned, established a Provisional Government, and hold it to be the only and lawful authority now in existence in Rupert's Land and the North-West which claims the obedience and respect of the people; that, meanwhile, we hold ourselves in readiness to enter in such negotiations with the Canadian Government as may be favourable for the good government and prosperity of this people. In support of this declaration, relying on the protection of Divine Province, we mutually pledge ourselves, on oath, our lives, our fortunes, and our sacred honor, to each other.

Issued at Fort Garry, this Eighth day of December, in the year of our Lord One thousand eight hundred and sixty-nine.

John Bruce, Pres.
Louis Riel, Sec.

What do you think?

1. Why did the Red River settlement proclaim a provisional government?
2. According to this document, what image of the Dominion government did the Red River settlers have?
3. Under what circumstances do you think distinct regions would be justified in proclaiming their own government? Explain.

LIST OF RIGHTS, 1869

A "List of Rights" had been drawn up on December 1, 1869, but it underwent several revisions before it was presented to the Federal Government at Ottawa by a delegation from the provincial government on March 22, 1870.

I.   THAT the Territories heretofore known as Rupert's Land and the North-West, shall not enter into the Confederation of the Dominion of Canada, except as a Province; to be styled and known as the Province of Assiniboia, and with all the rights and privileges common to the different Provinces of the Dominion.

II.   THAT we have two Representatives in the Senate, and four in the House of Commons of Canada, until such time as an increase of population entitle the Province to a greater Representation.

IV.   THAT the sum of Eighty Thousand (80,000) dollars be paid annually by the Dominion Government to the local Legislature of this Province.

V.   THAT all properties, rights and privileges engaged [sic: enjoyed] by the people of this Province, up to the date of our entering into the Confederation, be respected; and that the arrangement and confirmation of all customs, usages and privileges be left exclusively to the local Legislature.

VII. THAT a sum of money equal to eighty cents per head of the population of this Province, be paid annually by the Canadian Government to the local Legislature of the said Province; until such time as the said population shall have reached six hundred thousand.

X.   THAT the bargain of the Hudson's Bay Company with respect to the transfer of the Government of this country to the Dominion of Canada, be annulled; so far as it interferes with the rights of the people of Assiniboia, and so far as it would affect our future relations with Canada.

XI.   THAT the local Legislature of the Province of Assiniboia shall have full control over all the public lands of the Province . . .

XIII. THAT treaties be concluded between Canada and the different Indian tribes of the Province of Assiniboia, by and with the advice and cooperation of the local Legislature of this Province.

XIV. THAT an uninterrupted steam communication from Lake Superior to Fort Garry be guaranteed, to be completed within the space of five years.
XV. THAT all public buildings, bridges, roads and other public works, be at the cost of the Dominion Treasury.
XVI. THAT the English and French languages be common in the Legislature and in the Courts, and that all public documents, as well as all acts of the Legislature be published in both languages.

. . .

XVII. THAT . . . the Lieutenant-Governor, who may be appointed for the Province of Assiniboia, should be familiar with both the French and English languages.
XVIII. THAT the Judges of the Supreme Court speak the English and French languages.
XIX. THAT all debts contracted by the Provincial Government of the Territory of the North-West, now called Assiniboia, in consequence of the illegal and inconsiderate measures adopted by Canadian officials to bring about a civil war in our midst, be paid out of the Dominion Treasury; and that none of the members of the Provisional Government, or any of those acting under them, be in any way held liable or responsible with regard to the movement, or any of the actions which led to the present negotiations. . . .

What do you think?

1. *Did the provisional government have the right to negotiate with Canada? Why or why not?*
2. *What kinds of concerns are expressed in the Bill of Rights? Are they regional concerns? Explain your answer.*
3. *In what ways was the situation of the Northwest different from the situation of the other provinces before Confederation? Why was this the case?*

PROVINCIAL OR TERRITORIAL STATUS?

The Convention of Fort Garry, in revising the "List of Rights", had to decide for itself what the Red River settlement wanted from Canada. Central to the discussion was provincial or territorial status. The following is from a Convention session held February 4, 1870.

Mr. Riel—I was very nearly induced to adopt your view, expressed in committee, Mr. Ross, with regard to a Crown Colony. One important consideration which we must bear in mind, is, that as a Territory we escape a great deal of the heavy responsibility that may weigh on us as a Province. Of course it would be very flattering to our feelings to have all the standing and dignity of a Province. The exclusive powers to Provinces are considerable, and in themselves satisfactory, if we found them applicable to our case (Mr. Riel then read the Confederation Act to show the powers conferred on Provinces). He alluded specially to article 5, which provides that the management and sale of the public lands belonging to the Provinces and of the timber and wood thereon, is vested in the Province. This, he alluded to, as one of the most important, as far as we are concerned. In looking at the advantages and disadvantages of the provincial and territorial systems, we have to consider fully the responsibility of our undertaking. Certainly the North-West is a great pearl in the eyes of many parties. . . .

As to this question of a Province, let me ask, is it not possible for us to settle our own affairs in a satisfactory manner? . . . I have ample confidence in the good sense of our people for managing all matters wisely; and as to matters of a general nature, they will be managed by the Dominion. . . .

Mr. Ross—For my part, he said, I am perfectly satisfied that going in as a Province will do us harm. This question was considered in committee, and I understood we were to let it drop. Our position, if we entered as a Province, would be very different than that of the other provinces. They entered the Dominion entirely equipped with roads, bridges, court houses, etc. They entered as full grown men and having everything. We are here asking to be admitted as men, when, in respect to our equipment and outfit, the country is only in its infancy (cheers). We are in a position to ask, and of course can ask it. But I am satisfied we can never get it. . . .

What do you think?

1. *What was the argument used for provincial status? What was the argument used for territorial status?*
2. *Do you think that the granting of provincial status was a premature act on the part of the Federal Government? Why?*
3. *How does this debate reflect the concerns of the West today with respect to its role in Confederation?*

BISHOP TACHÉ COMMENTS ON THE RED RIVER SITUATION

The Roman Catholic clergy at Red River played an important role in the resistance. Bishop Taché advised the Canadian Secretary of State on March 11, 1870 on how to go about handling the situation both in the short-term and the long-term.

Sir,—The painful duty devolves upon me of communicating to His Excellency the condition of the country. . . . With the deepest regret I feel it my duty to state that, with very few exceptions, all who have come from Canada have acted as if their object was, not only to compromise the Dominion Government, but also to open out an unfathomable abyss. . . .

A Provisional Government is proclaimed, and is recognized not only by the French section of the population, but even also by the Scotch colony, and by most if not all the parishes where the English language is spoken. The Anglican Bishop and his clergy also recognized that Government, which was for the time a military organization resolved to cause itself to be respected. The idea of annexation, if at any time it existed, appears to have vanished; a large majority wish for union with Canada, but the Council desire to lay down their conditions, which will, perhaps, be different from those which were specified by the convention. . . .

You will easily understand the difficulty of my position under the present circumstances. It would be but too easy to cause a division, but I consider that this would be the greatest of misfortunes. I want, on the contrary, to labour for union and the re-establishment of peace, for the Indians would take advantage of such disunions. My action can be but slow, for the Government will easily understand that the utmost prudence is required under the circumstances. I have this day had an interview with the President in order to assure him of the just and generous intentions of the Government; I begged him not to attach any importance to the clamours of certain newspapers, to rest assured that Canada does not wish and cannot wish the destruction or the enslavement of the people of the North-West. The whole French population (except for a small fraction said to have been bought over) are convinced that the greatest misfortune that could have fallen to their lot would have been to fall under the government of Mr. McDougall, and of those who had accompanied or preceded him. People here believe in the existence of an organized plan, prepared without the knowledge of the Government (but which it ought to have foreseen and known), with the object of driving out of the country, or at least of reducing to a species of servitude within it, the French Canadian half-breeds of the Red River and of the whole North-West. It is this idea that exasperates the people. Time and kind treatment can alone heal the deep and fearful wound which has just been inflicted. Therefore it is that I take the liberty respectfully to state to the Government that steps must be taken to delay emigration, for, in the present exasperation of the public mind, the new comers would incur great danger.

. . . The matter hinges on the conviction entertained by the people that they cannot be forced to enter into Confederation any more than the other Provinces of the Dominion; that the people believe themselves in no way bound by the arrangements made with the Hon. The Hudson's Bay Company: that as a consequence the words "Rebels," "Insurgents," "Traitors," are so many insults which they repel with indignation. This is the root of the whole matter,—all the rest is merely accessory, and there exists no means of conciliation but to act in conformity with that principle. The people cannot tolerate the idea of having been sold, and this is the explanation of their discontent, as well towards Canada, for purchasing as towards the Company for their share of the transaction. . . .

I take the very great liberty of saying that these reasons are more than plausible, and that I am confident His Excellency's Government will take into favorable consideration the claims of the delegates who are to start on Thursday next, and that, in the meantime, Parliament will refrain from legislating for a country where its authority is rejected by the population.

What do you think?

1. According to Bishop Taché, why was the authority of the Dominion government rejected by the population of the Northwest?
2. "Time and kind treatment can alone heal the deep and fearful wound which has just been inflicted." How might the history of the West have been different if the disputing parties had heeded Bishop Taché's advice?

British Columbia

As the eastern colonies of British North America came together to form a nation, pressure was applied to the westernmost colony, British Columbia, to follow suit. As Canadian attention turned to the North-West, a vision of a transcontinental Dominion developed, extending from sea to sea and linked by a great railway. British Columbia had a number of options: it could remain a British colony, join the United States, or become a part of Canada. After some debate, British Columbia became the sixth Canadian Province in 1871.

BRITISH COLUMBIA USEFUL TO THE U.S.A.

Many Americans looked to the acquisition of Canada west of the Great Lakes to provide a land buffer between the United States and Russia. The following is from a speech by William Seward as reported by the New York Herald on January 25, 1861. As the United States' Secretary of State, in 1867, Seward arranged for the purchase of Alaska from the Russians.

I can stand here and look far off into the Northwest and see the Russian, as he busily occupies himself in establishing seaports and towns, and fortifications, as outposts of the empire of St. Petersburg, and I can say, 'Go in; build up your outposts to the Arctic Ocean; they will yet become the outposts of my own country to extend the civilization of the United States in the Northwest.' So I look upon Prince Rupert's Land and Canada, and see how an ingenious people, and a capable, enlightened government are occupied with bridging rivers and making railroads and telegraphs to develop, organize, create and preserve the great British provinces of the north, by the Great Lakes, the St. Lawrence and around the shores of Hudson's Bay, and I am able to say, 'It is very well; you are building excellent states to be hereafter admitted into the American Union.'

What do you think?

1. Why did some Americans want to gain control of British Columbia?
2. To what extent might American interest in the Canadian Northwest have influenced the plan of a transcontinental Dominion? Do some independent research to support your answer.

ANNEXATIONIST PETITION

Annexationist sentiment was not one-sided. An "Annexationist Petition" from which the following document is excerpted, was presented to the American President, Ulysses S. Grant, on behalf of the people of British Columbia on December 29, 1869.

To
His Excellency, the President of the United States of America.

Your Memorialists beg leave most respectfully to represent, that we are residents of the Colony of British Columbia—many of us British subjects and all deeply interested in the welfare and progress of our adopted country.

That those that are British Subjects are penetrated with the most profound feelings of loyalty and devotion to Her Majesty and Her Majesty's Government and that all entertain for Her, feelings of the greatest respect as well as attachment to the country.

That while we thus indulge such feelings, we are constrained by the duty we owe to ourselves and families, in view of the contemplated severance of the political ties which unite this Colony to the "Mother Country", to seek for such political and commercial affinity and connection, as will insure the immediate and continued prosperity and wellbeing of this our adopted home.

That this Colony is now suffering great depression, owing to its isolation, a scarcity of population and other causes too numerous to mention.

That we view with feelings of alarm the avowed intention of Her Majesty's Government to confederate this Colony with the Dominion of Canada, as we believe such a measure can only tend to still further depression and ultimate injury for the following reasons, viz:—

That confederation cannot give us protection against internal enemies or foreign foes, owing to the distance of this Colony from Ottawa.

That it cannot open to us a market for the produce of our lands, our forests, our mines or our waters.

That it cannot bring us population, (our greatest need) as the Dominion itself is suffering from lack of it.

That our connection with the Dominion can satisfy no sentiment of loyalty or devotion.

That her commercial and industrial interests are opposed to ours.

That the tariff of the Dominion will be the ruin of our farmers and the commerce of our chief cities.

That we are instigated by every sentiment of loyalty to Her Majesty, by our attachment to the laws and institutions of Great Britain and our deep interest in the prosperity of our adopted country, to express our opposition to a severance from England and a confederation with Canada. We admit the Dominion may be aggrandized by confederation, but we can see no benefit either present or future, which can accrue to us therefrom. . . .

The only remedy for the evils which beset us, we believe to be in a close union with the adjoining States and Territories, we are already bound to them by a unity of object and interest; nearly all our commercial relations are with them; They furnish the Chief Markets we have for the products of our mines, lands and waters; They supply the Colony with most of the necessities of life; They furnish us the *only* means of communication with the outer world; and we are even dependent upon them for the means of learning the events in the mother Country or the Dominion of Canada.

For those reasons we earnestly desire the ACQUISITION of *this colony* by the *United States.*

. . .

That in view of these facts we respectfully request, that Your Excellency will cause this Memorial to be laid before the Government of the United States, that that in any negotiations which may be pending or *undertaken* between Your Government and that of Her Most Gracious Majesty, for the settlement of territorial and other questions, that you will endeavour to induce Her Majesty to *consent* to the *transfer* of this *Colony* to the *United States.* . . .

What do you think?

1. *Why did these citizens of British Columbia prefer to be annexed by the United States rather than pursue the other two options open to them?*
2. *Do the arguments of the annexationists strike you as sound? Do they still apply today? Why?*

LOYALTY TO MOTHERLAND

The third option open to British Columbia was to remain a British Colony. The following verse illustrates the appeal of this option.

True Loyalty's to Motherland
And not to Canada,
The love we bear is second-hand
To any step-mama.

What do you think?

1. *Does this little ditty appeal to you? Why or why not?*
2. *Given what you have read about British Columbian sentiments about Canada up to this point, why might British Columbians have seen Canada as a "step-mama"? Explain.*

B.C. DEBATES UNION WITH CANADA

British Columbia debated the proposed terms of union with Canada in 1870. . . . The Hon. Mr. Helmcken said (member for Victoria City):—

Now, Sir, in the first place, it is necessary for the people to see that Confederation must be for the general good of the Colony. . . .

I believe it to be most inopportune. It is believed by most people that this Colony is on the verge of great changes. That the new gold discoveries will bring a large population to this Colony and that the slight despondency which now exists will be swept away, and that this Colony will once more enter upon an era of prosperity not inferior to that which belonged to it a few years ago.

I say, Sir, that this is an inopportune period to bring this question up, because when that population which is expected arrives, our position to negotiate for terms will be much better, because with a larger population and greater prosperity, we may demand far better terms than now; and, Sir, it is my firm conviction that if prosperity comes shortly the people of this Colony will not desire to change certainty for uncertainty.

Another reason there is that we ought to wait until after 1871. In that year Canada has to take a census of the population, and when that is taken we shall know the amount of the debt per head. I have no doubt it is greater now than when Confederation was first inaugurated. It is increasing, and I believe that instead of 22 cents per head it will now be 25 cents.

I should like, then to wait until after 1871, because we shall then have a better opportunity of knowing the financial condition of those with whom we would connect ourselves.

. . .

And now, Sir, let us glance at this Colony. I need not dilate upon what is known to all. I maintain, Sir, that this Colony is one of the richest portions of the world's surface; that it has unlimited supplies of lumber and spars; that it possesses coal, gold, and other minerals in abundance; that her waters teem with fish; that it is rich in everything. Take the climate; it is far better than that of England, far more temperate, far more bright and sunny, and, I may fairly add, far more healthy. . . .

. . . I say, Sir, that one cause of our want of prosperity has been the neglect of acquisition of population, and particularly of agricultural population. The next cause is that we have driven people out of the Colony.

I need only allude to our having deposed the Free Trade system. That deposition took population out of the Colony which has never been replaced. There was a depopulation of the cities without any attempt having been made to obtain a substitute rural population. We are now asked to undergo another revolution, which will ruin our farmers and do no sort of good to those engaged in commercial pursuits. . . .

. . . So far from Confederation benefitting the commercial community, I say it is much rather calculated to do them harm. No doubt if public works are undertaken, as we are told will be the case under Confederation, employment will be given for a time, but the supplies required will come from the United States, and our public works will actually be of more benefit to the United States, during their construction, than to this Colony. What we want, is an enlarged outlet for our resources. We want markets for our coal and lumber; we want our local industries fostered; and all of these can be obtained by a judicious arrangements of our own Tariff. Next, we want agricultural population, and any increase of this kind of population must depend upon the encouragement given. If our agricultural interests are left without encouragement, we shall not get an increased agricultural population; and, therefore, the country will not reap so much benefit from public works, as the supplies will come from the United States.

There can be no permanent or lasting union with Canada, unless terms be made to promote and foster the material and pecuniary interests of this Colony. The only link which binds this Colony to Canada is Imperial. The people must be better off under Confederation than alone, or they will not put up with it.

. . .

Confederation would make the Dominion territorially greater, but would, in case of war, be a source of weakness. It is people not territory, that makes a country strong and powerful. To be strong, the union must be of people, and in my opinion that condition is wanting. I feel certain that Her Majesty's Government has no wish to be put to the expense of defending the country; no wish to be involved in quarrels with the United States; no wish to keep Canada depending upon her support, but rather a wish to force her into independence—to get rid of her altogether.

. . .

It would be absurd for us to sacrifice our interest in order that laws may be made for us by a people who know little of our condition and wants, and who in fact must necessarily legislate for the greater number—the people of the Atlantic Provinces. It is dangerous to place ourselves at the disposal of superior numbers.

If we are united, or rather absorbed, everything will centralize in Canada, and the whole country will be tributary to Canada. The number of Representatives sent to Ottawa from other places would overwhelm the number sent from British Columbia. Even in the matter of appropriations, where the scramble always is, this Colony would be overborne; we should be laughed at by the victors for our pretentions. It is the case in all other Colonies, and would be here.

It is absurd to suppose that the same laws, whether civil, commercial, or industrial will be found equally advantageous to all parts of this great Continent. It manifestly cannot be so; the conditions are different. We know what is best for ourselves, and are able to legislate to effect that. We have no wish to pay Canada to do our legislation.

[The Hon. Mr. WOOD Said]:—

We want self-government, which means the protection of our own interests, and the establishment of our own welfare in our own way; the passing of our own Estimates in our own way; the selection of those who rule, and the subsequent meeting of our rulers, face to face, in open Council, that they may show us the results of their ruling. It means the imposition and collection of our own taxes, fostering our own industries, and the power of the purse. These are the elements of self-government, and they are reserved to the Dominion Government, and taken from the Provinces; hence my objections . . .

With respect to the applicability of the scheme of Confederation to this

Colony I have more special and particular grounds of objection. I consider such an union inexpedient on several grounds.

First, the remoteness of the Colony from Canada;
Secondly, the comparative insignificance of British Columbia;
And, thirdly, the diversity of its interest from those of Canada. . . .
. . .

The question has always appeared to me to be this:—Confederation with England, which we have, Confederation in its truest sense; Confederation with all the security of protection, and all the pride of self-government, now or hereafter to be, when the Colony shall have population and wealth sufficient: or Confederation—or, as it should be termed, "Incorporation"—with Canada. . . . Incorporation with all the humiliation of dependence, and to my mind the certainty of reaction, agitation, and discontent. Canada can never become the *assignee*, the *official assignee*, the *Downing Street official assignee*, of the affection and loyalty which exists between this dependency and the Mother Country. I am opposed to the political extinction of this Colony, and its subservience to the will of a majority of the House of Commons, at Ottawa, and the administration of its affairs by the political adherents of Canadian statesmen. . . .

Railway, or no railway—consent or no consent—the transfer of Legislative power to Ottawa, to a place so remote in distance and in interest, is an injustice and a political extravagance which time will most surely establish. . . .

[The Hon. Mr. DeCOSMOS, Member for Victoria District]:—We are engaged, I believe, in Nation-making. For my part, I have been engaged in Nation-making for the last twelve years—ever since I have been engaged in politics in the Colony. . . . The Hon. Registrar-General says that I have not made a Nation yet. I need only, in reply, quote for his enlightenment the old adage "Rome was not built in a day." . . . I have advocated the union of those three colonies, and in the union of two of them particularly I have taken a prominent part. For many years I have regarded the union of the British Pacific Territories, and of their consolidation under one Government, as one of the steps preliminary to the grand consolidation of the British Empire in North America. I still look upon it in this light with the pride and feeling of a native-born British American. From the time when I first mastered the institutes of physical and political geography I could see Vancouver Island on the Pacific, from my home on the Atlantic; and I could see a time when the British Possessions, from the United States boundary to the Arctic Ocean, and extending from the Atlantic to the Pacific, would be consolidated into one great Nation. . . .

We are here, Sir, laying the corner-stone of a great Nation on the Pacific Coast. When we look at past history, we find some nations that date their origin in the age of fable; some have been produced by violence, and extended their empire by conquest. But we are engaged in building up a great nation in the noon-day light of the nineteenth century, not by violence, not by wrong, but I hope, Sir, by the exercise of that common sense which the Honourable gentlemen who preceded me called statesmanship.

. . . I shall support the general principle of Confederation (Hear, hear), as I have always done, if we get to the discussion of the terms proposed. . . . B.C. Leg. Council Debate on the Subject of Confederation with Canada; Government Gazette Extraordinary of Mar. 1870. Victoria.

Supporters of Confederation in B.C.

Atty. General Hon. Henry Crease (Mar. 9, 1870)

Resolved, that this Council is of the opinion that at this juncture of affairs in British North America, east of the Rocky Mountains, it is very desirable that His Excellency be respectfully requested to take such steps, without delay, as may be deemed by him best adapted to insure the admission of British Columbia into the Confederation on fair and equitable terms, this Council being confident that in advising this step they are expressing the views of the Colonists generally. (p. 4)

. . .

We are sandwiched between the United States territory to the north and south—indeed on all sides but one, and that one opening toward Canada. Our only option is between remaining a petty, isolated community, 15,000 miles from home, eking out a miserable existence on the crumbs of prosperity our powerful and active Republican neighbours choose to allow us, or, by taking our place among the comity of nations, become the prosperous western outlet on the North Pacific of a young and vigorous people, the eastern boundary of whose possession is washed by the Atlantic. (p. 5)

. . .

I leave to others to dilate upon the advantages which Canada would derive from the connection, the possession of a Far West (Canada's great want) into which her rapidly increasing population may pour, instead of going to swell the bulk of the adjoining States. Those gentlemen will be able to show that the ultimate importance—nay possible existence—of the Dominion as a Nation may hereafter, in some measure, depend upon her Union with ourselves. (p. 6)

Mar. 10, 1870 J. W. Trutch Chief Commissioner of Land & Works.

To sum up my argument in support of the motion of the Honourable the Attorney-General, I advocate Confederation because it will secure the continuance of this Colony under the British Flag, and strengthen British interests on this Continent; and because it will benefit this community, by lessening taxation and giving increased revenues for local expenditure; by advancing the political status of the Colony; by securing the practical aid of the Dominion Government, who are, I believe, able to—and whose special care it would be to devise and—carry into effect measures tending to develop the natural resources, and to promote the prosperity of this Colony; and by affording, through a railway, the only means of acquiring a permanent population, which must come from the east of the Rocky Mountains.

What do you think?

1. *In the document you have just read the majority of speakers opposed Confederation. What basic arguments did they use to support their opposition?*
2. *Helmcken stated, "If we are united, or rather absorbed, everything will centralize in Canada, and the whole country will be tributary to Canada." What did he mean by this statement? Does this kind of sentiment still exist in B.C.? in other regions of Canada?*
3. *According to the various speakers, what conditions would have to exist in order to make confederation a viable choice for B.C.?*
4. *Mr. DeCosmos supported union with Canada, and saw himself as "engaged in Nation-making." Why did he approve of Confederation? What kind of Nation did he think would evolve as a result of union?*

THE TERMS OF UNION

The terms of union between British Columbia and Canada were finally negotiated, and the colony entered Confederation.

1. Canada shall be liable for the debts and liabilities of British Columbia existing at the time of the Union.

2. British Columbia not having incurred debts equal to those of the other Provinces now constituting the Dominion, shall be entitled to receive, by half-yearly payments, in advance, from the General Government, interest at the rate of five per cent per annum on the difference between the actual amount of its indebtedness at the date of the Union and the indebtedness per head of the population of Nova Scotia and New Brunswick (27-77 dollars), the population of British Columbia being taken at 60,000. . . .

4. The Dominion will provide an efficient mail service, fortnightly, by steam communication, between Victoria and San Francisco, and twice a week between Victoria and Olympia; the vessels to be adapted for the conveyance of freight and passengers. . . .

8. British Columbia shall be entitled to be represented in the Senate by three members, and by six members in the House of Commons. The representation to be increased under the provisions of the "British North America Act, 1867". . . .

10. The provisions of the "British North America Act, 1867", shall . . . be applicable to British Columbia, in the same way and to the like intent as they apply to the other Provinces of the Dominion, and as if the Colony of

British Columbia had been one of the Provinces originally united by the said Act.

11. The Government of the Dominion undertakes to secure the commencement simultaneously, within two years from the date of the Union, of the construction of a Railway from the Pacific towards the Rocky Mountains, and from such point as may be selected, east of the Rocky Mountains, towards the Pacific, to connect the seaboard of British Columbia with the railway system of Canada; and further, to secure the completion of such Railway within ten years from the date of the Union. . . .

What do you think?

1. Where was the most emphasis placed in these terms of Union? Why?
2. Why do you think the construction of a railway was an important priority? Do some independent research on this question.

The Future

6

The forces of regionalism have played an important role in our country's past and will continue to have a profound impact on Canada. This volume has examined some of the contemporary and historical manifestations of regionalism in Canada. No conclusions are drawn but the volume does assume that every Canadian should be concerned with understanding why regionalism exists and how it will affect our nation's future.

The basic question that lies ahead is whether it will be possible to accommodate regional aspirations and national goals within a Canadian Confederation. Are regional forces so strong and the union so fragile that Confederation will ultimately fail? Can any of the crucial issues raised by regional forces be resolved by changing the Canadian political and constitutional structure? If one part of Canada were to secede, would the rest of Canada stay united politically? Is it possible that one single issue or crisis would force all the regions to emphasize their common bonds rather than their differences? Are there solutions available that accept diversity and emphasize unity? Based on your knowledge of Canada's past, what sort of decisions do you think Canadians will make about regional issues in the future?

SEPARATISM IN THE WEST

How much injustice and inequity can one region withstand before it is forced to take the radical step of severing itself from the rest of the country? The urgency over one specific issue, or over accumulated grievances, leads many regional spokesmen to warn of the danger of separation. Here is a typical response, issued a few days after the federal election of July 8, 1974 by Gerald W. Baldwin, an influential Progressive Conservative Party Member of Parliament from Peace River, Alberta (Press Release July 15, 1974).

With the pundits rushing into print to deal with questions of cabinet reshuffling and leadership in the other parties, I am amazed that so few people here in central Canada have taken to heart, or given heed to the warning contained in the Western vote.

Almost half of the popular vote went to the Progressive Conservative Party; nearly ¾ of the people who voted in the West have decisively rejected, not just Trudeau and his liberals, but the Eastern Establishment.

Campaigning in several western provinces, I caught the strong pungent odor of this phenomena; a refusal to accept this rule and domination, and a determination that the true principles of a federalism, including the right of provincial self-determination in proper areas, must be retained in the West—OR ELSE! Which means there is more potential for a dissolution of the bonds of nationalism now in the western provinces than there ever was in Quebec where the economic consequences of separatism were always factors which prompted Québécois to vote to stay in Confederation.

The economy of the West is viable and could sustain an independent state with ease—and this is very obvious to westerners—and more of them are openly saying so.

At this stage of my political career I can make this comment as I have no vested interest in exaggerating this feeling, and certainly oppose promoting any movement leading to western alienation but, there are undoubtedly those who would have no compunction in doing so; and the situation is not unlike that of the tinder-dry-forest which needs only someone to strike a match to cause a conflagration.

And, thus, a need to file this caveat.

It warns against an attempt to use the big stick to deprive westerners of their equity in their own natural resources.

It warns that there is a limit to the delay in remedying the wrongs of the past and finding antidotes in relation to transportation problems and the establishment in western industry.

It warns that the West has had enough of such pseudo national and Eastern dominated organizations as the CBC, whose Toronto-based clique engages in patronizing put-downs of the West. Their blatant partisanship in the last election was such as to persuade me to consider putting down a motion for the next Parliament to the effect that each CBC news program should be preceeded by "this is a political program sponsored by the National Liberal Association and paid for by the taxpayers." If there can be a Quebec network which is virtually independent, maybe we should have a Western counterpart.

It warns that the devastating cost of the sickly programs of state-welfarism and guaranteed idleness emanating from Ottawa is unacceptable in the West.

But, the list is long and the hour is late.

The Prime Minister has a majority and a mandate in Central Canada. He has neither from the West. I and my colleagues and, of course, our Leader, are acquainted with the situation, and there is a duty to put the facts of life before the government. I am doing so at once on my own because there may be little time left.

We cannot wait because time does not wait. We cannot wait because delay could set in motion a course of events which could only lead to disaster.

What is meant by?

"a caveat"
"blatant partisanship"
"state-welfarism and guaranteed idleness"

What do you think?

1. *Why, according to Mr. Baldwin, are Westerners so unhappy with the Federal Government?*
2. *Why do some Westerners feel annoyed with what they regard as the policies of Central Canada?*
3. *In your opinion, would it be possible for a separate Western Canadian nation to exist? Support your point of view with a number of arguments.*
4. *As far as you are concerned do Westerners have more to gain than to lose by staying in Confederation? Why? Be specific.*

IF QUEBEC GOES, WILL THE EAST SUFFER EVEN MORE?

The following comments were taken from a document by Ralph Surette which appeared in Maclean's *Magazine on September 19, 1977.*

. . .

. . . What would happen to the Atlantic provinces if Canada split? What future for this clump of four half-forgotten footnotes to Canadian history—losing political clout with every census, getting shakier with every economic misfortune—should the final alienation of a physical cutoff occur? The most common answer amid a flux of conflicting opinions—often existing side by side within the same mind—is "disaster". In its simplest form it means that English Canada will lose the will to continue vital transfer payments and subsidies. The already poor Atlantic region would slip economically—some say to Third World status—and probably undergo another round of Depression-style depopulation.

. . .

. . . In the eyes of Atlantic Canada there is not one crisis over Confederation, but two: The threat of Quebec independence and economic disparity. The cultural problems of how Quebec will fit into Canada and the economic problem of how the Atlantic region will fit into Canada. This second crisis is the deepening dependency of the Maritimes and Newfoundland on transfer payments from Ottawa at a time when the federal capacity to continue transfers is under attack, an assault mounted not primarily by Quebec, but by the "have" provinces who want to keep more of their riches for themselves. The two crises become one when "decentralization" and "power to the provinces" are held out as the solution to the demands of both Quebec and the "haves". "That frightens me," says political scientist Murray Beck at Dalhousie University. "The Liberals, Conservatives—all have come out for decentralization. The kind of decentralization that Trudeau's talking about is frightening." Marty Dolan, research assistant to the leader of the Nova Scotia NDP says, "Quebec wants political separation with economic union. Alberta wants economic independence with political union. Alberta's more dangerous to us than Quebec. They can kill us."

. . .

June 21 and Nova Scotia Finance Minister Peter Nicholson was delivering the inevitable Rotary Club speech. He started with what sounded like an anti-Ottawa diatribe, complaining about "wrestling the federal government crocodile" and "getting blood out of Ottawa and other stones." Except that he finished by saying that "the authority of the federal government needs strengthening rather than diluting." What's this? Puffing up the crocodile that eats you! Another Maritime mind-bender? Masochism among the lobster-pots? Indeed, the dilemma. Despite the lack of emotion about Canada breaking up, no one needs Confederation more than the Atlantic provinces. "Of this province's $1.25 billion of estimated revenues and recoveries for the current fiscal year, $573 million comes from federal sources. In other words, 46%," Nicholson told his audience. He might have added that the story is roughly the same in the other three provinces. The matter of calculating who gets what from Confederation is known to have its hazards. But in balance-sheet terms, if anyone gains, it has to be the Atlantic provinces. The total federal transfer to the area in the current fiscal year is likely to reach more than $2.5 billion, . . . or double what it was only four years ago.

The thought of losing this federal largesse is what the word "disaster" means. . . . Then there's the crocodile part, which means that virtually nothing moves in the Atlantic area without federal money, without a fight with allegedly supercilious Ottawa bureaucrats. Or as Premier Regan has put it, "If you oppose them on one thing today, they'll get you on five more tomorrow." This is the resentment of dependency, a resentment made worse by the historical awareness of having gone from prosperity to poverty in 100 years. Blamed for this in large part are centralist economic policies starting with the national policy of protection tariffs in the 19th Century—a centralist bias in economic structure which many feel is poorly compensated for by equalization payments since the Atlantic area is not getting any less destitute.

What do you think?

1. *What is the primary cause of regional discontent in the Atlantic provinces according to Mr. Surette?*
2. *Why would Mr. Nicholson advocate strengthening the Federal Government?*
3. *What options are open to the Atlantic provinces if Quebec separates? Which is most likely in your opinion and why?*
4. *What role do you think the Federal Government should play in the National Unity debate and why?*

PROPOSALS FOR NEW MAP OF CANADA

One of the most frequent methods used to focus debate on the problem of regionalism in Canada is to suggest that Canadians redraw the present political boundaries of their nation. Here are two such attempts to create a new nation. The first proposal was made by the distinguished Canadian historian, A.R.M. Lower, in an article for the October 15, 1948 issue of Maclean's Magazine. *The Second is from a contest sponsored by* Maclean's *and published in its January 1970 issue.*

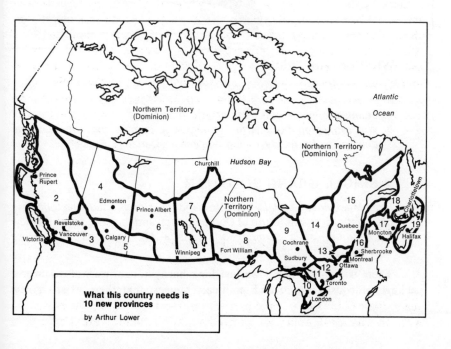

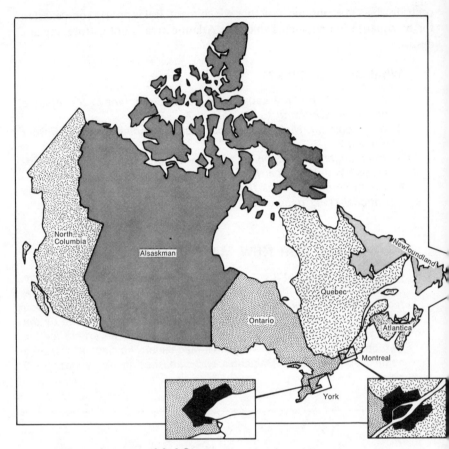

What do you think?

1. Which of the two proposed maps of Canada do you favour? Why?
2. How would you redraw the map of Canada? Give reasons for defining areas in the manner you propose.
3. Will redrawing boundaries in any way change the nature of the debate or the reality of regionalism in Canada? Explain.

A SINGLE GRAND SOLUTION

Flora MacDonald, M.P. for Kingston and the Islands, made the following observations on the future of Confederation and the possibility of a new constitution, at a seminar on Canada-U.S. relations at Harvard University, December 7, 1977.

There is a sense that if we just look hard enough, we will discover a package of constitutional and political changes; that there exists a new constitution, just waiting to be unearthed, a Canadian version of the Holy Grail, pulsing away with an eerie light, probably deep in some cave on Baffin Island.

But to talk of a single grand solution is misleading and maybe even dangerous. First of all, there may, indeed, be no solution, at least none which preserves the essential of a united confederation. It may even be impossible to resolve the multiple conflicts and cleavages which now divide Canadian society.

Secondly, different groups vary widely in what they would consider an acceptable solution, just as they differ widely in their *diagnosis* of the problems facing the country, and in their images of what they would like the country to be.

Thirdly, any solution is not likely to be a single neat package—a new British North America Act, for example. It is instead likely to be made up of a large number of diverse elements, including constitutional changes, changes in policy, and changes in attitude.

Lastly, and most importantly, it is misleading to talk of a solution as being one grand resolution of all our discontents, after which harmony would prevail far into the future. Politics does not work that way. In thinking about solutions, Canadians instead must realize that the goal should be to provide a *framework* and a set of rules, within which the continuing debate and dialogue between regional and national interests, and between French and English can go on in a civilized way. It is dangerous to put too much stock in search of a grand once-for-all solution. We also have to realize that in the short run at least, a new constitution cannot change old attitudes, and cannot alter fundamental realities. What it can do is recognize and reflect those realities, and make it possible to engage in a continuing search for accommodation and reconciliation.

So I will not attempt to set out a final blueprint here. But I will suggest some of the basic choices which are available, and some of the elements which might be part of any new accommodation.

Any solution that one proposes must also depend greatly on one's *diagnosis* of the nature and causes of the current political crisis in Canada, and of the longer-term dissatisfaction that has developed over many years as the federal system has grappled with the twin problems of reconciling the interests of French- and English-Canadians, and of accommodating growing regional discontent. The solution also depends on one's *values*, and on the kind of Canada one wants to create.

The problem facing us at the present time is one of reconciliation of three fundamental principles which have dominated Canadian political, economic, social and cultural life throughout its history. Indeed, our history is one of a constant tension and dialogue between these three drives, in which now one, now the other, tends to be dominant.

The first is *regionalism*, or province building, the recognition of the unique historical, cultural and economic attributes of each region, and of the desire of each to develop itself to the fullest extent possible.

The second is the search for a truly *pan-Canadian development*, building on shared values and attitudes, the common desires for national services, the desire to create an independent, integrated Canadian economy, and the need to develop an equitable sharing of resources among all regions of Canada.

The third might be called *two-nation building*, the recognition that sociologically Quebec is a distinct society and culture which exists alongside a less clearly defined English-Canadian nation. This drive reflects itself in the desire for equality between the two nations, and in the search for a distinct political role for the Quebec government.

So we have in Canada, one country, two nations, five regions, ten provinces, two territories and many cultures. Somehow our institutions must reflect and accommodate all of them, and be flexible enough to respond to changes in the underlying situation—as in the change from dominance of national aspirations and feelings during and after World War II, to the contemporary dominance and preoccupation with regionalism and even of two nations.

The character of regionalism is a complex one. Mackenzie King's statement that while some countries have too much history, Canada has too much geography, has a great deal of wisdom. Geographical factors account for many of our differences and for many of our problems.

But there is another aspect of Canadian regionalism which cannot be attributed to geography but belongs more properly to history. The different regions of our country were settled at different times by people whose values and attitudes were rooted in diverse societies. These transplanted values and attitudes have played a large role in shaping the political and social cultures of the regions, and thus of the country.

. . .

I firmly believe that until we truly understand these regional modes of thought and sets of values; until we really understand how they have come about and what makes them persist, then we will continue to concentrate on the problems of regionalism rather than on the potential it offers to a creative restructuring of confederation.

Canadian political debate has tended to concentrate almost entirely on the negative side of the regional dimension, stressing the grievances of every region against the federal government, stressing what it is that divides Canadians from each other rather than what unites them. That is a healthy and interesting development, but if carried too far, stressing how many pieces Humpty-Dumpty has broken into, we run the risk of simply not being able to put him back together again.

What do you think?

1. According to Macdonald, what principles have dominated Canada's history? Based on the articles you have read in this book, would you agree with her analysis of the Canadian situation? Why or why not?
2. What does Ms. MacDonald believe is essential for solving the problems facing Canada?
3. How might regionalism offer the potential for a "creative restructuring of Confederation"?

A New Constitution

On June 20, 1978 the Prime Minister's Office presented a proposal for a redrafting of the Canadian constitution. The following articles provide some background to the constitutional debate (June 21), the main proposals for the new plan (June 21), and some provincial reaction to it (June 24, by Jeffrey Simpson). The first and third articles are reprinted with the permission of the Globe and Mail—Toronto, and the second with the permission of CP.

IT'S TRUDEAU'S THIRD CONSTITUTIONAL TRY

For the third time in 10 years, Prime Minister Pierre Trudeau is attempting to mold a national consensus on constitutional reform.

Twice before—in 1968-71 and again in 1976—Mr. Trudeau unsuccessfully set in motion studies and conferences to produce concrete reforms.

But the urgency of presenting a reformed federalism to Quebeckers before the separation referendum and the need to respond to grievances in other parts of the country have prompted Mr. Trudeau to try again.

The white paper on constitutional reform and the bill tabled yesterday in the Commons pick up many of the themes aired in 1968-71.

In that period, Ottawa was responding to demands, particularly from Quebec, for constitutional change. After a series of conferences, the first ministers met at Victoria in 1971, having winnowed down areas of agreement to a document called the Victoria Charter.

The charter contained provisions for a charter of human rights, some provincial say in Supreme Court appointments, a preamble to the constitution setting out the aims of the Canadian federation and an amending formula.

All 10 provincial governments and the federal Government agreed to the provisions of the charter, but Quebec wanted provincial control over social policy included.

That demand from Quebec proved to be the charter's undoing, because Premier Robert Bourassa, under heavy pressure from within his own province, rejected the Victoria Charter.

Five years later Mr. Trudeau launched a new attempt to get the constitutional reform ball rolling with a letter to the premiers proposing agreement on repatriation of the constitution, provincial consultation on Supreme Court appointments and provision for court challenges to any federal actions that would harm the French language or culture.

Mr. Trudeau said that although he was ready to start from scratch in reforming the entire constitution, he preferred to go step by step.

At two meetings in 1976, the premiers reached a common position, touching the important redefinition of powers between the two levels of government. The provinces could not, however, agree on an amending formula.

The election of the Parti Québecois in November, 1976, ended the constitutional review process.

HIGHLIGHTS

Highlights of federal legislation to amend the constitution:

—A charter of rights would protect individual liberties and guard against discrimination for race, religion, sex or age—federally at first and regionally after ratification by the provinces.

—Guarantees for use of English and French, including the right to choose the language of education, would need provincial ratification to be fully operable.

—A preamble would state the country's aims, including the preservation of French culture and a federal system of government.

—A 118-seat House of Federation, half chosen by the provinces and half by the Commons, would replace the Senate.

—Justices of the Supreme Court of Canada, increased to 11 from 9, would be appointed with provincial advice and require ratification by the House of Federation.

—Measures to improve federal-provincial relations, with a requirement for annual conferences of the prime minister and 10 premiers.

—The Governor-General would be given powers to exercise authority in his or her own right instead of always acting in the name of the Queen.

PREMIERS WARY OF OTTAWA'S CONSTITUTIONAL PLAN

The initial reactions to Ottawa's constitutional bill are now in from provincial premiers across Canada, and on balance the response has been one of guarded pessimism.

Several have welcomed Ottawa's proposals, but most have worried about Prime Minister Pierre Trudeau's declared intention to proceed unilaterally if provincial agreement cannot be secured on those changes exclusively within federal jurisdiction.

Just what lies exclusively within Ottawa's jurisdiction has already emerged as an issue.

Premier Peter Lougheed, no friend of provincial appointments to the upper House, repeated his long-standing position that provincial agreement would be required before changing the Senate. The Alberta Premier, who said he would comment in more depth later, warned that any unilateral federal move would "not be in the spirit of Confederation."

In Saskatchewan, Premier Allan Blakeney, the chairman of the provincial premiers' organization this year, echoed the same theme. "Just how the federal Government proceeds is of the greatest importance," he said. "The extent to which the federal Government moves unilaterally and the extent to which there is effective consultation with the premiers are crucial."

In Manitoba, Conservative Premier Sterling Lyon continued his long-distance sparring with the federal Liberals, saying the surest route to reforming the constitution lay in "getting a new Government in Ottawa with which we can negotiate on a reasonable basis."

Mr. Lyon said parts of the federal bill have merit, but proposed changes to the monarchy "color the whole debate." These changes show "a continuation of the drift of Mr. Trudeau toward making a presidential republican system out of Parliament."

(The federal proposal would retain the Queen as sovereign of Canada, and Mr. Trudeau has repeatedly stated his constitutional proposals would retain the constitutional monarchy.)

Another negative response came from a man who would be premier, Quebec Liberal Leader Claude Ryan, whose opinion is watched carefully in other provincial capitals as a bellwether of federalist thinking in Quebec.

Mr. Ryan will announce his complete position this week, but his initial response criticized Ottawa for avoiding the question of dividing powers between the two levels of government.

Ottawa deliberately chose a two-phase strategy for its constitutional reforms; implementing those within federal jurisdiction by July 1, 1979, and those requiring provincial consent by 1981.

New Brunswick Premier Richard Hatfield said that by presenting a detailed bill Ottawa had made the already difficult task of constitutional discussions even tougher.

Mr. Hatfield would have preferred a detailed white paper, rather than a bill that implied future unilateral action by Ottawa. He also wondered about Ottawa's priorities, especially Senate reform.

"I don't think the Senate of Canada is one of the priority problems affecting the constitutional crisis in Canada," Mr. Hatfield said in an interview, adding that he would make a more detailed statement later.

Elsewhere, blanket opposition came from predictable quarters. Quebec Premier René Lévesque and Intergovernmental Affairs Minister Claude Morin breezily dismissed the proposals. Mr. Morin said they broke no new ground and that if he were a federalist, he would be disappointed.

Former Conservative leader John Diefenbaker objected to the "double majority" rule proposed for the House of the Federation whereby measures of "special linguistic significance" would require support from a majority of French-speaking and English-speaking members.

That idea, and giving Quebec four of 11 judges on the Supreme Court, would represent a form of special status for Quebec that mocks the idea of one Canada, Mr. Diefenbaker said. "That bill has as much chance of passing as I have of jumping out of this fifth-story window without hurting myself."

What do you think?

1. How does the proposal provide solutions to some of the regional concerns voiced in previous sections of this book? Which concerns are not dealt with?
2. What are provincial premiers' criticisms of the new plan? Do you think any of them are valid?
3. What effect might the new constitution have on provincial-federal relations and regional concerns? Explain your answer.

What do you think?

1. Events of November 1976 have altered the views of many Canadians about Canada, its federal system and Confederation. In general, what are Canadians saying about the options for the nation with regard to regionalism and federalism?
2. Of the many proposals you have read about restructuring Confederation, which appeals to you the most? the least? Explain your answer.
3. Of the various articles you have read about Canada's future, which ones are the most optimistic? the most realistic? Whose predictions do you believe? Discuss.

FOR YOU TO DECIDE

The following exercise is intended to help you sort out what you have read and to use the information to arrive at some conclusions about the issue of regionalism in Canada.

1. *List all the grievances expressed by representatives from each region in Canada. How important is each grievance? (For each region, rank the issues in order from most important to least important).*
2. *Do you feel it is possible to deal with regional grievances separately or must all these grievances be considered together? For each grievance listed, suggest how you would attempt to deal with the problem.*
3. *How might your solutions affect the other regions in Canada?*
4. *Could your suggested solutions be implemented so that every region would be satisfied with its role in Confederation? Explain.*
5. *What are the chances that your solutions might be the future course of action for Canada? Cite evidence to support your position.*
6. *What role can you play in determining Canada's future?*

Select Bibliography

ALLEN R., (ed.) *A Region of the Mind: Interpreting the Western Canadian Plains* (Regina, 1973)

BAILEY, A.G., *Culture and Nationality* (Toronto, 1972)

BECK, J.M., *The History of Maritime Union* (Fredericton, 1969)

BERCUSON, D. (ed.), *Canada and the Burden of Canadian Unity* (Toronto, 1977)

BREWIS, T.N., *Regional Economic Policies in Canada* (Toronto, 1969)

BURNS, R.M. (ed.), *One Country or Two?* (Montreal, 1971)

CAMU, P., Weeks, E.P., Sametz, Z.W., *Economic Geography of Canada* (Toronto, 1954)

FORBES, E., *The Maritime Rights Movement* (Montreal, 1978)

IRVING, J., *The Social Credit Movement in Alberta* (Toronto, 1959)

KILBOURN, W., (ed.), *Canada: A Guide to a Peaceable Kingdom* (Toronto, 1970)

MACEWEN, P., *Confederation and the Maritimes* (Windsor, N.S., 1976)

MACKAY, R.A. (ed.), *Newfoundland's Economic, Diplomatic and Strategic Studies* (Toronto, 1946)

MENZIES, H., *The Railroad's Not Enough: Canada Now* (Toronto, 1978)

MORTON, W., *The Progressive Party in Canada* (Toronto, 1950)

NEARY, P., *The Political Economy of Newfoundland, 1929-1972* (Toronto, 1973)

ORMSBY, M., *British Columbia: A History* (Toronto, 1958)

PUTNAM, D.F. (ed.), *Canadian Regions* (Toronto, 1954)

RAWLYK. G.A. (ed.), *Historical Essays on the Atlantic Provinces* (Toronto, 1967)

ROBIN, M. (ed.), *Canadian Provincial Politics* (Scarborough, 1972)

SCHWARTZ, M., *Politics and Territory: The Sociology of Regional Persistence in Canada* (Montreal, 1974)

SHARP, P., *The Agrarian Revolt in Western Canada* (Minneapolis, 1945)

SIMEON, R., (ed.), *Must Canada Fail?* (Montreal, 1977)

THOMPSON, J., *The Harvests of War: The Prairie West, 1914-1918* (Toronto, 1978)

WADE, M. (ed.), *Regionalism in the Canadian Community, 1867-1967* (Toronto, 1967)

WAITE, P.B., *The Life and Times of Confederation, 1864-1867* (Toronto, 1962)

WEALE, D., and Baglole, H., *The Island and Confederation: The End of an Era* (Charlottetown, 1973)

YOUNG, W., *Democracy and Discontent* (Toronto, 1969)

197

7242 χ 1